Critical Praise for John Douglas and Mark Olshaker's

MINDHUNTER

"This singularly important study [is] as readable as a mystery novel. . . ."

—*Publishers Weekly*

"Mr. Douglas and Mark Olshaker . . . have written a fascinating report on the criminal profiling program of the FBI's behavioral science unit and have provided a disturbing look at this country's most savage murderers. . . . Mr. Douglas sets out to produce a good true-crime book, but because of his insights and the power of his material, he gives us more—he leaves us shaken, gripped by a quiet grief for the innocent victims and anguished by the human condition."

—Dean Koontz, *The New York Times Book Review*

"One of the first to develop the specialty of 'criminal-personality profiling'. . . . Douglas is justifiably proud of its success. . . . Readable, popular. . . . [*Mindhunter* is] recommended for true-crime collections."

—*Library Journal*

By the Same Authors

Mindhunter
Unabomber: On the Trail of America's Most-Wanted
  Serial Killer

Books by John Douglas

Nonfiction

Sexual Homicide: Patterns and Motives
  (with Robert K. Ressler and Ann W. Burgess)
Crime Classification Manual
  (with Ann W. Burgess, Allen G. Burgess, and
  Robert K. Ressler)

Books by Mark Olshaker

Nonfiction

The Instant Image: Edwin Land and the Polaroid Experience

Fiction

Einstein's Brain
Unnatural Causes
Blood Race
The Edge

UNABOMBER

ON THE TRAIL OF AMERICA'S MOST-WANTED SERIAL KILLER

JOHN DOUGLAS
AND MARK OLSHAKER

A LISA DREW BOOK

POCKET BOOKS

New York   London   Toronto   Sydney   Tokyo   Singapore

An *Original* Publication of POCKET BOOKS

POCKET BOOKS, a division of Simon & Schuster Inc.
1230 Avenue of the Americas, New York, NY 10020

ISBN: 0-671-00411-5

First Pocket Books printing May 1996

10 9 8 7 6 5 4 3 2 1

POCKET and colophon are registered trademarks of Simon & Schuster Inc.

Cover photo courtesy of AP/Lewis and Clark Sheriff Dept.

Printed in the U.S.A.

CONTENTS

AUTHORS' NOTE

This book is a report on an ongoing case in which news continues to break virtually on a day-by-day basis. It chronicles and gives one perspective on the eighteen-year hunt for a notorious terrorist and serial killer, culminating in the apprehension of suspect Theodore J. Kaczynski.

But we must caution that Mr. Kaczynski is just that—a suspect. According to our system, he and everyone else must be presumed innocent unless—and until—proven guilty in a court of law. Everything that follows should be read in that context.

This book truly has been a team effort, and it would not have been possible without the diligent and devoted, practically around-the-clock efforts of each member of our team. Jay Acton, Ann Hennigan, and Carolyn Olshaker worked side-by-side with us from beginning to end, reading, researching, writing and rewriting, and generally keeping us going. It is no exaggeration to say that in many ways this work is as much theirs as ours. Special thanks also to Bennett Olshaker, M.D., for his insight, analysis, and interpretation of psychological and psychiatric issues.

On the publishing side, our intrepid editor and publisher, Lisa Drew, headed up a parallel team that included Pocket Books publisher Gina Centrello,

Julie Rubenstein, Tris Coburn, Marysue Rucci and a host of others, some of whom we've never even met, who all pulled together to make this book a reality literally in a matter of days after it had been only a concept. Special thanks are due to Simon & Schuster Consumer Books Division President Jack Romanos, who, along with Gina, originated that concept and pushed it forward.

Finally, we want to acknowledge all of John's colleagues at the FBI and the other law enforcement agencies—federal, state, and local—who worked so long, so hard, and so well to see this case through and see justice done. They have the undying gratitude of us all.

Special thanks also to Mark Morril and Emily Remes for fighting the good fight for us, and fighting it exceedingly well.

—John Douglas and Mark Olshaker
April 1996

Though this be madness, yet there is method in't.

—William Shakespeare, *Hamlet*

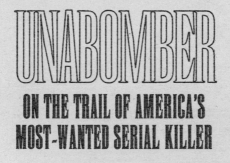

UNABOMBER

ON THE TRAIL OF AMERICA'S
MOST-WANTED SERIAL KILLER

PROLOGUE

ANOTHER DAY AT THE OFFICE

I just can't handle another major case, I said to myself. I don't know how I'm going to handle all the ones I'm working already.

It was late spring of 1980. It might have been a nice day in the rolling countryside or it might have been raining and dreary. I would have had no way of knowing. I was in my windowless office several floors belowground at the FBI Academy in Quantico, Virginia. I was the only full-time profiler in the Bureau, which was one agent too many as far as most of the brass at headquarters were concerned. J. Edgar Hoover had been dead only eight years, and his shadow still loomed large. The Hoover FBI had been interested in "just the facts, ma'am," and anyone who thought he could help solve a crime by claiming to describe the personality of some unknown perpetrator would likely have been suspected of witchcraft.

I hated to turn anything down. My colleagues at Quantico used to say I was like a prostitute who couldn't say no to a customer. On my desk were case

1

files from a series of horrifying murders of young black children in Atlanta, Georgia, that the local press was saying had to be the signature of some Klan-like hate group but which I felt was probably the work of a single young black male—not a popular opinion and not one likely to win me many friends. There was a guy in Wichita, Kansas, calling himself the BTK Strangler, for "Bind, Torture, Kill." At the same time I was trying to help Scotland Yard crack the case of the Yorkshire Ripper who was butchering women in north central England.

Those were just three of the hundred fifty or so active cases I was working on at the time. In addition, I was trying to convince anyone who would listen, both within the Bureau and at police departments from coast to coast, that we had something real and valuable to offer them. This meant meetings, consultations, lectures, and interviews all over the country. And any time I happened to find myself near a state or federal prison where there might be a serial killer, rapist, arsonist, or assassin for me to interview and learn from, I'd be there.

I wasn't spending time with my wife and two daughters. I was drinking too much, exercising like a fiend because I was too wound up to relax, and doing all the things I've always counseled the people who work for me not to do. I'd become obsessed with my mission, just like the people I was hunting. And driving everything was the overwhelming fear of failure. At this delicate stage of my program's development, it would take only one significant screwup to give the brass downtown the ammunition they needed to sink us. So not only did I have to take on more cases than one person could sensibly or responsibly handle, I couldn't afford to be wrong on any of them.

But when Tom Barrett, a special agent working in the Chicago Field Office called me that spring afternoon in 1980, I put down what I was doing and listened. Tom and I had been agents together in the

Detroit Field Office. Then, at the same time I was assigned to Milwaukee, Tom had gone to Chicago.

"We've had a bombing in Lake Forest," Tom explained. "June tenth. Percy Wood, the president of United Airlines, was injured opening a package addressed to him at his home in Lake Forest that exploded when he opened it."

Had the airline gotten any threats? I asked, beginning a series of standard questions.

"No. No ransom demands or anything like that. There's no apparent motive. I know you're doing a lot of work and research in sexual homicide and trying to profile the offenders. Do you think you could do anything on this type of guy?"

I thought about it for a moment. In addition to the work we'd been doing on serial killers and rapists, we were starting to delve into the backgrounds and personalities of assassin types. My research partner and Academy teaching associate, Robert Ressler, and I were in the process of interviewing such assassins as Robert Kennedy's murderer, Sirhan B. Sirhan; Arthur Bremer, who had shot and paralyzed Alabama governor and presidential candidate George Wallace; and Lynette "Squeaky" Fromme and Sara Jane Moore, both of whom had made attempts on the life of President Gerald Ford.

Just as there is no single profile for a serial killer, we were finding there was no single profile for an assassin. Those who did it up close and personal, like Sirhan, represented one type. Those who worked at a distance—anonymously—like the killers of President John Kennedy and Dr. Martin Luther King, Jr., represented another type. Those were the types I considered the most cruel and cowardly. I had already made a connection in my own thinking with arsonists and would later apply the same logic to product tamperers such as the craven Tylenol Poisoner.

As I listened to Tom Barrett describe the crime, I started thinking there could be a connection with bombers, too. A careful bomber will set or send his device and be nowhere nearby when it goes off. That had to tell me something about personality. And after all, I recalled, it was a bombing case that had really created the field I'd staked out for myself in the FBI.

"Okay, Tom," I said at last. "Let me see what I can do."

THE MAD BOMBER

It was the hunt for an elusive serial bomber terrorizing the public that actually began modern behavioral profiling.

By the mid-1950s, New York City had been racked for more than a decade by a series of explosions in such highly public places as train stations, movie theaters, and libraries. The earliest device had appeared on November 16, 1940, a crude pipe bomb found on a windowsill of the Consolidated Edison Company building on West Sixty-fourth Street. It was found before it went off. One blast in 1954 had gone off in Radio City Music Hall. Newspapers had dubbed him the Mad Bomber. The entire city lived in fear. I was a kid back then, growing up in Brooklyn, and I remember this case very well. Some of the devices exploded, causing injury and mayhem. Some of them were discovered and disarmed before they went off. And some just turned out to be duds. Fortunately no one had yet been killed. But two things were clear: the bomber's work had been grow-

5

ing in sophistication over the years, and anywhere you went in the course of a normal day, you could be the bomber's next victim.

Like other kinds of terrorists, many bombers feel a need to communicate with their intended victim, which is the public at large. That urge in the nature of the beast. Through neatly printed letters he had written to various newspapers, one important fact was known about the bomber: he had a grudge against Consolidated Edison, the New York City power company. His letters, signed "F.P.," were filled with florid references to Con Ed's "ghoulish acts" and "dastardly deeds," and he claimed that some unspecified ailment or injury from Con Ed and unspecified "others" had caused him "financial loss." He ended one letter to the New York *Herald-Tribune* with the statement, "I merely seek justice."

The problem with tracking down someone from this specific but scant evidence is that Con Edison was a huge but relatively new company, actually "consolidated" from the myriad other power companies that had served New York since the nineteenth century. Each of these companies had maintained its own records, many of which no longer existed. The ones that did were in no organized order. So while police and Con Ed clerical employees began poring over records of disability claims and complaint letters going back decades, they knew the chances of finding this particular needle in the haystack were remote. Even if the file existed and someone happened upon it, how would they know he was the guy?

Initially, the police had tried to keep a lid on the details of the crimes, figuring the more information they let out, the more they would encourage the bomber and the myriad copycats that inevitably crop up in high-profile cases. But as the Mad Bomber's work continued, there was little they could do to contain the public's outrage and hysteria. A bomb exploded inside Grand Central Station, nearly killing a redcap.

Then, just before 8:00 P.M. on December 2, 1956, as the city was gearing up for a typically festive Christmas season, a bomb ripped through the Paramount Theater in Brooklyn. Six people were injured, three critically.

That was the last straw. New York City Police Commissioner Stephen Kennedy announced that every resource would be thrown into the effort to trap the Mad Bomber and bring him to justice.

This was a publicly comforting pronouncement, but the fact of the matter was that NYPD had already thrown all of the traditional crime-solving resources into the hunt and so far nothing had worked. So Inspector Howard Finney, director of NYPD's crime lab, decided to try something new.

For more than a hundred years, fictional detectives such as Edgar Allan Poe's C. Auguste Dupin and Sir Arthur Conan Doyle's Sherlock Holmes had been solving cases by inferring, or profiling, the personality of the perpetrator. In the 1841 classic "The Murders in the Rue Morgue," Dupin had predicted a large ape as the killer when reason couldn't get any human type to fit his behavioral profile. But this was the stuff of books and movies until a cold December day in 1956 when Inspector Finney took two detectives with him and paid a visit to Dr. James A. Brussel, a Greenwich Village psychiatrist who also served part-time as assistant commissioner of the New York Department of Mental Hygiene. Though few in the department had any hope a civilian shrink could help crack a case in real life, Finney asked the psychiatrist if he could draw any conclusions about the bomber's personality from the details of the crime scenes or the style and content of the letters.

Brussel, as you might expect, knew little about bomb-making, so he started by asking the police officers to analyze the devices for him. They told him that the bombs represented highly skilled work, the product of an individual with some experience, and that they had grown increasingly powerful and sophisticated over the years. To Brussel, this certainly indicated that the unknown subject, or UNSUB, as we say in police terminology, probably had had a job involving electricity, metalworking, pipe fitting, or something related, which would have been consistent with employment with a large power company. Since these skills are often learned in the military and in 1956 many American males were veterans of World War II, it seemed likely he had some military background involving technical skills.

The one thing that could be said with some certainty was that the bomber believed Con Ed and the mysterious "others" were responsible for some accident or event that had left him chronically ill and that he had been obsessed with this belief for at least the last sixteen years. This obsession had probably been going on a lot longer than that, since Brussel knew from his psychiatric experience that most fixations take time to brew and fester before they are acted upon. But though the first device had been directed specifically against Con Ed, the bomber had quickly expanded his targets to a wide variety of public spaces, as if he was now trying to punish the public at large, and believed that everybody in New York City was potentially out to get him.

"What kind of man would harbor such a belief?" Dr. Brussel wrote in his memoirs, *Casebook of a Crime Psychiatrist.* "I was forced to a conclusion: the Mad Bomber was suffering from paranoia.

"Paranoia, to define it in textbook language, is a chronic disorder of insidious development, characterized by persistent, unalterable, systematized, logically constructed delusions. The definition fit the Mad Bomber, as far as I knew him, perfectly."

The bomber's communications with newspapers certainly demonstrated to Brussel a persistent, sys-

8

tematized, and logically constructed delusion. It seemed to have developed insidiously and, judging by the growing sophistication and lethality of the bombs, was continuing to develop. From his psychiatric perspective, Brussel knew this type of individual to be narcissistic, self-centered, and convinced of his own moral rightness, even if the whole world seemed to be allied against him. But for these hostile forces, he would succeed, conquer, flourish. Maybe it was Con Ed originally, but now everyone was the enemy.

That was not to say you could pick this guy out of a crowd from his behavior. Quite the contrary, except for his directed antisocial behavior—in this case the bombings—he might be expected to behave in a legal and proper fashion. After all, he was the one who had been wronged, and far be it from him to stoop to the level of those beneath him. He could be expected to write letters making all sorts of bizarre legal threats, but in his own context, that would seem absolutely proper. He would never, for instance, threaten someone directly. This, interestingly enough, was a trait we were later to see over and over again in serial killers. The one they actually felt they had the grudge against—mother, girlfriend, boss—was often the last person they could bring themselves to confront.

In a sense, Brussel surmised, the Mad Bomber probably saw himself as both victim and avenging angel. Such people are tough to treat from a psychiatric point of view because they don't believe there's anything wrong with them. The problem is with everyone else.

Inspector Finney found this discussion interesting, but he hadn't heard anything he couldn't have figured out on his own, and nothing so far to help him get closer to the bomber.

"Is there any way you can describe him to us?" Finney asked.

Brussel hesitated. He wasn't a cop. He hadn't examined physical evidence. He didn't know any bombers personally. But the police had come to him for help, and he thought he'd take a shot.

"He's symmetrically built," he began, "neither fat nor skinny."

The three cops exchanged skeptical glances. "How did you arrive at that?"

Actually, it had been a statistical guess, Brussel later admitted in his memoirs. He had followed the work of the noted German psychiatrist, Ernst Kretschmer, who had studied thousands of psychiatric patients in an attempt to match physical build with personality type. Kretschmer's study suggested that about 85 percent of all paranoiacs had a symmetrical, or athletic, body. As weird or baseless as this might at first sound, follow-up studies by other pioneers such as psychologist William Sheldon have shown a certain validity to this approach. We've found, for instance, that manic-depressives tend to be heavyset and nervous; high-strung people tend to be thin.

So, emboldened by this first step, Brussel continued. The Mad Bomber would now be in his early fifties. Paranoia is a slowly developing disease, the doctor explained, usually not coming into full bloom until the mid-thirties. They knew that the bomber had been at work for at least sixteen years, and that his latest activities marked the blossoming, not the planting, of the initial seed.

The communications Finney showed Brussel were the work of a neat, obsessively meticulous man. Every letter of every word was carefully penned and precise. If and when his Con Ed personnel file was found, it would reveal a solid, reliable, cooperative worker. He would have been polite, punctual, and neatly dressed—up until the day that the perceived injustice occurred. Then his world would have turned upside down.

The level of articulateness of the letters suggested the bomber had some education—probably not college, but high school. More significant, though, was his use of the "dastardly deed" type of phrase, which hadn't been in popular usage since Victorian melo-dramas. Also, he continually referred to "the Consolidated Edison" or "the Con Ed." He had obviously been around since before 1940, yet most New Yorkers routinely referred to the company simply as "Con Ed," without the definite article. This suggested someone of a European background, to whom English was not a first language. In spite of the letter writer's obvious anger and passion, there was a formal, stilted tone to each paragraph. In fact, this guy, in his meticulous, obsessive fashion, was probably thinking in his native language, then translating into English.

The way Brussel was evaluating the letters was a precursor of what we now refer to as psycholinguistic analysis, and as we shall see, a trained and experienced profiler can reach a rich lode of information this way.

On a related front, something else about the handwriting struck Brussel as significant. While twenty-five letters of the alphabet were consistently sharp and blocky, the *W*'s were oddly but consistently misshapen into twin rounded forms the psychiatrist speculated might subconsciously represent the female breasts or the male scrotum.

"His censoring conscience kept all his other printed characters standing rigidly at attention, but there was something inside him so strong that it dodged or bulldozed past his conscience when he penned a *W*."

The method of planting bombs in theaters—slashing the undersides of seats—represented the same kind of deep, hidden motivation. Brussel thought this could have something to do with an Oedipal tendency the bomber didn't want to face. From there, Brussel constructed a portrait of a man who'd never gotten past the Oedipal phase, who would have no close friendships with men and no meaningful relationships with women. He would not be married and might likely still be a virgin. Brussel guessed he'd never even kissed a girl. He would live alone or with a female relative who reminded him of his mother— either an aunt or sister. Since the police had already concluded that the types of tools the bomber used probably required a house-size workshop rather than something that could be crammed into an apartment, this suggested that he lived with female relatives rather than alone. This was not the type of person who would live alone in a house.

So, putting it all together, Brussel described a symmetrically built, neat, and clean-shaven middle-aged white male of European background, a polite but friendless loner who lived with a sister or aunt in a house. There would be nothing flashy about his appearance. When he was employed, presumably by Con Ed or one of its precursors, he would have done his job well but would not have mingled with other employees. He would have eaten lunch alone and would not have attended company picnics or other social events.

Both from the psycholinguistic analysis and from the types of weapons used, Brussel was willing to bet the Mad Bomber was not only European but Slavic. A Slav would be more likely to use a bomb than a gun to settle his scores, Brussel felt. If he was a Slav, he'd probably be a Roman Catholic, and if his religious devotion fit in with the rest of his life and habits, he'd be a regular churchgoer.

As to where he lived, Brussel focused on Connecticut. Most of the letters had been postmarked either in New York City or in Westchester County. A man as fastidious and careful as this would never make so basic a mistake as to mail his communications from his own town or city. He would mail them either in New York, where he was setting his bombs, or somewhere between his home and New York. On his forays into the city, he could drive partway and then take either a commuter train or subway the rest of the way in. Brussel knew there was a large Polish community in Bridgeport, Connecticut, and that the state in general had many residents of Slavic origin. To get from Bridgeport, say, to New York City, he would have to go through Westchester.

The man believed he had a chronic illness that was Con Ed's fault. Whether it actually was or not would be hard to determine. The facts wouldn't necessarily get in the way of this guy's logic. But again playing the odds, Brussel felt there were three good possibilities: heart disease, cancer, and tuberculosis. Cancer was a long shot, due to the time that had obviously elapsed since the first incident. If it was cancer, he would either have been cured or long since dead. With the antibiotics available in the mid-1950s, tuberculosis was treatable and manageable. That left heart disease. Since this covers such a multitude of causes and effects, both physical and emotional, Brussel's profile called for someone who either had, or thought he had, a chronic heart condition.

As a wrap-up, Brussel told the detectives that whenever they found this middle-aged, foreign-born white Slavic male with a heart condition who lived in a house in Connecticut with his sister or aunt, he would be fastidiously but not flashily dressed.

"When you find him, chances are he'll be wearing a double-breasted suit. Buttoned."

So that was the profile James Brussel gave to the frankly stunned police officers. But then what? Many times I've given highly detailed profiles to local police departments around the country, only to have someone respond, "Okay, Douglas, but what's his name and address?" As much as the people in my unit and I may resent working our asses off helping someone with a case that's primarily their responsibility, not ours, there is a point to this. A profile, if you have faith in it, might help you limit your suspect pool, but it only goes so far. What the profile should suggest is a proactive strategy for using it.

And that was, in fact, what Brussel did in this first

real-life profile. He suggested to the police that they use every means at their disposal to publicize his evaluation, forcing the bomber into the open to respond or comment. On one level, he was having the satisfaction of terrorizing the public and outfoxing the police, proving to himself what he had believed all along—that he was smarter than everyone else. But on another level, in his everyday life, he was still this insignificant nobody who probably got ignored at lunch counters and department stores. The increasing size and complexity of his bombs spoke to Brussel of the bomber's growing frustration at not being recognized. A part of him wanted to go public, to let the world see him in all his glory.

Finney pointed out that the department had maintained a policy of letting out as little information as possible. But "by putting these theories of mine in the papers," Brussel recalled saying, "you might prod the bomber out of hiding. He'll read what I've said about him. Maybe a lot of my theories will be wrong, maybe all of them. It'll challenge him. He'll say to himself, 'Here's some psychiatrist who thinks he's clever, thinks he can outfox me—me, the Bomber! Well, he's all wet, and I'll tell him so.' And then maybe he'll write to some newspaper and tell how wrong I am. He might give his correct age and other clues—who knows? It's an outside chance, but it's worth trying, I think. And if my theories are anywhere close to the mark, there's a chance somebody might recognize him—a mail carrier, a local merchant, a fellow employee. . . ."

The police did take Brussel's advice, though they may have been sorry they did. For weeks, everyone saw the Mad Bomber—in the neighborhood, on the train, in movie theaters and libraries, in parks and supermarkets. A special Bomb Investigation Unit was established under the direction of a veteran and well-respected chief inspector named Edward Byrnes. Throughout late December and into January of 1957,

Byrnes's unit handled between fifty and a hundred bomb reports a day!

As Brussel imagined, with all this publicity, the bomber would feel compelled to show off his cleverness and expertise. Early in the afternoon on December 24, an unexploded bomb, obviously the Mad Bomber's handiwork, was found in a phone booth at the main branch of the New York Public Library at Fifth Avenue and Forty-second Street. Four days later, another was found in a seat at the palatial Paramount Theater in Times Square.

Brussel himself got a taunting phone call in the middle of the night from a caller identifying himself as "F.P." Brussel and the police had been prepared for such a possibility, but the caller was smart enough to get off the line before a trace could be initiated.

Meanwhile, as they had the time, various Con Ed employees were slowly and laboriously plowing through the mountains of employee claim records. But now with Dr. Brussel's guidance, at least they had some idea what they were looking for.

At the company's main office at Fourteenth Street and Irving Place, south of Gramercy Park, three secretaries were reading through injury compensation files whenever their other duties allowed. By the second week in January 1957, they were up to files from the late 1920s and into the 1930s that had belonged to some of the companies that had been consolidated into Con Ed. There were so many liability claims, so many disgruntled employees, so many individual incidents that their eyes tended to glaze over with the details.

Late on Friday, January 18, one of the three women, Alice Kelly, came upon a file folder marked "Metesky, George." According to the record, George Metesky had been employed as a generator wiper at the Hell Gate plant of United Electric & Power, one of Con Ed's precursors, beginning in 1929. On September 5, 1931, a backdraft of hot gases from a boiler had knocked him down. Though doctors found no serious or permanent injury, Metesky insisted that the incident had left him permanently disabled. At first the company let him stay home and gave him sick pay, but eventually he was perceived to be malingering and was dropped from the payroll. United Electric seemed to be one of the "others" F.P. referred to in his letters.

In a claim filed before the Workmen's Compensation Board on January 4, 1934, Metesky asked for permanent disability pay, stating that the accident had left him with tuberculosis. The claim was denied, and over the next three years Metesky wrote increasingly volatile letters demanding his rights, bitterly complaining about the "dastardly deeds" perpetrated against him by the company. But then he became silent and disappeared. The last entry in the file was dated 1937.

Recognizing the phrase "dastardly deeds," Kelly dug out the rest of Metesky's personnel files and sifted through them carefully. Mr. Metesky had joined the marines after World War I and had been trained in the service as an electrician. He had had a sterling employment record up until his accident—everything Brussel had predicted. His age at the time would make him fifty-four if he was still alive. He was a Roman Catholic born in Poland. His last known address was 17 Fourth Street in Waterbury, Connecticut. Other than the fact that he'd dismissed tuberculosis in favor of heart disease, Brussel's profile seemed right on the money. And if this was the UNSUB, he'd provided enough information for a reader to recognize a hot file when she saw it.

Byrnes's Bomb Investigation Unit asked the Waterbury police for a check on the specified premises, but at first they couldn't find any George Metesky. It had belonged to a Mr. Adam Milauskas in the 1920s and had been deeded over to his son, George Milauskas, who had owned it during the time in question. A discreet check in this rather shabby neighborhood of

Irish, Italians, and Middle Europeans revealed that though he'd never changed it officially, George Milauskas had, since grade school, gone by the name Metesky. Neighbors described him as polite but "strange," a loner with no known close friends.

The clincher came on Monday morning when a letter from F.P. arrived at the office of the New York *Journal-American*. It made reference to a date he must have figured would be meaningless to the paper and the police but which would demonstrate his own superior knowledge and understanding: September 5, 1931—the date of George Metesky's accident at the Hell Gate power plant.

Late that night, four New York City detectives drove up to Waterbury, Connecticut, and knocked on the door of number 17 Fourth Street. George Metesky, a man of medium height and average weight, answered the door in his pajamas. He was unfailingly polite to the detectives and willingly complied when they asked for a sample of his handwriting. It matched the angry and taunting letters exactly.

"What does F.P. stand for?" one of the officers asked.

"Fair play," Metesky replied.

The detectives placed him under arrest and asked him to get dressed for the ride into the city. He left the room to do so and to inform the two unmarried sisters with whom he lived. When he returned, he was wearing a double-breasted suit, neatly buttoned.

Normally, when a suspect is subjected to what police call the "perp walk," where he is paraded past the hungry press on his way to appear before a judge or magistrate, you see a glazed expression, an attempt to hide his face or place a coat over his head, or you will hear shouted claims that he is innocent or the wrong man. The newspaper photos of the captured Mad Bomber show a smiling man with a twinkle in his eye who is clearly enjoying all the attention and publicity. I find this very significant.

Metesky was kept in custody in Bellevue Hospital, where medical tests revealed that one lung was actively tubercular. A course of antibiotic therapy was instituted, and gradually, Metesky's condition improved. In reviewing his own reasoning process and his exclusion of tuberculosis, Brussel saw his analytical mistake: his failure to realize that many paranoiacs would mistrust a doctor as much as they would mistrust anyone else, feeling they knew more, and therefore would not go for treatment.

Brussel visited Metesky several times over the years at Matteawan State Hospital, which has a facility for the criminally insane. He was always neat, proper, and very cordial.

The police in various cities continued to call on Dr. James Brussel, including such celebrated cases as the Boston Strangler and the Coppolino murder.

Special Agent Howard Teten, who taught applied criminal psychology at the FBI Academy, became interested in Dr. Brussel's work in the late 1960s and early 1970s and began corresponding and consulting with him, trying to apply Brussel's observations and principles to the police understanding of criminal behavior.

When I came to the Academy as a young agent, fresh from a couple of years as a field agent in Detroit and then Milwaukee, Teten and his associate, Dick Ault, were the FBI's recognized masters of what was then referred to as behavioral science. Behavioral profiling, in the sense that Brussel practiced it, was strictly an informal activity Teten practiced in his spare time when police colleagues who had been through his course at the Academy would ask his hunch on a particular open case they were working on. Eventually, police students began asking for help from some of the other behavioral science instructors, including Ault, Jim Reese, Dick Harper, Tom O'Malley, Bob Ressler, and the new guy, me.

I was in my early thirties when I was assigned to the

Behavioral Science Unit, teaching classes to police officers often a generation older than me. It used to scare the hell out of me that I might be standing up there in front of the class, imparting the FBI's received wisdom on a particular case to a group of hardened cops, and I'd have one raise his hand and say, "Hold on a minute, Mr. Douglas. I worked that case and that's not the way it went down at all," or "I arrested that guy, and he was nothing like what you say."

Where did we get off, I wondered to myself, telling cops their own business? If we were going to say anything meaningful about a case or a type of crime, we'd better damn well know what we were talking about.

Not all of the training took place at the Academy. We also conducted week-long "road schools," in which usually two of us would go to a local police or sheriff's department or an FBI field office and teach for a week, then move on for a week at another location before heading back home. Bob Ressler and I used to do a lot of these road schools, and I recall one time in 1978 we were in Sacramento. I remember commenting to him that away from home, there are only so many margaritas you can drink and only so much television you can watch. As long as we were out on the road anyway, why didn't we go into the prisons wherever we were and interview some of these guys we'd been talking about in class? Get the story straight from the horse's mouth, as it were. That way, we could start to see what really made them tick and tell the cops and other agents something valuable.

I already had something of a reputation as a blue flamer in the Bureau, but Ressler went along with me, even though we both knew this was something Headquarters was unlikely to applaud or instantly approve. Even more than "Just the facts, ma'am," the primary principle by which we all lived was "Don't embarrass the Bureau." We both knew that if anything we did came back to cause embarrassment to the Bureau, they'd hang us out to dry like surplus laundry.

The first subject we interviewed was Edmund Kemper III, an inmate at the California State Medical Facility at Vacaville, between Sacramento and San Francisco. As a teen, Kemper had shot and killed both his grandparents, had done time in a juvenile facility, had been released, and was regularly reporting his psychological progress to a therapist while he was picking up, raping, and murdering college coeds and other young women in and around the University of California at Santa Cruz. He had finally worked through his displaced anger and rage and killed the one person he really felt had messed up his life—his mother—and then a close friend of hers. Having gotten this out of his system, he turned himself in to police. Certainly this is an oversimplification of Kemper's story, but those are some of the basic details.

Kemper is a giant of a man with an equally large intellect. He spoke to us for several hours on several occasions and gave us tremendous insight into the mind of a serial killer. We went on to interview many other violent offenders and eventually compiled a rigorous study with Dr. Ann Burgess of the University of Pennsylvania. Eventually we published two books based on our work: *Sexual Homicide: Patterns and Motives,* and the *Crime Classification Manual.*

Gradually but steadily I became more and more involved in profiling and less and less involved in teaching until I was the only full-time profiler in the unit. But as I've implied, what I and such other colleagues as Special Agent Roy Hazelwood, another instructor who became interested in profiling, were doing was far from FBI or forensic science orthodoxy.

In one murder case in New York, for example, the police had no idea after a year who had strangled a young woman on the stairway landing of her apartment building. Their only lead was a pubic hair from a black male, which had been found in the body bag. I looked at crime scene photos and told them their UNSUB was a white male in his early twenties who was unemployed, had no driver's license, lived within a mile of the scene, was related to someone in the building, would be disheveled in appearance and nocturnal by habit, would spook easily, had been institutionalized, and was on medication. He had no college education, military experience, or serious criminal record, I told the police, and he had undoubtedly already been interviewed in the normal course of the investigation. And I turned out to be right.

We needed successes like that to make our potential clients, as well as our bosses and fellow agents, into believers. And when Tom Barrett called me from Chicago to tell me about an unknown bomber, I was very much looking for believers.

TYPES OF BOMBERS

Before you can come up with an accurate profile or effective proactive strategy, you have to know what kind of crime you're dealing with. It may be a murder, but there are many types of murders and murderers, and unless you know how to classify the one before you, you're not going to get very far. The classification system my Quantico colleagues and I developed was based on firsthand knowledge from the experts—the offenders themselves. Before our study, there were a lot of suppositions based on academic teachings and psychological theory, but no one could actually say what aspects of those suppositions came from real-world experience.

In classifying a bombing, the critical elements to us are victimology, crime scene indicators, victim-offender relationship, type and/or construction of the bomb, and any elements of staging.

Then we ask a number of questions. The more of them we can answer, the more complete our product can be.

Under victimology: Is the victim known to the offender? What is the risk level—that is, how strong were the victim's chances of becoming a victim? What is the offender's risk level of being identified in or around the scene? For example, if he places the bomb in the middle of a full football stadium, his risk level is obviously very high. If he mails it to a private home, his risk level is obviously considerably lower. And either of these circumstances will tell you something meaningful about the bomber.

Were the targets chosen discriminately or indiscriminately? To make the determination you review the delivery system used by the bomber. For example, was the bomb addressed to a specific person or was it addressed to the university or to an individual department?

It is more difficult to assess the motive of the offender if the bombs are sent indiscriminately. In assessing a series of cases, you are looking for common denominators or threads that link the cases together. Unfortunately, a single bomb is more more difficult to use in assessing motive than a series. In assessing cases, more is generally better.

How many crime scenes are there? Are they clustered in one limited geographical area or are there many locations?

Criminals are no different from law-abiding people when it comes to being creatures of habit. We feel comfortable in areas where we work and live, and so does the bomber. Consequently, the first set of cases will be in one of these familiar areas. And he will remain there as long as he believes his identity will not be revealed or his personal safety compromised.

What about specific place and time? Indoors or outdoors? Daylight or nighttime? Urban, suburban, or rural?

We consider all of these factors when we are attempting to place a label on the motive as well as to develop personality characteristics of the offender.

Was the bomb delivered by mail, planted by the offender, or carried by a third party? Sending a package bomb through the mail requires much more technical ability. The package bomb must be detonated by the intended victim when the package is opened, not before.

In most cases in which a third party is involved, such as terrorist airplane bombings, the carriers do not know they are delivering a bomb and in many instances they are killed or injured by the blast.

All of the aforementioned factors are gauged to help determine the risk level on the part of the offender and victim. Offenders begin to increase their risk level over time. Psychologists and criminologists will sometimes state that the reason for this change in behavior is that they want to be apprehended. It has been my experience, on the other hand, that at a certain point offenders begin to feel invincible or uncatchable. As I point out frequently, they feel they are above the law and smarter than the authorities. This is a positive change in favor of law enforcement, because sooner or later the bomber will make a mistake.

How many offenders are there? Many bombers are no different from extortionists who send some form of communication to the intended victim or law enforcement agency. In this communication they almost always use the plural "we" or "our" to imply that they are part of a larger group or organization.

If the assessment determines that the motive is group-caused, there will be more than one offender. However, due to their paranoia, typical bombers they almost always act alone. Why? Because they don't trust anyone.

We also have a number of statistical factors that we

must plug in, such as race and gender. Historically, most bombers have been male, and most have been white. Over the years we occasionally have had female bombers, but their targets tend to be family members or close associates. Very rarely, if ever, will they go for an unknown or indiscriminately chosen target.

Most bombers are single or involved in a marriage of convenience. The wife or girlfriend is made to feel subservient to the bomber.

What about staging? Many crimes are staged. That is, there is an attempt on the offender's part to deflect the investigation away from the logical suspect. During the course of my career I have done many analyses and testified in cases where a husband or wife has killed his or her spouse. An attempt is subsequently undertaken to make the scene look as if the spouse died at the hands of a burglar or rapist.

Since we know a lot more about the subtle details of how each type of crime is "supposed" to look than the offender, staging often gives us a lot of good behavioral evidence to go on. (So I'll just say parenthetically here that if you're thinking about killing your spouse and trying to make it look like some other type of crime, forget it. It won't work.)

The bomber will often stage his crimes by sending a communiqué. The analysis should determine if the crime fits the message that the bomber wants us to believe. We must always be suspicious. He may be setting us up, particularly if he has left few clues and has eluded law enforcement for some considerable period of time.

What are the forensic findings? This evidence will be critical in linking any potential suspects to the crime.

Crime detection has become much more sophisticated over the years. Blood, hair, fiber, fingerprints, and psycholinguistic analysis may link a suspect to a bombing. Psycholinguistics, as I've implied earlier, is a fancy word for the process of analyzing language with the purpose of assessing the personality and critical choices of the author of the communiqué.

If letters or packages are sent, we have added evidence that can be assessed forensically. Though the capability didn't exist back in 1980 when we started profiling Unabomber, now we can often subject licked stamps to DNA analysis.

As for the bomb device itself, what level of expertise was necessary to construct it? Is the bomber a technician who's had certain vocational or educational experience? Or could he have gone to the nearest library and checked out one of the many books that have been published describing and depicting how a bomb can be made?

Are there unique components? Unique workmanship? Unique design? Are the bomber and builder the same individual?

Another important factor to assess is the risk level to the offender in constructing the device. By talking to forensic bomb experts we must learn if making the bomb created any degree of danger to the bomber or if the risk level was low.

When we have a mobile offender with bombings occurring over a wide geographical area, motive is often the thorniest issue to resolve. The classification of the bomber initially may fall into one or more categories. It could be a criminal enterprise, a personal cause, a group cause, a psychologically disorganized individual, or a mix of these elements.

We know from some cases of extortion, arson, and product tampering that the offenders may be driven principally by a desire for power. Their otherwise drab and colorless lives seem more exciting if they can get this kind of reaction out of so many people, mobilize large police and fire and rescue resources, and generally have a public effect.

Traditional motives are clearly related to normal,

though hideously exaggerated, emotions. Anger, hatred, and love are typical. Revenge or retaliation can be methods of acting out these feelings. In cases of extortion, product tampering, arson, and bombing, the motive is not always clear.

A criminal-enterprise bombing may be undertaken for material gain, such as insurance or inheritance. On November 1, 1955, twenty-three-year-old Jack Gilbert Graham drove his mother, Mrs. Daisie King, to the airport in Denver and put on her United Airlines Flight 629. Eleven minutes after takeoff, the DC-6 exploded in midair and thirty-nine passengers and five crew members plunged to their death. The cause of the explosion was a bomb planted by Graham in his mother's suitcase. At the airport he had taken out several hefty policies on his mother's life from insurance vending machines. Graham, who was convicted of first degree murder and executed in the Colorado gas chamber in 1957, had once commented to a neighbor, "I'd do anything for money."

Under the heading of personal cause, we would include bombings that aren't motivated by the quest for material gain and are not sanctioned by a group of, say, political terrorists or by some hate organization. It is the underlying emotional conflict that propels the bomber to act out his anger and/or frustration.

On December 16, 1989, in a suburb near Birmingham, Alabama, Mrs. Helen Vance was wrapping Christmas gifts when the mailman brought a package addressed to her husband, Federal Court of Appeals Judge Robert Vance. The bomb contained in this package exploded with such force that the judge was killed instantly.

Then, in a room of the Atlanta, Georgia, Federal Court of Appeals, an X-ray check intercepted a second bomb. A third device turned up in a Jacksonville, Florida, office of the National Association for the

Advancement of Colored People. In Savannah, Georgia, a fourth bomb went off, killing Robbie Robinson, a lawyer who had done legal work for the NAACP.

After seventeen federal judges across the Southeast received threats and another communiqué warned that more NAACP officials would be murdered, panic spread.

Walter Moody, Jr., a brilliant and charming chameleon of a man was indicted and later convicted of homicide. Nearly seventeen years earlier, Moody had been one of seventy-four subjects arrested for bootlegging whiskey in Georgia. For years, Moody had complained to ATF Agent Chet Bryant about the perceived mishandling of the bootlegging case. Bryant later recalled that Moody's wife, Hazel, was maimed in an explosion.

Moody targeted his victims because of the paranoid belief that he was somehow wronged by the judicial system. Moody's "personal cause" was revenge.

A group cause, on the other hand, pertains to two or more people with a common ideology who sanction the act committed by one or more of its members.

On February 26, 1993, at eighteen minutes past noon, a massive bomb exploded in an underground parking garage beneath the Twin Towers of the World Trade Center near the tip of Manhattan. Of the 50,000 people in the 110-story towers, six individuals were killed and over a thousand sustained some injury.

Two days after the explosion, one of the ATF's explosive experts found the remnants of a medium-size van that evidently had been used to transport the explosives. Found on its chassis were the remains of a vehicle identification number, which allowed the van to be traced to a Ryder Truck Rental Company office in New Jersey. Sheik Omar Abdel Rahman, a blind radical Egyptian cleric, was directly linked to the bombing. Rahman, along with three conspirators, was charged and convicted.

The disorganized and sometimes mentally unstable bomber almost always acts alone. A disorganized bombing incident or site may be the work of a youthful offender, a subject under the influence of alcohol or drugs, or someone who lacks criminal experience and/or sophistication or mental stability. Consequently, disorganized bombers are much easier to identify.

They may also experience delusions and hallucinations, and they will take little care to hide or mask themselves. While we see this type of individual more frequently in other serious crimes, including murder, it is rare to see one in a bombing due to the technical experience level required to make a bomb effectively and safely.

The last category is a catch-all classification used when the motive is not clear. We speak of this category as "mixed." An example of this type might be an abortion clinic bombing. Is this a group-cause crime perpetrated by an extreme pro-life organization? Or is it a personal-cause bombing for which one individual is responsible, whether or not he is also be part of a group?

If a motive cannot be clearly established, then proactive techniques might be used to try to flush out the bomber. The area of focus for these techniques should be within in the geographical area of the first bombing or cluster of bombings. Investigators focus on the very first case or first few cases because the offender can be linked directly to that area and because the subject is generally less criminally sophisticated at first and is not yet likely to have a well-defined modus operandi.

Let me say a few words about search-warrant considerations.

If you've gotten to the point where you have a potential suspect and are going for a search warrant, you should be looking for some specific things. Among them would be books on making bombs, possibly books or articles on political philosophy to support or justify intellectually his actions, scrapbooks or clippings of previous cases, and of course tools and materials to make the bombs.

If you've been accurate in your classification, you shouldn't have too many surprises.

THE MANHUNT

The most expensive manhunt in United States history, ultimately costing upward of $50 million, began with a relatively insignificant event. On May 25, 1978, what appeared to be a lost package was found in a parking lot on the campus of the University of Illinois at Chicago. Addressed to a professor of engineering at upstate New York's Rensselaer Polytechnic Institute, the package had the return address of a professor from Northwestern University and so was forwarded to Northwestern to be returned to its presumed sender, Buckley Crist, a professor of material sciences. The explosion that injured Terry Marker, a police officer on the Northwestern campus the next day marked the beginning of the eighteen-year search for the mysterious bomber whose case the FBI would dub "Unabom."

That first bomb, built of match heads and other

wooden components held together in a simple wood box, gave little indication of the complexity of the devices that would follow. Police were left with no apparent motive, no witnesses, and no clues other than the remains of the bomb itself—that is, until another bomb exploded in the same area almost exactly a year later.

In the second incident, another member of the Northwestern University community was injured—this time a thirty-five-year-old graduate student of civil engineering. John G. Harris suffered minor cuts and burns when he picked up a curious-looking cigar box, taped shut, that he found in a common area in the school's technological institute. Although shocking to the college community, the bombings were not yet big news outside the Chicago area. This was just one among many that occurred every year in the United States, and not a particularly noteworthy one on its own.

In November of that year, though, the stakes grew higher with the bomber's next target: American Airlines Flight 444, in flight from Chicago to Dulles International Airport over the Virginia countryside outside of Washington, D.C. Although the bomb did not explode as intended, it caught fire in a mailbag in the cargo hold and forced an emergency landing. Twelve people on the plane had to be treated for smoke inhalation.

The bomber had moved beyond targeting one person at a time. He'd gone outside a university setting and was enlarging his base past the immediate Chicago area.

Tom Barrett and Chris Ronay, an FBI bomb expert who would go on to become chief of the Explosives Unit, focused on the airplane bomb's improvised detonator and showed the evidence around to other experts to see if they felt this was related to the previous explosions. There was a consensus that they were. The detonator was nearly unique.

But federal explosives specialists who studied the device recognized that the construction of the bomb was more sophisticated than investigators had imagined the university bomber capable of—the bomb's trigger was an altimeter, set to explode when pressure in the cabin reached a critical level.

The first two bombs at Northwestern—one placed in a handcrafted wooden box, the other in a cigar box—had earned the UNSUB the nickname "the Junkyard Bomber" at the FBI Crime Lab because the internal parts were constructed from leftover materials such as furniture pieces, plumbing pipes, and sink traps.

Seven months after the American Airlines incident, on June 10, 1980, another bomb was targeted at the airline industry, this time arriving at the Lake Forest, Illinois, residence of Percy Wood, the president of United Airlines. Wood suffered injuries on his hands, face, and thighs when a package bomb exploded in his suburban Chicago home. It was hidden inside *Ice Brothers,* a novel published by Arbor House, a company that used a tree leaf as its trademark. Given the name of his latest victim, the leaf trademark, and the construction of his bombs (usually largely fabricated from wood), investigators began to speculate that his message might be tied to an obsession with wood. Still, they were no closer to establishing a specific motive for the bomber's attacks.

It was at this point that Tom Barrett called me. And it was at this point that the multiagency task force was assembled.

* * *

A number of traditional forensic people were working the case, so if I had anything to contribute, it would have to be in the area of the unknown bomber's behavior.

Traditionally, police have used modus operandi, or M.O., as their primary guide to serial-crime linkage. In other words, they study the method by which the crime was accomplished—the use of a particular weapon, a note used by a bank robber, a technique for disabling a rape victim—in determining whether a series of offenses was committed by the same individual or group of bad guys. But as we studied more and more serial offenders and developed our profiling methods, we came to realize that while M.O. was important, in certain types of crimes it wasn't nearly as important as what I call "signature"—the unique aspect that was critical not so much to accomplish the crime as to *satisfy the perpetrator emotionally.* A sexual sadist, for example, might bind one victim with rope and take her home or use duct tape on another and place her in the trunk of his car, but his reason for abducting each of them is the same. Or he might use a whip on one and a pair of pliers on another, but in each case his signature is torture. He does what he has to do to acquire his victim, but what satisfies him emotionally is the torture and ultimate murder of that victim—his ability to manipulate, dominate, and control her. So while modus operandi is adaptable and evolutionary for a successful criminal, it's something he'll learn from and improve upon from crime to crime, whereas signature is relatively static. It's a clear indication of motive and therefore, to my way of thinking, a much more reliable indicator of serial-crime linkage.

My feeling has always been that if you can get into a case fairly early in the series, after the signature has been established but while the M.O. is still in the working-out stage, you get your clearest insight into the UNSUB and your best chance of catching him.

Just as there is a behavioral signature to many sadistic and violent serial crimes, there is also a physical signature to such hand-art crimes as bomb-making.

By the time I got involved in the Unabomber case, the FBI lab in Washington had already established distinctive links among the four cases. According to our experts, whom I personally believe to be the best in the world, all four bombs displayed a similar signature, an indication of the type of flair the maker obviously found emotionally satisfying: there was a high degree of handcrafting of elements that could have easily been bought in a hardware store; the experts also thought they had found a written signature of sorts on the bombs' bases: the initials "F.C." Immediately I thought of George Metesky's "F.P." and wondered if this bomber was a student of history.

In this case, unlike in the Metesky case, the problem was that there was no communication from UNSUB to victim, no clear or obvious relationship between the subject and any of the victims, and no apparent motive. Other than the physical forensic connections established by our labs, the only thing that stood out was that the first two targets had been *UN*iversity-related and the second two had been *A*irline-related, hence the FBI case code: *Una*bom.

The first task was to come up with a motive for the bombings. There was a combination of specific and nonspecific targets—that is, we had two bombs intended for particular individuals, and two that were essentially left for anyone to find. With no clear common denominator, how would we classify these crimes? Group? Personal Cause? What? And why had the subject shifted from universities to airlines?

I wondered if the subject had experienced some

precipitating event that prompted him to switch gears. Had he been traveling and felt he was slighted in some way by people working for the airlines? Since he had changed his focus like this, I thought perhaps the crime had become a personal cause. He was already motivated to cause harm to nonspecific victims; if he perceived he'd been mistreated by some company, individual, or group, that feeling could have led him to narrow or change his target.

On the federal, state, and local level, the United States has more than 17,000 separate law enforcement agencies. So as often happens with major cases, something of a turf war was brewing with Unabom. In addition to the FBI and the various police departments in places where the crimes had taken place, the Bureau of Alcohol, Tobacco and Firearms and the Office of the Postal Inspector also had legitimate interests. The multiagency task force was established to include all the key players.

In analyzing a crime from a behavioral perspective, we try to figure out what actually happened between the attacker and the victim. For example, my colleague Roy Hazelwood has shown how, in rape cases, the attacker's acts have a lot to do with how the victim reacts. This is not to say we can prescribe a specific way a victim should behave if she's unfortunate enough to be involved in a rape attempt, since there are various types of rapists. But if we can get a good interview with the victim afterward, we're going to know a hell of a lot about her attacker.

This applies across the board. When we analyze a murder, we try to find out as much about the victim as we possibly can. Victimology, as we call it, is as important as any other single aspect of our analysis. So in bombings, as in other more up-front and direct crimes, we needed to know as much about the victims as we did about the bombs. As background, I looked into what was going on in the Chicago area around that time—in the news generally and in politics, industry, academia, and airlines.

The early bombs were fairly unsophisticated but very carefully made. The risk level to the bomb-maker was low—that is, the devices were unlikely to blow up during construction. Likewise, the early bombs were not as deadly as the later ones turned out to be. They could blow your hands off if they exploded at close range, but they probably wouldn't kill you.

At that time, bombing was a relatively popular crime, although I hadn't been involved in many of the investigations. The FBI and ATF lab work, though, clearly differentiated F.C.'s work from all the others.

Some of the original suspects in the Chicago area were a group of college students who belonged to a Dungeons & Dragons club. But when they were brought in to the FBI office for questioning, it was clear they weren't going to pan out. Drawing on my experience with related types of crimes, I felt certain the bomber would be a lone subject. Like George Metesky and most other cowardly "distance crime" offenders, he wouldn't be comfortable around other people, certainly not to the extent that he would trust them.

Our research has shown that various types of crimes tend to begin at various ages. Therefore, we generally take age twenty-five as our starting point and add or subtract years depending on the details and specifics of the case. Based on the level of sophistication, I profiled a white male in his late twenties to early thirties. I thought he would be white because of the types of targets: airlines and universities. Culturally, I thought a black, Asian, or Hispanic individual would have other targets for his rage. And I thought the bomber was a male because female bombers were extremely rare and when they surfaced at all, they would typically target loved ones—or, should I say, former loved ones.

Like Metesky, he wouldn't be antisocial. Rather, he'd be asocial. He'd be the type of person who might hold a night job because he felt more comfortable when there weren't a lot of people around. It was unlikely he belonged to any sort of organized political group or movement, but if he did, he would be the guy in the background, not a demonstrator type. He'd be a secondary player or a gofer, sending out the letters or writing the flyers. He would also keep diaries, detailed notes, obsessive lists. He would trust only himself, so he would maintain an active self-dialogue.

For this reason, I didn't expect him to have a criminal record. He would, quite the contrary, be very careful to stay on the right side of the law at all times.

I visualized this subject as an obsessive-compulsive, a very rigid personality. As with most bomber and assassin types, the elements of his everyday life, such as eating habits and personal hygiene, would be in complete disarray. But what is really important to him would be immaculately kept. His library would be well organized. His garage and/or workshop would be kept under lock and key. All of his tools would have a specific, carefully labeled place. His bomb work area would be in perfect order, matching his rigid, ritualistic style. When the four NYPD detectives drove up to Connecticut to arrest George Metesky, for example, he proudly showed them his well-ordered workshop.

When an individual commits his first violent crime, there is almost always a "trigger." Something happens, some stress, that makes the person lash out, often against people he doesn't even know. There can be many different kinds of triggers, but the ones we've uncovered most often in our interviews with convicted offenders and our study of cases are loss of a job and the end of a relationship with a significant other person. Sometimes those two things will come together, as they did in a case my colleague Jud Ray handled in Anchorage, Alaska. In that one, an angry and emotionally volatile young man was jilted by his girlfriend, who immediately took up with his boss. The boss then fired him to be rid of the interference. Rocked by this double whammy, the young man brutally killed his aunt and two young girl cousins, whose stable and happy life he resented.

We had no real idea what the Unabomber's initial trigger might have been, but we were sure there was something.

As I've indicated, I believe a subject's earliest crimes are the most telling. He's fulfilling himself emotionally, but he has not yet perfected himself or his crime. If you understand the early crimes, you can study the subject in process. Therefore, despite the relative crudeness of the bombs, I felt we were dealing with someone with a strong connection to the academic world, either to Northwestern or the University of Illinois at Chicago, or both. Maybe he was an instructor who'd been turned down for tenure. Maybe he was an "ABD"—All But Dissertation—a frustrated, long-suffering grad student who just couldn't get it together to finish. Maybe he had some other type of grudge. But I was relatively certain this wasn't a blue-collar type. This guy was well educated and intellectual, with a strong grounding in the sciences.

There was some talk in police circles that our UNSUB was probably a Vietnam veteran and that he learned his bomb-making skills in the service. But from what I understood of his devices, it didn't appear that he would have needed a superior skill level to construct them. An intelligent person with some science background, as I expected him to be, could have gotten all he needed out of such readily available publications as *The Anarchist's Cookbook,* for example.

This is not to say I originally pegged the bomber as brilliant. Initially I just figured him to be of above average IQ. The longer his crime spree went on, however, the more respect I gained for his intelligence.

There is a danger in investing too much significance in the initials F.C. It was highly unlikely they stood for a name, so expending manpower combing records looking for names that matched up would be a huge waste. The letters meant something only to the user. Maybe they stood for "Fuck Computers" or something like that. Computers were a sufficiently universal symbol of our age that someone who felt on the outs with society enough to want to blow things up might possibly focus on the computer as the source of all ills. But that was just a guess.

Sometimes you have to hold something three feet from your face instead of three inches. When I interviewed serial killer David Berkowitz, the Son of Sam, in Attica, I asked him the significance of the wavy and curly lines at the bottom of some of his letters. Several psychiatrists had speculated that they might represent female breasts, specifically the breasts of his biological mother, who gave him up for adoption in infancy and whom he later tracked down. But he simply smiled and said, "I just liked the way it looked."

If the UNSUB had a car, it would be well maintained, given his level of technical expertise, but it would be an older, unflashy type of vehicle. This person would not have the money for a new car.

I thought the subject would be single and would have severe difficulty maintaining relationships with both men and women. It was possible that later in life, in his forties or fifties, he could have a relationship with a woman and even marry, but the marriage would be one of convenience. His wife or girlfriend would have to be someone who would always obey him if, for instance, he told her always to stay out of a particular room in the house. This pattern is fairly common. We had one serial killer who kept body parts from his victims in a large freezer in the garage. When his submissive and unknowing wife wanted a particular cut of meat to prepare for dinner, she had to ask him to get it for her. While she might have suspected something from her husband's secretiveness, she would never have challenged him on it.

All in all, though, I would expect this guy to remain single throughout his life.

The offender would be similar in many ways to arsonists I had studied. Like other types of criminals, there is a range of arsonists, from the nuisance type to someone intent on hurting people. Bombing is also like arson in the sense that most of the evidence goes up in flames, making analysis difficult.

Still, from the victimology, I could see no apparent motive or common denominator to this bomber's crimes.

I thought a good first step would be to go to newspapers in the Chicago area, including college papers, to look for letter writers. Before the subject decided upon his course of criminal action, he would likely have signed his real name to his letters, since he wouldn't yet have had anything to hide.

In focusing on the early crimes, I noted that the first incident took place around Memorial Day. Although not apparently meaningful to others, this day could hold some significance to him.

Going public with this profile of the guy, focusing more on pre- and post-offense behavior than on specifics such as age can be an important investigative technique. People don't just wake up one morning and say, "I'm going to be a bomber." An arsonist might do this, although he probably wouldn't. But while anyone can light a match, bombing is something one has to learn and practice first. There are earlier steps that someone close—a parent, a teacher, a neighbor—would recognize if, for example, the kid next door has been setting nuisance fires or mistreating the neighborhood cats.

In 1980, I'd only been at this game for about three years and the FBI wasn't ready for a full-court press. In an organization as large and complex as ours, "analysis paralysis" can easily set in if you have to explain your methods or get permissions to try proactive techniques such as working with the media or using a decoy. This was several years before the Wayne Williams–Atlanta Child Murder case really spotlighted our proactive techniques, giving them national attention and public authentification.

There was also the feeling in a lot of Bureau circles that since we couldn't use a behavioral profile as evidence in court, what good was it? Why bother?

This tussle between the operational people and the behavioral people will probably always be ongoing, though I like to think it can be resolved to everyone's satisfaction. Years later, for instance, my people and I were deeply frustrated by the events at Ruby Ridge and Waco, where we felt our message based on our knowledge of profiling either wasn't being listened to or wasn't being understood. But it doesn't have to be this way. In my career I've experienced many examples of terrific and productive cooperation between us and the front-line police troops and forensic guys.

Finally, I felt certain the Unabom crimes would continue to grow in sophistication and dangerousness as the UNSUB perfected his craft. There was a good chance we'd start to see some social or political justification for his violence and an even better chance that he would move his operations farther outside the Chicago area.

On October 8, 1981, sixteen months after the blast that injured Percy Wood, another bomb was found by a maintenance worker in a business classroom at the University of Utah at Salt Lake City. A bomb squad got to it and was able to diffuse it before it went off. When it was analyzed in the lab, the report came back: Unabomber had struck again. And he had moved outside the Chicago area. Still, we had little more to go on than we'd had the previous year.

The next mysterious wooden box was received May 5, 1982, addressed to Professor Patrick Fischer, a computer scientist at Vanderbilt University in Nashville, Tennessee. Tracing the path to the intended victim of this bomb was a little more complicated, though. The package was addressed to Fischer's previous place of work at Pennsylvania State University, a position he'd left two years earlier. Someone had forwarded it from Pennsylvania to Nashville. But how the package even got as far as the Pennsylvania address was something of a mystery, since the bomber had used canceled stamps when he mailed it in Provo, Utah. It appeared that this bomb was intended to work like the very first bomb, the one that injured the Northwestern campus security officer: the intended victim may have been the person named in the return address. In this case, that was Brigham Young University electrical engineering professor LeRoy Bearnson. Although the link with Bearnson was no more apparent than with Fischer or any of the other recipients thus far, we were interested to learn that Bearnson's middle name was Wood.

But the package never made it "back" to Bearnson. Instead, Fischer's secretary, Janet Smith, was injured and had to be treated for lacerations when the bomb inside the parcel exploded.

Only a couple of months later, on July 2, a professor at the University of California at Berkeley became the victim of the next bomb. A professor of engineering and applied physics, Diogenes Angelakos, went to move a package, described as a "green container with wires hanging out of it," or perhaps a can of some kind left in the faculty lounge.

It was relatively early in the morning, around eight o'clock, and Angelakos thought the container might have been left behind by construction workers or by a student. Another nonspecific target of the Unabomber, Angelakos suffered severe burns on his right hand when the small pipe bomb exploded.

The next few years were quiet, with no more of the distinctive bombs making an appearance until May 15, 1985. Unfortunately, the bomber now seemed intent on making up for lost time: a total of four Unabom devices exploded before the end of the year, including the first lethal explosion.

Berkeley was targeted again for the first bombing of that year. Engineering graduate student John Hauser, an aspiring astronaut and air force pilot, casually picked up a box along with a stack of notebooks he'd found in a second-floor computer lab. The booby-trapped bomb, sitting under a black binder, took off parts of several fingers on Hauser's right hand and tore apart his forearm, opening two main arteries. As part of his hand blew off, Hauser's Air Force Academy ring burst across the room with such force that it left an imprint of the word "Academy" in the plaster of a wall.

This bomb was clearly more powerful than the previous devices. In addition to the signature wood, it contained a mixture of ammonium nitrate and aluminum powder.

Although Hauser survived the explosion and went on to earn his Ph.D. and eventually become a professor, the Unabomber had destroyed his dreams of space flight as he continued to terrorize the Berkeley community.

It was apparently just an extraordinary coincidence that Professor Angelakos was across the hall when the bomb went off injuring Hauser. He heard the explosion and fashioned a tourniquet out of a colleague's tie for Hauser's arm. Angelakos, whose wife had died of cancer one month after his brush with the bomb, is the only known dual recipient of the Unabomber's work.

It was after this blast that the Unabomber made his first contact with the media. In a letter addressed to the *San Francisco Examiner,* he identified himself as part of a terrorist group known as the Freedom Club, whose initials, F.C., would continue to show up on nearly all the later bombs. The only clue to the offender's motivation and target selection was the letter's emphasis on the club's political and antitechnology-antiscience sentiments. Despite his mention of the Freedom Club, this was not inconsistent with a single person.

And this bomber was progressing with his crimes like many of those I'd interviewed. The bombs were getting stronger and more deadly because the bomber's fantasy of power and control was growing. The more frightening the explosions, the more power he holds. After seriously injuring Hauser, this bomber would not be satisfied with match heads and smokeless gunpowder. We all felt strongly that we had to get this guy, because he wasn't going to stop on his own and he wasn't going to get less dangerous.

When a subject moves his target, the investigation can be hampered. FBI Headquarters shifted the investigating office of origin from Chicago to the San Francisco Field Office. Although Tom Barrett continued to be consulted, Chicago had become merely an auxiliary office for the case.

In Chicago by this time the agents were busy with their own current cases, burned out on Unabom with no viable leads, and probably glad that it was now San Francisco's baby. From San Francisco's perspective, this was an old unsolved case from Chicago. The task force was also moved to San Francisco since, based on the postmarks on his packages, this was where it was assumed he lived. Tom Barrett remained my point of contact with Unabom.

The danger in this type of case from an investigative perspective is that if it drags on too long, it loses momentum and tends to become reactive. I believed that Chicago should have remained the base of operations because that was where it had all started. The first crime is almost always the most important, the most indicative. It's the one that occurred before the UNSUB perfected his M.O. That's where he would have made his greatest mistakes. That's where someone might recognize him.

Maybe, like many other types of killers, he somehow injected himself into the investigation to try to stay on top of it and find out what the police knew. Maybe the police had already interviewed him and given him a clean bill of health. Maybe that was why he'd moved away.

Less than a month after the second Berkeley bomb, on June 13, 1985, the next bomb arrived by mail at Boeing's Fabrication Division in Auburn, Washington. This time the device was discovered and defused before anyone was hurt.

On November 15, another package bomb was sent, this time to the home of Professor James McConnell, a well-known psychology professor at the University of Michigan at Ann Arbor. A one-page letter post-marked in Salt Lake City was taped to the outside of the package. It read, "I'd like you to read this book," and advised, "Everybody in your position should read this book."

Both McConnell and his research assistant, twenty-five-year-old Nicklaus Suino, who actually triggered the bomb while trying to open the package, were injured when the device exploded. McConnell lost some of his hearing, and Suino suffered powder burns on his arms and legs and shrapnel wounds to his body.

Up to this point, while the geography of the bombings fluctuated, the targets had remained fairly consistent. All the victims of the linked events had been involved with a university or airline. And while there had been several serious injuries, no one had been fatally wounded by the mysterious bomber's devices.

Both of those factors changed on December 11, 1985, when a bomb, hidden in a paper bag, exploded outside a computer store in Sacramento, California. The thirty-eight-year-old owner of the business, Hugh Campbell Scrutton, was killed. His right hand was torn off by the blast, and a hole was blown out of his chest, leaving his heart exposed.

Just as I'd feared, the subject was apparently getting greater satisfaction out of deadlier, more powerful explosions. The bomb that killed Hugh Scrutton was filled with pieces of nails to maximize the devastation to the victim.

The Sacramento bomb, bearing the hallmark F.C., was a particularly cruel and deadly one. It had a gravity trigger, which meant it would go off as soon as it was touched. Our bomb experts found remnants of two independent systems of batteries and wires—a backup failsafe mechanism—installed to make sure the bomb would work.

George Metesky had told police interrogators his bombs were not intended to kill anyone. The Unabomber would never be able to make a similar claim.

Given the situation and the cruelty involved in this latest case, I didn't think the subject had just picked a store at random. He had probably checked it out, visited it to get the lay of the land, perhaps even shopped there or nearby. His picture could have been recorded by surveillance cameras, I thought, or someone who had waited on him might remember that he asked questions about a particular piece of equipment. This would be especially true if the bomb was hand-delivered. The subject would want to make sure of the landscape.

The next bombing, too, took place outside a computer store, although this one had a less tragic outcome for both the victim and the authorities. On February 20, 1987, computer store owner Gary Wright was injured when a bomb exploded in the parking lot of his store, Caams Computer Store, in Salt Lake City.

The investigation of this bombing yielded a valuable clue: the first possible eyewitness to the Unabomber.

From a window overlooking the parking lot, a woman saw a man carrying something that looked to her like a bag full of wooden boards. With curly rusty-blond hair and a mustache, wearing a hooded sweatshirt and sunglasses, the man appeared to leave the bag in one of the parking spaces. The potential witness knocked on the window, and the man left. Within the hour, the bomber's latest victim was injured when he picked up a bomb set up to look like pieces of two-by-fours.

The location of this bomb, carefully designed to

looks like a road hazard in a parking space, meant that any Good Samaritan could have been his latest victim, which frightened people greatly. I was convinced the bomber got off on designing explosives and situations. For him, orchestrating public fear was the ultimate power trip. But maybe this time the control had shifted into our hands: at least now we had a description of our man.

Investigators searched the Salt Lake City area, circulating the now-famous composite drawn from the witness's description. There was another flurry of activity in the media and in law enforcement circles, but then—nothing. No more bombings, no more communications of any kind. It was as if the Unabomber had just disappeared.

When there's a long break in any series of crimes, or when a series seems suddenly to stop, there are a number of possible explanations. Given the type of offender we think we're dealing with, it's possible he has committed suicide. It's also possible he's been arrested on some other, possibly lesser charge and is doing time on that charge while the authorities are unaware they've actually got a much bigger fish than they think. Of course, with all the police jurisdictions in this country, it's also possible that the arresting agency just hasn't communicated with others that have been involved in ongoing investigations.

A sizable segment of the law enforcement community did believe he'd either committed suicide or, more likely, been arrested for some other unrelated charge.

I didn't feel this way, however, mainly because of the circumstances of the Salt Lake City case. I thought the reason we weren't hearing anything else from the Unabomber was that for the first time, he'd actually been scared by what had happened. For the first time, he'd had a close call. Someone had seen him and had connected him to a bomb explosion. For the first time, he was literally only several feet away from someone who had the power to end his career.

"I'm not going to do that again," I imagined the guy saying to himself. I saw him growing more careful and calculating rather than doing something else antisocial or daring that could get him arrested.

Remember, bombers are by nature cowardly. No matter how skillful, intelligent, or cunning this subject was, he was not the type who, if caught in the act, would turn on a witness with a knife or gun and get rid of the threat. These things scared him.

He would go back to wherever he lived—not necessarily the San Francisco Bay area—and lie low for a while. He would go back to reading newspapers and magazines and watching television to see if anyone had any good leads on him. If he felt they did, he would go even deeper underground.

Then he would go back to working on bombs, but he would change his M.O. to something safer and more efficient. When George Metesky's bomb blew up inside Radio City Music Hall in 1954, before he'd had time to get far enough away, he was shaken not by what he'd done but by the fact that for the first time, he had come close to getting caught. He had not meant for the bomb to detonate so soon. As he thought about his M.O., he resolved not to end his campaign of terror but to construct all future bombs with more precise fuses.

I knew the Unabomber would have made a similar resolution. The bombs themselves, meanwhile, would probably continue to grow more sophisticated and deadly. He knew from the press reports that he had killed. Killing again wouldn't be a huge emotional hurdle.

In an interesting side note, years later the Unabomber himself would confirm part of my "time off" theory. While he would never admit that the last incident had scared him, he did admit to going underground for a while to perfect his technique. In a letter he sent to the *New York Times* years later, he explained, "Our early bombs were too ineffectual to attract much public attention or give encouragement to those who hate the system." He said he'd taken "a couple of years off to do some experimenting. We learned how to make pipe bombs that were powerful enough, and we used these in a couple of successful bombings as well as in some unsuccessful ones."

I've never placed too much emphasis on the composite drawing. While they can be better than nothing, they are fairly generic. In the Unabomber composite not much of the actual face was showing. There would be too much of a tendency to rule out individuals who didn't have curly hair and wear sunglasses and hoods. I've interviewed guys in prison who told me they breathed a sigh of relief as soon as they saw the published composite because they realized it looked like any man on the street. It didn't resemble them enough to trigger an identification. Also, if we didn't catch the bomber right away, the composite would have less and less meaning as he aged, yet that image would be—as, in fact, it has been—fixed in people's minds.

But there probably would be another dimension to his thinking now, I believed, a dimension we've seen in a lot of violent offenders. And that is the justification or rationalization of the crimes.

I've spent a lot of time interviewing felons incarcerated in prisons and penitentiaries across the country. Before I go in, I try to review the subject's entire record. That way I know exactly what he's done, and I can concentrate on asking him why he did it. My point here is that before I go in to an interview, I know enough about the case and the offender's M.O. to know he's guilty.

Yet over and over again, and I'm sure this comes as no great surprise, these guys will tell me that they didn't do it, or at least they didn't do it the way the record shows. Sometimes their stories were so convincing that after the interview session, I would go back to the files for corroboration, wondering if maybe this guy was framed.

Very few people think they're bad or that what they're doing is evil. I'm sure Hitler and Stalin didn't wake up in the morning and say, "What can I do today that's truly monstrous?" or "What can I do today that will cause misery and suffering to as many individuals as possible?" As evil and perverse as we know them to have been, from our own perspective, each of those men had to be able to justify what he was doing in his own mind and soul.

I've interviewed rapist-murderers of children and teenagers whose presence made me sick to my stomach. Yet many of them could tell me with a straight face that he didn't seek out that young girl, but you know, the way she was parading around all the time in that sexy little cheerleader outfit, what did she expect? Or "That woman was wearing a see-through blouse without a bra, but after I said something to her, she turned me off as if she hadn't been asking for it all along. I mean at that point, the way she'd led me on, I couldn't turn back." Everyone has a justification. Everyone wants to blame someone else.

And that was exactly what I thought our UNSUB would be doing during his hiatus. He wouldn't be off catching butterflies. He'd be obsessed with what had become his main mission in life. He would be constructing some elaborate justification for the death and injury and destruction he had caused and would probably continue to cause in the future.

I also thought there was a chance he'd visit scenes related to his earlier crimes, either the universities themselves or sites related to one or more of the victims. He might want to see how his bombing had changed the situation, to find out if the people were now living in fear or taking extra precautions. If this turned out to be the case, it could give us some strong insight into possible relationships between the attacker and his victims.

In murder cases, for example, the killer often returns to, say, the grave of one of his victims, usually at night or when he thinks he will be alone. He doesn't necessarily do this to show remorse, as used to be generally thought, however. More often, it's to relive the thrill of the crime or to solidify in his own mind the relationship between himself and the victim.

The forensic evidence gathered from the early bombs indicated that this guy had some sort of fixation with wood and nature. This mind-set probably served as his rationale for setting the bombs off, his substitute for whatever deeper psychological problems had actually caused him to commit the crimes. A lot of violent terrorist activity is the result of political beliefs, but at the same time, I've never seen a violent terrorist yet who I didn't feel had deep psychological problems and a serious character disorder.

And this man was diabolical. Repeatedly, the Unabomber had carefully disguised his bombs to look like ordinary objects or packages—a notebook in one case, a pile of wood in another. But he was even cleverer than that. In at least two cases, he put insufficient postage on his mail-bomb packages, apparently so they would be sent back to the listed sender, who in fact was the bomber's real intended target. Whatever delusional system he might be operating under, it was clearly not one that rendered him irrational or erratic. While clearly disturbed, he was a sane individual with the ability to organize, plan, and think many steps ahead.

Given the time he was now devoting to his sabbatical, I expected the Unabomber to elaborate on his original rationalization and construct in his own mind a complex idea system that would not only justify the taking of human life but also point toward the kinds of targets he would pursue in the future. That way, he wouldn't really have to think too hard any longer about whether or not to commit a given crime, whether or not to send a bomb to a particular address, and I felt pretty sure his M.O. would shift back to sending rather than delivering his packages. The rationale was already formulated. The blame had already been projected onto the appropriate people or groups.

Just as George Metesky felt he had every right to place bombs in Grand Central Station or Radio City Music Hall because of the dastardly deeds that "the Con Edison" had done to him, the Unabomber would feel he had every right to keep on blowing up his own favorite targets. Not only did he have a right, he had a responsibility. Only in this fashion, from this godlike perspective, could the ills of society and his own personal grievances be properly addressed.

In fact, I suspected we would see another communication to that effect at some point, possibly even before the next device was exploded, just to give society time to straighten out before this avenging angel was forced to do his work.

It may be that the bomber felt compelled to get back in the limelight after others had moved definitively into center stage. The mammoth World Trade Center towers were bombed on Feb. 26, 1993 by Islamic terrorists in New York City. The FBI engaged in a six-week standoff with the Branch Davidian sect in Waco, Texas, before the entire compound went up in an apocalyptic blaze on April 19, 1993, just as its messianic leader had predicted.

For whatever specific reason, the Unabomber reentered the criminal arena with two bombings in the same week. On June 22, 1993, geneticist Charles Epstein at the University of California, San Francisco, was seriously injured by a package bomb mailed to his home in Tiburon. He lost several fingers, sustained a broken arm, and suffered severe damage to his stomach.

Just two days later, Yale University computer scientist David J. Gelernter received a package bomb at his office in New Haven, Connecticut. The blast, which seriously wounded him in the abdomen and chest, also left him with permanent injuries including the loss of part of his right hand, the vision in one eye, and the hearing in one ear.

It was around this time that the U.S. government began to offer a million-dollar reward for information leading to the Unabomber's arrest and prosecution. They set up a twenty-four-hour toll-free hot line to handle tips: 1-800-701-BOMB. Eventually more than 20,000 calls would be logged on this line.

To add insult to Professor Gelernter's physical injury, the bomber later sent him a taunting letter. This was good news to us, however, since it gave us more behavioral and psycholinguistic clues to work with.

In the letter, the bomber blamed computers for a variety of problems, ranging from invasion of privacy to "environmental degradation through excessive economic growth." Notwithstanding the "Freedom Club" reference, maybe I'd been right all along about F.C. meaning "Fuck Computers" to this guy, at least subconsciously.

He also railed against genetic engineering and

mocked his victim: "People with advanced degrees aren't as smart as they think they are. If you'd had any brains you would have realized that there are a lot of people out there who resent bitterly the way techno-nerds like you are changing the world and you wouldn't have been dumb enough to open an unex-pected package from an unknown source."

In the meantime, the bombs were getting deadlier as the UNSUB's skill level evolved. The crime scene analyses suggested that each bomb took more than a hundred hours to construct. Although the bomber would not have had to have been in the military to learn this skill, the sophistication of the bombs indi-cated that he was a real technician. These crimes suggested a level of training and education higher than the original blue collar profile.

As the profile is updated it is also adjusted for age. Assuming we were correct in our initial evaluation of his age, what an investigator can expect behaviorally from a suspect evolves as the suspect ages.

The Yale and U.C. bombings again pointed to a suspect who had had something to do with academia. There was a good chance that he considered himself an innovative intellectual pioneer who was bitter because he hadn't made tenure or been given due credit for his discoveries.

The renewal of the Unabomber's activities put tremendous new pressure on the Bureau and the other agencies working the case. George Clow, the FBI's assistant special agent in charge, or ASAC, for nation-al security in San Francisco, was appointed by FBI director Louis Freeh to head up the task force. Today Clow is assistant director of the training division. He called me at my office in Quantico and asked me to recommend someone he could bring out on a TDY, or temporary duty assignment, to work on the behavior-al aspect of the investigation.

I told George he didn't have to bring out any-one, that he already had the perfect guy right there in the San Francisco Field Office, and that was Bill Tafoya.

Special Agent William Tafoya had a Ph.D. in criminology and, among many other assignments, had served as the FBI's resident "futurist" at Quantico. Bill was the one who analyzed current statistics, sociological issues, and trends in crime and tried to predict what law enforcement might expect in the coming years. He had a lot of fans within the Bureau as well as a fair number of disbelievers, partly because, while he was very tough on law-and-order issues, he wasn't exactly the traditional cop's cop. He didn't advocate hiring a new army of police officers to deal with the growing crime wave; he did advocate hiring an army of social workers. He would preach to anyone who would listen, either within law enforce-ment or on Capitol Hill, that if we really wanted to reduce crime and violence, we needed to spend mon-ey and deploy resources as we had done during the Gulf War. And we had to pursue that effort, Bill felt, for at least ten years.

In the fall of 1991, Tafoya left Quantico and was working foreign counterintelligence out of the San Francisco Field Office, so I thought he'd be the natural choice to join the task force. Also in the San Francisco Office was Mary Ellen O'Toole, a very bright and capable young special agent who was the office's profile coordinator. That meant that she did profiling for the Bay Area law enforcement agencies as well as referring major cases back to Quantico. We thought so highly of her work that in 1995 we re-quested she be detailed to the Investigative Support Unit in Quantico, where she now works. Coinciden-tally, both Bill and Mary Ellen were in the same profiling class in Quantico that I taught back in 1985, yet when they got together in San Francisco, neither remembered the other.

There was some concern on Bill's part that Mary Ellen might resent his intrusion into her turf, since he would now be the senior behavioral person on the task force, while she would continue her field office duties and interact with the task force only on a part-time basis. As it turned out, however, they worked extremely well together.

In the first week the task force had about ten members, in the second week another ten, and in the third week another ten. By the time it was fully staffed, around fifty people were assigned full-time, mainly agents from the Bureau, ATF, and the Office of the Postal Inspector.

The San Francisco Field Office is in the federal building on Golden Gate Avenue in the heart of the city's tenderloin district. The joke was that all you had to do was walk outside the door to see a crime in progress. To make room for all the new people on the building's twelfth floor, it was necessary to displace an equal number of people from their assigned space. It wasn't a comfortable arrangement for anyone.

Not only were there files from San Francisco and Sacramento, but there were all the case records from Chicago, Salt Lake City, and Seattle—as well as anyplace else where a lead had been investigated. Like a lot of people who ended up working the Unabom case, Clow had worked in foreign counterintelligence and so had probably never even set eyes on the files before this assignment was dropped in his lap.

At first morale on the task force was very high, since these people knew they had been handpicked because of their skills and expertise. But as the weeks dragged on, many task force members began to feel like glorified file clerks, and morale plummeted. Though no one from the FBI bailed out, several people from the other agencies found ways to get themselves reassigned.

At one point the task force brought Tom Barrett out from Chicago for a meeting, but generally they pursued matters on their own without much input from the original guys. If there was an institutional memory in the group, it was Tony Muljat, a postal inspector who was an expert in bombing matters and who had been working the case since the Berkeley bombing in 1985. He had done a lot of work with Barrett in the early days of the investigation and was so dedicated that he actually delayed his retirement to follow the Unabom case through to its conclusion. If anyone asked why the task force didn't follow some approach or other, Muljat would know whether it had been done before and what the results had been.

Though Bill Tafoya was a seasoned agent, he'd never worked on Unabom prior to being assigned to the task force. Therefore, he had no preconceptions about the case, including the behavioral aspect, other than the well-known fact that they were dealing with someone who was antitechnology. He would head up a six-person team, including Mary Ellen O'Toole, that would analyze the victimology and try to make connections among the victims or between the victims and anyone who might have known more than one of them.

By this time there were a lot of previous theories about the case, for example, the original Dungeons & Dragons lead. Tafoya was to come up with his own analysis before turning to any of the earlier theories, including mine. He studied all relevant case materials, crime scene reports, and forensic analyses. He also worked with the two 1993 bombings, which had occurred before I created my most recent evaluation.

It's always been a publicly stated policy in my unit

that when a local police force asks our help in constructing a criminal profile or providing crime-scene analysis, we want as many facts and as much documentation as it can give us, but what we don't want is a suspect list or the case investigator's own theories on who the subject might be. That way, we can remain unbiased in our analysis. On major or hot cases, a technique I've always believed in has been to let each man or woman working on a behavioral analysis come up with his or her own analysis or opinion before discussing it as a group.

By the same token, any case that goes on as long as Unabom is likely to employ the talents of several profilers over the years, each one updating and building on the work of his or her predecessors. But equally important, I feel, is for each one to take a fresh look at the evidence, data, and all relevant case materials to come up with an independent, unbiased, and fresh analysis. For a long time, what my colleagues and I did was referred to as behavioral "science," but to my way of thinking, "art" or "skill" is probably a more descriptive word.

And part of the art is to try to come up with various proactive techniques that are appropriate to the profiled offender. This could be something as simple as having the police encourage a local newspaper to run a story on one particularly sympathetic victim, all the way up to a sophisticated effort to "harden" likely targets of a bank robber so that he is more likely to hit the bank you want him to.

When you think you have an intelligent, proud subject, one technique I've always liked and found effective is to try to get him to focus on one particular person who becomes, in effect, the bait. For example, if someone from my former unit comes to town to consult the local police on a serial murder case, we might try to get that individual designated the "super-cop" by the local media. The agent might then make statements intended to lure the UNSUB into a "dialog," or provoke an arrogant killer into making a move. In the Mad Bomber case, the police used Dr. Brussel this way. Metesky actually called Brussel at his office after this. Telephone trap and trace were still primitive in those days, but if, say, Brussel had a published book, as he later did, I might recommend watching libraries in certain areas to see who was taking it out.

Whenever I teach or lecture on the subject, I stress that we always prefer such a low-risk, high-gain strategy if at all possible. A high-risk scenario might jeopardize an undercover agent or force a suspect to go further underground, and we take all of this into consideration as we're deciding whether or not to try it. But something like the "supercop" approach has little risk associated with it. It might or might not work, but if it did, we could hit the jackpot.

One problem in going this route is that it doesn't exactly fit what I interpret as the FBI corporate culture. In its earlier days, it was well known both inside and outside the Bureau that there was supposed to be only one supercop, or "Efrem Zimbalist, Jr.," as we used to say after the FBI television series. And that was J. Edgar Hoover himself. After he died, no one was supposed to take over that mantle, even on a temporary basis.

The Unabom behaviorists had plenty of proactive ideas of their own. But one of the key things they had to do was try to help the investigators learn as much as they could about the Unabomber, his habits, the people he thought about, the circles he traveled in.

So Tafoya turned his attention to creating what

turned out to be a sixty-three-page interview protocol to be used in questioning victims. It was based on the kinds of documents we'd developed at Quantico but tailored to the specifics of this case. Tafoya also served as an ongoing resource to the task force, consulting members individually and addressing them as a group, trying to determine the behavioral implications of each new lead or piece of evidence.

Tafoya kept trying to get across his point that the UNSUB had to be someone not only from academia but with a hard science background. It seemed clear to him that the concepts the Unabomber was employing to develop his bombs came right out of the hard sciences. Tafoya also questioned whether the subject actually lived in the Bay Area, thinking it might be somewhere considerably more remote. The Unabomber was undoubtedly testing his devices—he actually alluded to such tests in later communications—and so he had to be in a place where his tests wouldn't attract a lot of attention.

William Megary, from the Baltimore Field Office, was brought in to supervise, among other efforts, the work of the victimology team. (He's now the special agent in charge of the Washington, D.C., Field Office.) All of the behavioral people on the team say to this day that he deserves special notice for the support he gave them and for advocating their approach.

Most of the other agents, once they got through the monumental task of evaluating the existing case files, began exploring their own leads, evaluating new tips, deciding which new avenues to explore, and conferring with other field offices around the country to point them in directions that had been decided upon in the course of the investigation.

Meanwhile, the Unabomber was still communicating—in more ways than one. One scrap of wrapping paper, recovered from the scene of a package bomb sent in 1993, seemed to carry a clue: the almost imperceptible imprint of a message. Authorities tried to trace the handwriting and the subject of the note, which read "call Nathan R Wed 7 pm."

On the other hand, this might have been a red herring, planted by an offender smart enough to want to jerk the FBI's chain. "Nathan R" might not mean anything. But if the notation was written in the Unabomber's hand, it could have its own peculiar significance.

Robert O'Block, a psychologist, criminologist, and founder of the American College of Forensic Examiners, now tells me what he did was analyze the handwriting. But the clue itself—not just the handwriting style—could have represented a potential break and no one wanted to let it slip through the cracks.

This type of clue can sometimes be of critical forensic significance. During the 1985 hunt for the killer of Shari Faye Smith in Columbia, South Carolina, in which I participated, the high school girl's abductor had forced her to write a letter to her parents on sheets torn from a writing tablet. A faint impression of what appeared to be a partial phone numbers, picked up by a sophisticated machine at the offices of the South Carolina Law Enforcement Division, led to home in which the killer had recently house-sat. The combination of good police work, good profiling and proactive techniques, and good forensic science brought Larry Gene Bell to justice.

Maybe the same thing would work in Unabom. FBI investigators began checking out approximately 10,000 Nathan R.'s located throughout the United States. But this lead, which seemed promising at first, yielded nothing.

* * *

There was a strong feeling that the Unabomber must be blue-collar and a mechanic of some type. Analysis of his techniques in creating the bombs prompted some of the experts to insist that he worked for one of the airlines or aircraft manufacturers; that was the only way he would have picked up these skills.

Had anyone asked me, I wouldn't have agreed with this. We always felt that an intelligent person could learn the skills. The whole orientation pointed away from the blue-collar conclusion. The San Francisco and Yale bombings made me even more convinced of this.

Murder investigation isn't a neat and orderly puzzle. Most of the pieces are ragged or incomplete. And there can be serious conflicts between the forensic evidence and the behavioral evidence. Just about the time I was called into the Unabom case, I was helping NYPD investigate the murder of Francine Elveson, a young special education teacher who had been brutally raped and murdered in her Bronx apartment building one morning as she was leaving for work.

The case had gone unsolved for months. Elveson had been strangled with the strap of her pocketbook, which told me it was a crime of opportunity rather than premeditation, but there was very little hard evidence to go on. The only solid forensic evidence the police had to work with was a single Negroid pubic hair found on her body by the medical examiner.

Despite this, I was absolutely convinced from the behavioral indications I saw in the crime scene photos that the offender was a white male in his early twenties. Fortunately for the nascent profiling program, I was right. Police arrested and got a conviction of a man who matched our profile. It turned out that the body bag used to transport the victim's body from the scene had previously contained a black male shooting victim.

It was frustrating not to be able to get our point across more strongly to everyone else. The devices were becoming increasingly sophisticated, increasingly powerful, increasingly deadly. He was not repeating his history. Rather, he was learning from his earlier devices and experience, in terms of both chemical components and packaging. An airline mechanic, no matter how sophisticated, was unlikely to be able to quickly grasp and assimilate the math, chemistry, and physics concepts involved in the opening and exploding of the bombs.

The maker had to have been extremely careful in putting them together. These were dangerous and volatile devices, and only someone who really knew what he was doing could get by without blowing off a hand or two.

Ironically, a variation on this scenario was something to be concerned about. At any time, the bomber could blow himself up. Unless he happened to have some incriminating evidence on the premises, he might never be connected to the Unabom crimes. Or worse yet, if he were an academic, and if he killed himself accidentally he might go down as another Unabomber *victim!*

As we had throughout this long and frustrating investigation, my unit at Quantico continued to press for a more proactive behavioral approach to flushing this guy out and bringing him to justice. Dave Icove, who had a Ph.D. in engineering and who was manager of the arson and bombing program at Quantico, took an independent look at the case. He agreed with the original profile and felt it would continue to be valid as the subject aged.

In some cases you want to keep the profile within the law enforcement community because tipping your hand might give the UNSUB additional advantage. But in other instances the profile can prove to be a tremendous proactive tool.

Some years ago we were called into the case of the rape and murder of a young woman who worked as a stenographer in one of the FBI field offices in Texas. Jim Wright and Roy Hazelwood flew down from Quantico and examined the woman's apartment while the scene was still intact. From the behavioral evidence they were able to glean, the two agents thought they had a pretty good idea of the type of person who had done it, and that he would likely confide the crime to one other person close to him. Since the killer would then feel vulnerable and would also be prone to sudden outbursts of rage, whoever he told consequently would be in some danger. Wright and Hazelwood gave out their profile and this observation to the local media, withholding a few select details they wanted to retain as controls. Within a few weeks, the UNSUB's armed robbery partner turned him in.

In a serial arson case in Seattle, publishing key details of the profile in the local papers actually led the arsonist's family to recognize him and turn him in.

I felt Unabom was the type of case in which publishing information on the bomber's likely behavior could have some effect. I thought it was important to stress the behavior we'd be looking for rather than the specific details—age, weight, and physical build, for example. If we made a big deal about the age and turned out to be off, even by a few years, a neighbor might not turn in the guy who lived next door. But he would recognize behavioral clues if they rang true.

I worked with Eugene Methvin of *Reader's Digest*

on a story about the profile, hoping the readers would recognize something about it. Methvin had written a story on the Shari Faye Smith case back in 1989, and I admired his work. I knew that his aims as a journalist and mine as a cop wouldn't conflict.

At the same time, I wanted to check with professors who'd received bombs to find out if any of them had received phone calls or other communications telling them that something was coming. They might possibly have ignored or misinterpreted the warning at the time. The more behavior we had to analyze, the more we would know about our bomber.

In November 1994, Bill Tafoya left the task force. He was transferred to the field office's Child Abduction Unit to serve out his final year until retirement. "I clearly wasn't being persuasive," he said. "I thought my usefulness to the task force was over."

Truth to tell, many members of the force, as well as their superiors in Washington weren't terribly sorry to see him go. In many ways, he'd been at cross-purposes with the goals and directions of the group. The profiler who replaced him was much more to their liking, concluding from the evidence that Unabomber was, in all likelihood, a blue-collar airline-industry worker. During its existence, the task force managed to interview or focus on virtually every mechanic who had worked in the airline industry since the late 1960s.

Meanwhile, the elusive bomber grew still more dangerous. Another year of silence was broken on December 10, 1994, when advertising executive Thomas Mosser, fifty, was killed instantly by a bomb sent to his home in North Caldwell, New Jersey.

Just two weeks before Christmas, at around eleven o'clock on a Saturday morning, Mosser was waiting for his wife and daughters to get ready to go

Christmas-tree shopping. He'd been away on business and had only returned the night before, so he decided to pass the time by going through the mail that had stacked up for him. The bomb, in a package about the size of a videocassette, could have been opened earlier by his wife, his thirteen-year-old daughter, or even the fifteen-month-old baby. These details, combined with the fact that no one in advertising—let alone anyone in New Jersey—had been targeted before, served more to fuel the public's terror than to provide us with additional insight into how this UNSUB was choosing his victims. The only immediately apparent link was the victim's street address on Aspen Drive, but that seemed too weak to be convincing.

As with the Fischer case, the bomber seemed to have gotten his information from an outdated source. He sent his package to Mosser at Burson-Marsteller, where he had been an executive. Having since been promoted to vice president and general manager of Young and Rubicam, the other firm's parent company, Mosser hadn't worked at Burson-Marsteller for nearly a year.

We felt sure we were dealing with an antitechnology Luddite, and this latest murder only strengthened our conviction. We felt that a deep inadequacy about his own life and contribution lay behind the bomber's philosophy. Perhaps he had failed in his work or in getting recognition for it, and that his job had something to do with science and technology, hence his brutal turn against it.

Thomas Mosser, a molder of public opinion, therefore represented the ultimate threat. While working at Burson-Marstellar he had achieved a high profile promoting various technologies. This latest bomb appeared to be a way to attack someone who was getting recognition and credit for science and technology, the very things we speculated the Unabomber craved.

Less than five months later, on April 24, 1995, the bomber killed again. Forty-seven-year-old Gilbert Murray, president of the California Forestry Association, a timber trade organization, died instantly when a bomb exploded in his office at the group's headquarters in Sacramento. The package Murray opened was addressed to the association's former president, William Dennison. The force of the explosion was so great that the pieces of Murray's body, when retrieved, filled eleven bags. *Newsweek* reported that evidence was presented to the coroner "in paint cans."

Another executive at the association described the force of the explosion as so great that it pushed the nails partly out of walls in other offices in the building. The victim's office smelled like chemicals, with shrapnel all over and complete destruction of walls and carpeting. Ironically, the Unabomber's latest victim had lived through two tours of duty in Vietnam but was unable to survive as a timber trade group executive in California.

And this bombing could have been even more tragic. Two other employees were close to the bomb just before Murray opened the package; one of them was a pregnant assistant who brought him the scissors he used to open the package. She was heading back down the hall to her office when the bomb exploded.

Significantly, this event occurred just five days after the deadliest incident of terrorism in American history: the horrific bombing of the Alfred P. Murrah Federal Building in Oklahoma City, which killed 168 people. After this bombing, apparently for the sake of his ego, the Unabomber had to get back in control. He had to show the public that the Oklahoma bombers were Johnny-come-latelies and amateurs while he was the experienced professional. Bombing was the thing that defined this otherwise insignificant nobody in the public's mind. He couldn't let anyone else steal his thunder.

If authorities had earlier questioned whether the bomber intended to kill or merely maim his victims, the lethality of these last two bombs, and the severity of the last blast in particular, left no doubt.

A transformation of sorts seemed to occur during the spring and summer of 1995. That spring, around the time the bomber sent his package to his last victim, he also mailed to the *New York Times* a "rambling and detailed letter" that offered an interesting glimpse into his rationale. In the letter, received at the end of April, the Unabomber offered an apparent motive for having targeted one of the victims. "We blew up Thomas Mosser," he wrote, because he worked for Burson-Marsteller, "about the biggest organization in the public relations field. This means that its business is the development of techniques for manipulating people's attitudes. It was for this . . . that we sent a bomb to an executive of this company."

In his letter to the *Times,* the bomber also derided the efforts of investigators, and of the FBI in particular. "Clearly we are in a position to do a great deal of damage. And it doesn't appear that the FBI is going to catch us any time soon. The FBI is a joke." Of course, I never thought the FBI would catch *"us* any time soon." I knew this was just one guy and that he would never be more alone in his life than when we did catch him.

With letter to the *Times,* the bomber included threatening notes for two more prominent scientists.

Dr. Richard J. Roberts and Dr. Philip A. Sharp had independently discovered the concept of split genes in the 1970s, changing the then-current understanding of DNA and, in the process, sharing a Nobel Prize. It was unclear to the scientists and investigators why Roberts and Sharp had received written, and not explosive, communications from the bomber, but it was clear that the letters came from the same person.

According to Sharp, his note warned that "It would be beneficial to your health to stop your research in genetics." This message was reportedly included in his letter and in the letter to Roberts. Interestingly enough, after he read the manifesto, Sharp concluded that its author didn't know his molecular biology. Sharp felt his work with gene-splicing did not fit in with the kinds of technology decried in the manifesto.

Then, within the span of a few weeks, the bomber mailed a series of letters to various individuals and news agencies, providing more insight and clues to his identity than he'd left behind in seventeen years of violent criminal activity.

The end of June 1995 marked another step in the evolution in the Unabomber's M.O. For the first time, he made a direct threat against a specific target in advance, although it was a large target. The *San Francisco Chronicle* received a letter on June 27, bearing this return address: *F*rederick *B*enjamin *I*saac Wood, 549 Wood Street, Woodlake, California. The letter included the following notice: "WARNING. The terrorist group F.C., called unabomber by the FBI, is planning to blow up an airliner out of Los Angeles International Airport some time during the next six days. To prove that the writer of this letter knows something about FC, the first two digits of their identifying number are 55."

This was just one more indication to the task force and investigators that Unabomber must be a disgruntled airline-industry worker.

The timing of this threat seemed significant to me: just before the July Fourth weekend, the bomber was flexing his muscles, demonstrating his power again through his acts of terrorism.

Federal authorities tightened security at California airports, delaying flights and forcing many travelers to change their plans.

In a public release, the Federal Aviation Administration explained that "The precautions were instituted in response to a letter received on June 27 by the *San Francisco Chronicle* from an individual known as 'UNABOMBER.' In the letter, the individual threatened to 'blow up an airliner out of the Los Angeles Airport sometime during the next six days.'

"'The safety of airline passengers is the FAA's highest priority. We must—and we will—continue to implement whatever actions are necessary to safeguard the traveling public,' said David R. Hinson, administrator of the FAA. 'These security measures will remain in effect as long as they are deemed necessary.'"

The Unabomber's threat interfered with national and international flights (Los Angeles International Airport is the fifth busiest airport in the world, moving about a million passengers each week) and halted all airmail in northern California, since he was still presumed to live in the Sacramento area. That delay was more than a little inconvenient: airmail represented about one-third of all the mail destined for delivery in that area. Before air delivery resumed, the U.S. Postal Service assigned forty additional inspectors to sort through packages.

The individual airlines were also being extra careful: a United Airlines 747 jet was evacuated shortly after landing a Los Angeles–Sydney, Australia, flight when crew members noticed a suspicious-looking transistor radio in the back section of the plane. A passenger on another flight was temporarily detained for interrogation because he slightly resembled the composite drawing of the Unabomber and had been "acting suspiciously" on a flight from San Francisco: apparently he kept his sunglasses on during the flight.

Unfortunately, we knew only too well that the Unabomber had the skills and cunning to make good on his threat. We remembered the early explosive device on the American Airlines flight in 1979. He had gotten away with that one, and that was early in his career, when he was just beginning to develop his expertise.

Then, in the letter to the *New York Times,* he declared that the LAX threat was just a hoax. "Since the public has a short memory we decided to play one last prank to remind them who we are," he wrote. Despite his assertion that he had not "tried to plant a bomb on an airliner," the extra security precautions continued. In fact, the office building housing the *San Francisco Chronicle* was evacuated on June 29: someone had noticed a toolbox left unattended outside the building. Police cordoned off the three blocks around the building, but fortunately the toolbox proved to be nothing more than what it seemed.

I was pretty sure I knew why the Unabomber had announced his intention to blow up an airliner and then called it off. The first part was obvious. He felt he was losing his grip on public attention and wanted to manipulate, dominate, and control the lives of millions of people. This person, who was an insignificant nobody in real life, was addicted to the power his Unabomber persona gave him.

I believe he called off the threat because he got more than he'd bargained for—that is, when the airlines and government authorities tightened security to such a degree, he became afraid he might get caught up in the web. This doesn't necessarily mean he was afraid he'd be caught with a live bomb by an airport metal detector, or even that he intended to fly out of a California airport that week. What he was afraid of, I felt, was that with security awareness of all means of travel throughout the United States at such a high and nervous state, he himself could be stopped and questioned. And even if he wasn't carrying a bomb or bomb-making equipment, authorities knew enough about him from the profile that he might trigger an inquiry.

But the letter to the *New York Times* announcing the airline hoax offered a stunning new development in the case. He repeated his antitechnology, anti-industry themes, but made an offer no one would have predicted and few, if any, truly believed: if the *Times* or another national news organization would publish a 29,000- to 37,000-word paper he was working on, he would stop the killing.

The Unabomber gave them three months to decide.

I thought this was one of the most intriguing aspects of the case. Ultimatums are normally issued only hours or days ahead of time. We all remember the old cowboy-movie cliché, "You've got till sundown to get out of town!"

And yet here was someone saying, in effect, "Okay, guys, you'd better have an answer for me in three months or I'm going to get angry."

People don't get angry over a period of months. The deadline didn't make sense. The reason for the time length had to have something to do with the Unabomber's own plans and personal schedule.

I considered several possibilities. We'd long believed his key professional tie was to academia. The time frame of the ultimatum roughly equated with academic summer vacation. Could it be that our guy was some prominent professor who would be overseas or somehow otherwise engaged until the next school year began? Whatever it was, I felt some personal consideration had to be at the root of the time limit.

Without promising to run the treatise, *Times* publisher Arthur Sulzberger, Jr., stated publicly on June 4, that the paper would review any manuscript that came in and "make a journalistic decision about whether to publish it."

Penthouse magazine publisher Bob Guccione reacted to the bomber's offer by advertising an offer of his own in the print media and on the Internet: he promised to publish any article submitted by the bomber. But no manuscript was immediately forthcoming to either the *Times* or *Penthouse*.

Investigators considered the apparent change in the bomber's M.O. They speculated, as we had, that the flurry of correspondence was inspired by the bombing of the Murrah Building in Oklahoma City on April 19, which pushed the Unabomber outside the spotlight.

This theory seemed to be supported by the recent letters: the bomber had never previously been so prolific or forthcoming, and the recent letters contained sections that were crossed out, unlike the meticulously prepared letter the *Times* had received two years earlier.

To me, the crossed-out sections didn't mean too much in and of themselves except to support my theory that he'd felt the need to contact the press in a hurry. But I was glad to see continued written communication. Down the road, if his style changed and the writing became illogical—if the words and ideas became disjointed, for example—that could show he was in a cycle in which he'd be likely to make mistakes. Mentally and emotionally, he would be growing sloppy, careless.

The promised manifesto finally surfaced at the *New York Times* on June 28 and at the *Washington Post* the next day. Accompanying the document, which came in at around 35,000 words, was a letter requesting that it be published in full and that the publishing newspaper follow up by printing three similar documents he would provide on an annual basis. In addition to the legal and ethical dilemmas facing the editors, the document—at sixty-two pages of single-spaced academic text, including about eleven pages of footnotes, estimated by the *Times* to fill about seven full newspaper pages—was hardly a quick read.

Along with this communication came letters addressed to other publications, including *Scientific American* and Guccione's *Penthouse*. All the letters touched on the Unabomber's favorite themes, including the blatant incompetence of the FBI.

In one letter, the author denied having an obsession with wood, asserting he had used it in his devices for practical purposes only, since it is light and strong. He also noted other areas where he perceived the Bureau had made mistakes. He pointed out that news reports based on information provided by the FBI contained inaccuracies, and used as an example published reports stating that forestry association president Gilbert Murray had been killed by a pipe bomb. The writer carefully explained that the bomb that killed Murray included a "home-made detonating cap." It was as though his obsessive-compulsive nature and pride in his workmanship would not allow these inaccuracies to stand unchallenged.

In his letter to the *Washington Post,* the Unabomber also bragged about the meticulous care he took not to leave evidence: he not only wiped off any fingerprints from his bombs but even sanded his devices to erase subsurface oils that might have gotten into the wood or metal. This guy really wanted us to understand that he was in control of his game.

To Mr. Guccione, the bomber explained that the *Times* and the *Post* were given "first claim on the right to publish," given their greater respectability, but that *Penthouse* could publish the document if the other two declined his offer. But there was a catch: in addition to leaving the door open for continued bombings as acts of sabotage (the document defined his perception of the difference between sabotage and terrorism), his price for having his words printed in a second-choice publication was high—he reserved the right to bomb another individual.

As he explained in his letter to Guccione, "To increase our chances of getting our stuff published in some 'respectable' periodical, we have to offer less in exchange for publication in *Penthouse.*"

Guccione countered by offering him one full page for a monthly column if he would stop his bombing.

In another one of his letters, the Unabomber once again distanced himself from the Oklahoma City amateurs, stating, "We strongly deplore the kind of indiscriminate slaughter that occurred in the Oklahoma City event." He went on to deny that that incident had prompted the upsurge in his activities.

Interestingly enough, the Unabomber said in the body of the manifesto itself that since the system had to be eliminated, "almost any means that may be necessary for that purpose are justified, even if they involve risk to innocent people."

As much fuss as he made about not being influenced by the Oklahoma City event, most of us felt he was arguing the case a little too hard to be believed. After that bombing, the *San Francisco Chronicle* published an article that included a quote from Tom Tyler, a social psychology professor at Berkeley. In the article, which appeared on May 1, Tyler asserted that the Oklahoma City bomber and the Unabomber were both individuals who had inflated thoughts and tremendous paranoia about the government being "out to get them." Apparently the Unabomber disagreed with that description strongly enough to send Tyler a letter—with a copy of his manifesto—at the same time he mailed the document to the *Times* and the *Post*. Investigators figured he had seen the *Chronicle* article, because he responded to its subject matter and because the article had Tyler incorrectly identified as "head of the social psychology group" at the college, which is how he was addressed in the Unabomber's letter. He requested that Tyler read his manifesto, presumably to better understand his true motivations.

As it turned out, the manifesto was a confirmation of the profile. From the manifesto's complex text I could see right away that the bomber was operating with a highly organized delusional system—that is, his argument was logical and convincing if you could accept his basic premise, just as Charles Manson's "Helter-Skelter" pronouncements to his followers made sense if you accepted his basic premise, in which case you could justify killing innocent people in the most savage manner imaginable.

Publishers and media leaders agonized over whether to print the manifesto. Theoretically, they had three months to make their decision, during which time the bomber implied he would refrain from criminal activity. But there had been the Los Angeles airline threat. Who wanted to risk trusting this guy?

Both the *Times* and the *Post* issued initial statements that they were considering the bomber's offer. The *Times* pointed out that in addition to the lives weighing in the balance, they were confronting the possibility of a continued long-term relationship with this man if he made good his demand for further publication.

Representatives of the Department of Justice sat in on meetings involving leaders of the *New York Times* and *Washington Post*. Should they print this terrorist's ravings in the hope that he would keep his word and not kill again? Or by doing so would they be playing right into his hands and in the process offering up world-class news organizations as forums for any criminal or madman narcissistic enough to want to get his message out?

This was one of those questions with no clear correct answer. A reasonable person could have defended either decision—to publish or not to publish. After a lot of consideration, the FBI advised them to publish. It was figured that there had to be a lot of people out there who had come in contact with this UNSUB over the years. And after carefully going through the manuscript, Bureau officials believed that if it was published, someone—perhaps in the academic community—might recognize the writer's style, phraseology, and favorite subjects. While publication was clearly a risk, they felt it was a chance worth taking.

So, apparently, did the publishers. The manifesto was printed as a special section included with the *Washington Post* in mid-September. The financial cost was split between the *Post* and the *New York Times*.

I'm sure the publishers finally arrived at their decisions independently, but this cooperation between the media and law enforcement in a difficult situation, in a way that did not compromise the goals or principles of either entity, was gratifying.

Meanwhile, there was despair in various quarters that this case would ever be brought to a successful conclusion. The FBI's former Explosives Unit chief,

Chris Ronay, who had retired in September 1994, told the San Jose *Mercury News* he doubted after all this time that the UNSUB would ever be caught.

"You have to find physical evidence, or somebody has to tell you where to look," Ronay stated. "If he doesn't give us anything and if luck doesn't intervene—if he doesn't pay his rent, for example, and his landlord comes in and finds a bomb factory—I don't see on the horizon anything leading to him."

Unlike me, Ronay seemed to be taking the Unabomber at his word that if the manifesto was published, he would stop his crimes and that would make it even tougher to find him; he'd just fade away.

The article, which cited the still unsolved Zodiac and Green River murders, noted that in both the World Trade Center explosion and the Oklahoma City bombing, materials found at the bomb sites had quickly aided in finding the perpetrators. But the Unabomber, said Ronay, didn't use "materials in his bombs that can be traced back to him, or even to a manufacturer."

In December of 1995, months after I'd retired from the FBI, Scribner's published my memoirs, *Mindhunter,* and sent me on a promotional tour around the country. In the media interviews and at book signings, I was repeatedly asked about Unabomber and the ongoing quest to find him. While I was no longer up-to-date on details of Bureau and task force activities, I had confidence in the profile and had seen nothing in the published manifesto to make me change my opinion. I still feel that in many cases, proactive techniques have the best chance of success.

I remember being at book signings, particularly in the San Francisco area, glancing around me and wondering if any one of the strange-looking guys standing off to the side could be he. More than once people passed me envelopes in which they had written down their tips on who Unabomber might be. In some cases, a letter writer struck me as a more likely suspect than whoever they were fingering, but of course I turned over all these leads to the task force.

Midway through the tour, when I was back home for a few days, a close friend and colleague of mine from Quantico came to my house one evening. After chatting for a while and beating around the bush, he said that the task force and the Bureau media representatives in Washington had asked him to talk to me. They were afraid my talking in public could jeopardize some of the leads they were working up.

"Wait a minute!" I broke in. "I'm not doing anything to jeopardize the investigation. You know as well as I do that we should be going much more proactive on this. All I'm doing is describing the pre- and post-offense behavior people might recognize, concentrating on Chicago, where it all began."

While I was talking, my friend was nodding in agreement. He was just the messenger. "Well, can you just call this guy at Headquarters and smooth his feathers?" he asked.

"I'm not going to call him," I replied. "If he wants to talk to me, let him call me. But you can tell everyone I'm not doing anything that's going to hurt the case. The only way he's going to be caught is if he happens to commit some major screwup or if someone from his past or present recognizes something in the profile or the manifesto."

That, we think, is just what happened.

THE SUSPECT

The boy his parents called Teddy John was born in Chicago on May 22, 1942, to Polish immigrants Wanda Theresa (*née* Dombek) and Theodore R. Kaczynski. Neither parent went to college, but they were both fiercely interested in learning and education and vowed that their children would have every opportunity to pursue it. When Ted was six his father's best friend, child psychologist Ralph Meister, gave him an IQ test and reported that the young boy had scored between 160 and 170.

Ted was baptized in the Roman Catholic church, following his father's Polish Catholic roots, though friends have said that Wanda was an atheist. Theodore, whose nickname was Turk, worked as a sausage-maker at his cousin's plant on the South Side of Chicago. He told a friend that his greatest disappointment in life was not obtaining two sausage-making patents he felt he deserved.

When Ted was six months old, a severe allergic reaction to medication sent him to the hospital, where his parents could not stay with him or hold him. Family friends and relatives report that prior to this incident Ted had been a happy and easygoing child. When he returned home, he seemed different—more distant, less happy and trusting. One of the words used to describe him was "flat."

"There was a significant personality change as a result of the hospitalization," the *Washington Post* quoted one of those familiar with the case as saying.

An incident like this so long ago is difficult to evaluate, but studies on early childhood separation and its attendant anxieties certainly indicate that an event such as this can have a marked effect on a child's outlook and behavior. The first two years are crucial, according to most child psychiatrists, in establishing the fundamental security and comfort with others that will sustain an individual throughout life. When that security is breached, they believe, the results can be long-term and far-reaching.

Wanda had left her teaching job to raise Ted and then David, who was born seven years later. After David was born, Ted seemed to change again, an aunt told the *Daily Southtown,* a newspaper in Chicago. He became even more withdrawn.

Unlike others in their generally conservative and hidebound neighborhood of Evergreen Park, Wanda and Turk Kaczynski were avid readers who supported many different social causes and frequently expressed their views in letters to local newspapers. Turk was still writing to the *Chicago Tribune* as recently as 1988, praising Social Security, unemployment insurance, the GI Bill, and other social programs.

But the family was apparently happy in its modest three-bedroom frame-and-brick house that looked so much like the homes around it. Wanda, who tended to wear little makeup and dressed modestly, liked to sit on the porch and read to her sons from such publications as *Scientific American.* Turk, a liberal-minded pipe smoker, would take Ted and later his brother, David, hunting and fishing. They also practiced wilderness survival skills. It seemed to be a source of pride for the parents that in addition to their intellectual skills, the boys could live by their wits in the wild, catching their own food. These skills would later prove to be of critical importance to Ted: at his Montana cabin he killed animals for food, from squirrels and porcupines to coyotes, and cooked them over a fire in his yard. During his childhood, however, even these activities seemed to take a back seat to his studies.

A neighbor recalls that Ted once skipped a fishing trip with his dad to stay home and read a calculus textbook. Math was an area of pure truth, a realm in which Ted could interact solely with his own mind, exclusive of other people.

But young Ted's intellectual pursuits made it difficult for him to make and keep friends. He was also the oldest of all the kids in the neighborhood, placing him in the awkward position of being intellectually more on par with the adults, who expected him to play with the other children. The family's next-door neighbor, Dorothy O'Connell, recalled Ted playing Scrabble with her, his mother, and another adult when he was eleven. His vocabulary was already so highly developed that he outplayed all three women. While this incident may have been exciting for him as an opportunity to exhibit his intellectual prowess, it nevertheless underscored an awkward social situation.

He studied nearly all the time. Even an uncle found it odd that he seemed to have no time for close friends or for girls. He had formidable academic skills but few social ones.

Russell Mosny, one of his few childhood friends, recalls the two of them playing in the school's chemistry lab with nitrogen triiodide, a chemical compound that is stable in liquid form but explosive when it dries. Dale Eickelman, who is now a professor of anthropology and human relations at Dartmouth College, told a reporter that he and Ted would detonate small bombs in an open field and even in the metal trash cans in the Kaczynski house. These blasts would rock the rafters.

While engineering a similar blast, Ted caused some trouble in high school. His classmates recalled the details differently, but they all agree on the basics of the incident. At least one other student in Melvin McCaleb's chemistry class asked Ted for the formula to create a small explosion, which he provided. Ted was, however, the only one knowledgeable enough to assemble the ingredients in the proper amounts safely, and the ensuing blast was larger than planned: it blew out the windows in the classroom lab.

One classmate, Jo Ann De Young, remembers his peculiar brand of practical joke. He once gave her a "little hand bomb" he'd constructed out of a few chemicals and a rolled up piece of paper. It made a small pop when she opened it. Another time she caught him watching her open her school locker only to find that the skin of a cat had been left inside. There was no proof he was the one who had put it there, but animal skins were used to make friction in the advanced physics class, according to Evergreen Park Community High School math and science teacher Robert F. Rippey. Ted would not have known any other way to interact with girls in high school, however, since he was several years younger than they were chronologically and no doubt emotionally younger still.

But Ted's overriding passion was studying. He skipped one grade in grammar school and another in high school. He was one of five National Merit scholars out of Evergreen Park High's class of 181. He also found time to play trombone in the band and was, at various times, a member of the math club, the German club, and the coin club.

The photograph of Ted in his high school yearbook shows a young man with the swept-back pompadour of the 1950s, staring out and seeming to contemplate his next move.

Lois Skillen was his guidance counselor in high school. She recalls what a brilliant student he was and how much potential he had. He could have gone to virtually any college in the nation but narrowed his choices to MIT and Harvard. Wanda wanted him to have the liberal education she'd been dreaming of for him for so long, so he accepted the invitation from Harvard, complete with scholarship.

But the shy, reclusive student didn't fit in any better at Harvard than he had in Evergreen Park. During his freshman year he was one of only seventeen students housed at 8 Prescott Street, a location said to be "on the wrong side of Harvard Yard." Two housemates of his, who presumably would have remembered him, given the small size of the dorm, had no real recollection of him. And things only got worse the second year, when Harvard traditionally moves advancing freshmen into upperclass houses.

Ted and his roommates were assigned to a suite of rooms that had originally been maids' quarters on the fourth floor in preppy Eliot House. And, as in high school, none of his classmates can remember him having had either a date or close friend. Suite mates in N-43 recall him rushing in from class, sweeping past them, and quickly closing the door to his bedroom behind him. He spent hardly any time in the suite's common area.

Patrick McIntosh, one of the suite mates, remembers Ted banging his chair against the wall repeatedly as he studied, disturbing the other students. He was also known to play his trombone late into the night.

Other students remember the trash, old food, and even older milk cartons in his room growing so odiferous that the house master and then the cleaning crew had to be summoned.

Wayne Persons, another suite mate, said, "I can't recall him being involved in anything."

A couple of other class members offered similar tales of Ted going out of his way to avoid them, striding across campus, looking straight ahead and unsmiling.

But most people at Harvard didn't remember him at all. "When the news about him broke," one member of Kaczynski's class reports, "a bunch of us got on the phone and started calling each other, trying to see if anyone remembered him or knew who he was. Not one of us could remember seeing him or anything about him."

Ted Kaczynski graduated from Harvard in three years, just another face in the crowd. *New York Times* columnist Frank Rich, himself a Harvard alumnus, ruminated in an Op-Ed piece after Kaczynski's arrest in Montana that "what's fascinating about Mr. Kaczynski's Harvard pedigree is not its existence but that anyone might be surprised by it."

In 1962, Ted enrolled at the University of Michigan at Ann Arbor. He received his master's degree in 1964 and his Ph.D. in 1967. The subject of his seventy-five-page dissertation was boundary functions, an obscure topic in pure mathematics that is not recognized to have much, if any, practical or real-world application. He also managed to write and publish six articles in prestigious mathematics journals. He told no one about these articles, but some of his classmates and professors did happen upon them while reading the various publications. He did not join any of the national math societies, nor did he participate in the social events on campus or in the department.

In five years of teaching six hours a week, assisting professors as they graded papers, and conducting his research, Kaczynski left nothing of himself behind: no entry in a yearbook, no photos. It was as though there was nothing to him beyond the mathematical genius.

In grad school, as in high school and college, he

filled his days studying abstruse mathematical puzzles. In fact, he solved math problems even his own professors could not master. His dissertation won the Sumner B. Myers Prize as Michigan's Thesis of the Year.

Most students who do advanced academic work spend a great deal of time with their doctoral advisers, but not Ted. He preferred to work alone, printing out all his proofs in perfectly spaced, neat letters, with overly detailed explanations.

Ann Arbor in the mid-1960s was becoming a hotbed for student and academic radicalism. SDS—Students for a Democratic Society—was founded there in June of 1962 with the issuance of the Port Huron Statement. SDS promoted "participatory democracy" and urged students everywhere to get involved with the system and to change it meaningfully. Over the years, a number of SDS members became involved in radical antigovernment activities, eventually evolving into the Weather Underground, a faction that used bombs, purportedly as a way of altering society.

Two close advisers of Ted's, Allan Shield and Maxwell Reade, had signed a manifesto along with approximately seventy other mathematicians throughout the country, urging students and colleagues not to take jobs or engage in research that might somehow support the American war effort in Vietnam.

Yet all of this seems to have had little outward effect on Ted. He attended classes, worked on the math problems that interested him, and kept to himself. Perhaps his greatest gesture of protest, though we cannot even be certain it was that, was to wear a jacket and tie around campus at a time when most others sported jeans and sweatshirts.

In 1967, at about the time he received his doctorate, Kaczynski won a coveted tenure-track position as an acting assistant professor of mathematics at the

University of California, Berkeley, thought by many to be the outstanding math department in the nation.

According to the course catalog, he was actually named an assistant professor before he received his Ph.D. People in the know about such things take this as a sign of just how much confidence the university had in Kaczynski's abilities.

Again, he seems to have made few if any friends among his colleagues or students in the four courses he taught at Berkeley. In fact, when the media converged upon former students after Kaczynski's arrest, they were hard pressed to find anyone who even remembered him. Throughout the 1967 Summer of Love, Ted Kaczynski didn't have a single date.

During his time at Berkeley, Kaczynski taught Introduction to the Theory of Sets and Number Systems on the undergraduate level and courses in general topology and function spaces to graduate students. The student-published course-evaluation guide to Math 120A labeled him a poor teacher who was intellectually arrogant, a generally poor communicator who showed little interest in his students. They complained that he gave them no support or encouragement, that he didn't seem to be at all interested in them. His students gave Kaczynski one B, one C, one D, and three F's.

He seemed to sabotage himself even in situations where his genius and abilities were recognized. After an impressive presentation to the faculty one day, Kaczynski was asked to join the group for pizza and beer, a customary ritual at Berkeley after such gatherings. Characteristically, he declined, presumably preferring instead to return to the single-story bungalow he lived and studied in, about six blocks from the college campus.

Although he still chose not to join the National Mathematical Association or other other professional organizations, as others did, he continued to publish papers on such topics as the "curvilinear convergence of a continuous function defined in the interior of a cube," a subject that was perhaps symbolic of the defined interior existence he was already beginning to create for himself.

In a city and campus caught up in the 1960s social revolution, Ted Kaczynski couldn't turn to the math department for stability. Professors petitioned President Johnson to bring an end to the Vietnam War, a top professor participated in a strike with non-teaching staff, and an assistant professor avidly worked on the presidential campaign of Eugene McCarthy. But the few who remember Kaczynski's existence there have no recollection of him ever expressing a political opinion in any direction.

Then suddenly, and apparently without warning, he quit his teaching position at Berkeley. His simple notice read: "Dear Professor Addison: This is to inform you that I am resigning at the end of this academic year. Thus I will not be returning in Fall, 1969. Sincerely yours, T. J. Kaczynski."

The distinguished department chairman, John Addison, tried to talk him out of his decision, stating that Ted had a brilliant career as an academic mathematician ahead of him.

But he refused to be persuaded, admitting he didn't know where he would go or what he would do with his life after June 30, 1969, his last day at Berkeley. The only thing any observer could be sure of was that he was voluntarily giving up a coveted job he had worked toward his entire life, with nothing specific to replace it.

In 1971, following his flight from Berkeley, Ted Kaczynski moved to Lincoln, Montana, a town about sixty miles northwest of Helena.

Montana is Big Sky country, a place in many ways different from the rest of the United States. I went to Montana State in Bozeman for a year in the early

1960s, and it was quite a change from the urban environments of Brooklyn and Long Island where I grew up.

To gain some perspective on the next part of the story, I think you to have an appreciation of Montana itself.

James Grady is a former investigative reporter, screenwriter, and highly successful author of such novels as *Six Days of the Condor* and the current *White Flame.* He was born and raised in Montana and went to the University of Montana in Missoula. His family has been there since the turn of the century. According to Grady, "Montana is two different places: the geographic and political reality, and also the legend, going all the way back to the days of Lewis and Clark."

The Montana environment creates extremes. Winters can be 40 degrees below zero at night, and summers can be 110 at high noon with everything but hurricanes in between. The state has always been a victim of outside domination. For years it was mainly the province of cattlemen, sheepherders, and Indians. Then, in the 1800s, gold and other minerals were discovered. After all the pioneer miners pulled out, financiers moved in to take control. During the Homestead Movement, railroad magnate James Hill encouraged thousands of easterners to move in, lured by the offer of 160 free acres. Within a few years, most of them had been starved out. This continues to be true. Most of the people who come in from outside eventually leave.

By the 1920s much of the state and its resources were controlled by the Anaconda Copper Company, which created the fortune of Senator George Hearst, father of newspaper baron William Randolph Hearst. During World War I, federal troops occupied Butte six times in an effort to keep wartime copper production at an acceptable level.

Tension with outsiders was always high. In Butte on August 17, 1917, a national labor organizer for the International Workers of the World, known as the Wobblies, was dragged from his bed by five men and hanged from a railroad trestle. Interestingly, a few days earlier the contract for his murder had been offered to a Pinkerton detective named Samuel Dashiell Hammett. Hammett, later dropped his first name, went on to become the father of the hard-boiled detective novel, and refused to name names before the House Un-American Activities Committee. He turned down the offer of the murder contract, and according to some of his biographers, this incident marked the beginning of his political alienation.

According to James Grady and others who have closely observed the state, it was the movies that largely created the legend of Montana—the rugged individualism and romantic adventure of the cowboy and the Old West. "That legend is almost completely devoid of reality," Grady observed, but "because of it, Montana has always been a magnet for dreamers."

What did have a reality, based on history, was the fact that Montanans didn't trust outside authorities or anything that didn't have obvious inherent value. Well into the 1960s the only really trusted currency there was was the silver dollar.

In Montana you didn't ask too many questions about those around you. Whatever their reasons for being there, they were just as valid and just as private as yours. When you're stuck in that harsh an environment, you don't want to get too far into your neighbor's business, because if you have a disagreement, he can't let it fester; he'll have to do something about it. If there's bad blood between you and your neighbor and a blizzard comes in, you could both be in trouble if you can't cooperate.

"Friendly situations can go to homicides with no in-between," Grady observed. "I've seen it three or four times in my life."

The town of Lincoln, at a curvy bend in the road, was originally a way station for mountain travelers. Most people who lived there were in some way tied to the industry of serving the highway. Visitors tended to stay only a matter of hours, or a day at the most. Geographically and spiritually, Lincoln is midway between two college towns: liberal intellectual Missoula and conservative agricultural Bozeman.

The people who come from outside to live in or near a place like Lincoln generally do so because they are fed up with the urban angst of most of the rest of modern America. They may carry their own devils with them, but they've come to get away from another kind of life. But for whatever outside forces he brought into the equation, a guy like Theodore Kaczynski could have hidden out in a place like Lincoln forever.

In the rough foothills of Baldy Mountain about five miles out of town, along a glorified dirt trail called Humbug Contour Road, Ted Kaczynski purchased an acre and a half from Cliff Gehring. The Gehring family owned the local sawmill. Ted's younger brother, David, cosigned on the purchase. For a guy like Kaczynski, with no job or apparent means of support, rural Montana was an economically possible place.

The Internal Revenue Service computers have no record of income tax returns filed for Kaczynski after he left his teaching position at Berkeley in 1969, but the law does stipulate that persons earning less than $6,400 a year are not required to file income tax returns. Despite his subsistence-level existence, however, the real estate taxes on the cabin were paid promptly over the last few years, with the exception of last year, for which Kaczynski apparently still owes $110.

David—himself an Ivy League grad, from Columbia—also lived in Montana for a time, in a small brick apartment house on Sixth Avenue North in Great Falls. He worked as a tank man at Anaconda

Copper for about a year, then in the refinery laboratory. Ted stayed with him from time to time, and once took a job at the Kibbey-Corner Truck Stop in the tiny town of Raynesford, about thirty-five miles east of Great Falls.

After two weeks he quit, angrily accusing the owner, Joe Visocan, of overstating how much money he could make. Significantly, the accusation came in a letter in which Ted threatened to complain to "the authorities" if his payment check was not forthcoming. In this letter, he also took pains to explain that this alleged misrepresentation on the owner's part was the reason he quit abruptly, without giving notice.

He closed the letter, "Love and kisses, Ted Kaczynski."

At first Ted lived on the Baldy Mountain property in a tent, eventually building a ten-by-twelve-foot cabin. The cabin Ted Kaczynski built in the mountains near Stemple Pass had thin plywood walls and a leaky tarpaper roof. Its location, I think, is another element that supports a diagnosis of paranoia. Kaczynski's shack was well out of town, in the midst of difficult terrain and hidden among dense trees in a place where it didn't need to be hidden for privacy and in an area where people are conditioned not to look. You might even speculate that the person Ted Kaczynski was trying to hide from was himself, just as the Unabomber's manifesto suggests an individual who cannot face the hard and cold realities of his own soul.

Kaczynski's water came from a stream located a short walk from his shack, and his shower consisted of bottles hanging from a tree. Another tree on the property had a ladder going up its side to a tree stand, which could have been used as a lookout for the animals he hunted and for unwanted outsiders.

The shack itself was a metaphor for his paranoia. The interior was cold and dark. During the day, sunlight had access through just two small windows, each about one foot square. One of the windows was too high to serve as a normal window, but people could look out—or in—through the other one. His one door was protected by three locks. Since he had no phone, his family couldn't reach him quickly in an emergency. If they needed him, they would write and mark the envelope with a red line underneath the stamp. Otherwise, me might ignore it for weeks or fail to open it at all. He was accessible only to the degree that he allowed, within limits that he set. Neighbors recall running errands for him on occasion or helping him with something, but then not being invited inside.

In 1990, census taker Joe Youderian, a volunteer fireman, was one of the few known visitors to Kaczynski's cabin. He observed piles of books all over, including the works of Shakespeare and Thackeray, along with tools, but nothing suspicious was left out when Youderian was there. In fact, he and Ted had a rather lengthy conversation that left him thinking Kaczynski was an intelligent man. In all the interviews with folks around Lincoln, this seems to be about the only recollection anyone has of a long, face-to-face interaction with Kaczynski. In some respects, he was still running through the common areas, racing to get back to the safe solitude of his room, shutting the door quickly.

Even during the long, cold winters Kaczynski would ride a dilapidated bicycle to town to read obscure texts the library had secured for him. His tiny shack had no electricity or indoor plumbing. At home, he read by the light of candles he made himself. He also grew potatoes and parsnips, which he fertilized with his own feces. It was in the root cellar where he stored the home-grown food he'd need over the winter that agents found what they believed to be an early draft of the Unabomber's manifesto.

Lincoln itself numbers only some five hundred

residents. A few times each year Kaczynski would hitch a ride to Helena with a mail carrier and would occasionally stay overnight in the Park Hotel's cheapest room—fourteen dollars a night. The few residents who did know him in Lincoln found him mostly unkempt, smelly, and taciturn. The few odd jobs he took he would quit after a few days.

But despite his disheveled appearance and lifestyle, Ted Kaczynski remained as meticulous and precise as he'd been back in his days on campus, carefully writing out his mathematics proofs. When the local newspaper in Lincoln held a contest to see who could find the most mistakes in an issue, he won hands-down, sending in his copy nearly completely marked up with corrections. He was proclaimed the winner, having found 147 errors.

James Grady is pretty certain he encountered Kaczynski one day in the early 1980s when he was driving from Missoula to Shelby, where Grady's family lived. "It was a typical spring day," he recalled, "which means patches of snow, sixty-five degrees, and mud everywhere. I had to slow down at the curve in the road which is Lincoln, and all of a sudden I see this bizarre figure on a bike in front of me. He was gangly and bearded, with a bad haircut, and I thought to myself, This character belongs in Missoula, not Lincoln. In those days, everyone was riding around on ten-speeds with drop handlebars. But he had this cheap, tacky single-speed bike without gears that couldn't have possibly made the trek around here. I remember turning and looking at this guy with completely out-there eyes, and it was like he was looking right through me."

Grady noticed him, but by then, for the residents of Lincoln he would have blended into the community. Anyone who noticed him at all would just have thought of him as the local hermit.

Kaczynski had constant money problems and

found himself on the receiving end of checks from his mother and brother for $1,000 and $2,000. Wanda was reportedly embarrassed that her brilliant son was now a Montana hermit. She told friends that Ted was working on a big book and when it was published, everyone would see how smart he really was. But it was clear that both parents were deeply disappointed that this son, in whom they had invested so much of themselves and their dreams, was not living up to his own potential or their expectations for him.

According to *Newsweek*, Ted may have written his mother as many as a dozen letters, his preferred method of interpersonal communication, over the years, blaming her for his inability to have normal relationships and for his becoming a recluse. *Newsweek* goes on to say that he told David he wanted nothing more to do with their parents, though after this Ted is known to have hosted his father on a camping trip to Montana.

For a time in 1978, Ted moved back to Lombard, Illinois, where his family now lived, to earn some money. He got a job at Cushion-Pak, a company that manufactured foam-rubber products. His father had managed another larger Cushion-Pak plant in Lisbon, Iowa, where he and Wanda had moved in 1966. They moved back to Lombard in the early 1970s and the elder Theodore Kaczynski continued to work for Cushion-Pak.

Ted's job at the plant was to cut foam with a saw. One of his supervisors was his younger brother, David.

Another supervisor, according to the *Washington Post,* was Ellen Tarmichael, with whom Ted appears to have had one or two dates before she quickly ended the relationship which, she told the press, was never a romantic one. Ted, however, continued to be infatuated with her. Their unfortunate breakup produced fallout for David as well. According to reports, Ted made crude remarks in front of the woman and other workers and posted dirty limericks around the plant. David told him to stop doing this. When Ted persisted, David fired him, severely straining the relationship between them.

His failed romance was one of the few relationships between Ted and a woman the Kaczynski family could recall. The only other one they could think of was a very brief association with another woman in the early 1960s while Ted was pursuing his graduate degrees.

After leaving the foam-rubber company, Ted worked briefly at another manufacturing job in a factory that made restaurant machinery before returning to Montana during the summer of 1979. Interestingly, David continued to send him support money from time to time.

Investigators believe that Ted used some of this money for travel expenses and that several of these payments, ranging from $1,000 to $2,000, correspond to Unabomber incidents. For example, Ted received a $1,000 money order from his brother in late 1994. Shortly after that, advertising executive Thomas Mosser was killed in his North Caldwell, New Jersey, home. In 1995, David sent Ted $2,000. In April of that year, California Forestry Association president Gilbert Murray was killed while opening a mail bomb at the group's headquarters in Sacramento.

Ted apparently met Ellen Tarmichael about a month after the first bombing at Northwestern University—May 26, 1978. He was still in the Chicago area on May 9, 1979, when a second bomb exploded at Northwestern.

In profiling and behavioral analysis, we look for an inciting incident or trigger that bridges the space between the rage, anger, or fantasy that's been building up in the subject and his decision to act out this emotion or escalate the acting out. From our research

and experience, the two most common triggers—
overwhelmingly—are loss of job and loss of love. In
this case, the rejection might have provided the
"reinforcement" to the suspects evolving anti-social
behavior.

Another intriguing possibility surfaced on April 30,
1996, when ABC News reported that Northwestern
University math professor Donald Saari had met a
young man in 1978 he was virtually certain was
Theodore Kaczynski. Saari said the young man asked
his help in getting a manuscript published having to
do with modern technology. When other faculty
members at both Northwestern and the University of
Illinois at Chicago declined to support the publication, the young man became enraged and promised to
"get even." Five weeks later, the Unabomber's first
bomb exploded at Northwestern, where it had been
sent to its supposed return addressee after being
found in a parking lot on the campus of the University of Illinois.

There is evidence that Kaczynski did leave his
mountain refuge from time to time, including an
apparently fairly extended trip through Latin America, where the highly educated former academic taught
himself to read and write Spanish. But whatever job
he took never lasted longer than a few weeks at most.

Once, he sought a job from Butch Gehring, whose
family owned the sawmill. Gehring gave him a job
stripping bark from logs before they went to the saw.
But Kaczynski decided the work was too hot and quit
before the end of his first day.

In 1983, David Kaczynski bought a thirty-acre lot
in the Chalk Mountains of west Texas near the Big
Bend National Park. Before building a small cabin
without running water or electricity, he lived alone for
months in a cellar covered with metal roofing material. According to a neighbor in Brewster County, he
was at that time very proud and even somewhat

envious of Ted's ascetic lifestyle. But David was not asocial like his brother. He was also apparently more liberal than Ted—or at least more willing to express his liberal views. He even debated with native Texans about the need for guns and about vegetarianism, which neighbors figured fit in with his Buddhist beliefs.

David stayed in west Texas for six years. His brother never came to visit him.

The question often comes up in my line of work as to whether violent criminals are born or made. Which is the determining factor—nature or nurture? Of course, there's no easy or hard-and-fast answer to this. Most complex aspects of life—and human behavior is among the most complex of all—are multidetermined; they have more than one cause or set of causes. But based on my twenty-five years of experience and the extensive primary research my colleagues and I have undertaken, I have had to come to the conclusion that violent offenders are made rather than born. Virtually every one I've studied has had a troubled background of some kind, been subjected to some sort of abuse, or witnessed some form of dysfunction in his family, or endured some other emotional stress growing up.

Does that excuse the criminal behavior? Absolutely not. People with emotional burdens, even severe emotional burdens, are capable of separating out right from wrong and are able to conform to the standards of society if they choose to do so.

One of the tests we use to prove this point, as articulated by such leading psychologists and experts on criminal behavior as Dr. Stanton Samenow, is to study the siblings, particularly the brothers, of individuals who have pursued lives of crime. In most cases, the sibling will have been subjected to very similar emotional conditions, yet the life outcome is almost always very different. Of course, with anything as complicated as human behavior we have to allow for a multitude of variables, and parents do not and cannot treat all of their children exactly the same way. When a second child comes into a family, the family dynamics are inevitably and permanently changed. But the fact remains that cases such as the Menendez murders, in which two siblings both "go bad," are the rare exception rather than the rule.

Whatever emotional stresses Ted and David Kaczynski might have experienced as children or teens, whatever the influences in general, it seems that up to a point they had a similar effect on the two brothers. Then, at a certain juncture in his life, Ted went off to Montana and lived in a shack in the middle of the woods. At a certain juncture in his own life, David went off to Texas and lived in a glorified hole in the ground. Psychologically speaking, they appear to have been reacting to life in similar ways, based on similar emotional experiences.

But if Theodore Kaczynski is proven in a court of law to be the Unabomber, then we can safely say the two brothers' lives took dramatically different turns. David reached out to other people, found love, got married, moved to New York State, and pursued a career as a social worker, one of the most giving and caring of all professions.

Ted, on the other hand (again, *if* this is proven in a court of law), remained a recluse and filled the frustrations and emotional emptiness in his life by creating bombs to hurt and kill people he'd never met or knew only vaguely, and to upset the workings of a society with which he interacted poorly, if at all.

What made David come back to civilization from his west Texas hideaway, so similar in its Spartan simplicity to his brother's Montana quarters? The answer, as we've said, seems to be love, one of the things that had always eluded Ted, just as he was trying to elude so much else of life.

David married his high school sweetheart, Linda

Patrik, who was now a philosophy professor at Union College in Schenectady, New York. The two had a Buddhist wedding in 1991 and David moved to nearby Albany to take a job as a social worker. His specialty was dealing with runaway kids. He has also worked at a group home for the disabled.

From this point on, the brothers' paths seem to have diverged for good, not only emotionally but physically as well. Ted did not attend David's wedding, or his father's funeral the year before. His father had visited him in Montana a year before he died, reporting proudly upon his return how able a woodsman his son was. At this point, it might have been the only thing left his father could brag about his older son.

There may have been some rationalization on his father's part, as Turk Kaczynski apparently had his own explanation of how his son ended up in the wilds. He reportedly told people his son had left Berkeley and quit math altogether because he didn't want to help students learn how to design nuclear weapons.

Later, when his lung cancer had spread to other parts of his body and was diagnosed as terminal in 1990, Turk got his personal affairs in order and held a family meeting. Ted was not present when they discussed his future plans and so was perhaps less prepared than the others when his father ended his life with a .22-caliber rifle on October 2, 1990.

Wanda and David informed Ted by mailing him a letter with a red line under the stamp, indicating the urgency of the communication and inducing Ted to open it. There are conflicting accounts of whether Kaczynski felt that his father's death warranted using the code. The *Los Angeles Times* reported that Ted responded that it was not an appropriate use, but *Newsweek* subsequently reported that he praised his family for its appropriate use.

In any event, the relationship between Kaczynski and his father must have had an influence on at least some of Ted's life choices. According to neighbors, Theodore R. Kaczynski may have played a role in instilling some of his antitechnology leanings in his children, although the elder Kaczynski is said to have been a pacifist. When Theodore and Wanda moved to Iowa to be near his job with Cushion-Pak, neighbors report that they immersed themselves in local politics.

Democratic State Representative Dick Radl was one of their neighbors, along with Paul Carlsten, then a professor of political science at Cornell College in Mount Vernon, Iowa. According to a report in the *Chicago Tribune,* Carlsten recalls Theodore Kaczynski's interest in a controversy brewing over whether Amish children from a nearby community would attend public schools.

"Kaczynski really admired the Amish, the way they lived," Carlsten was quoted by the *Chicago Tribune* as saying. "He saw how technology could subvert the world—just like the Amish did."

Ted's father was also described as an "ardent supporter" of the antiwar, left-leaning 1968 Democratic presidential candidate Eugene McCarthy. He seemed to buy into the argument that one of the forces keeping the Vietnam War moving was technology, and was concerned that "the best minds were being recruited into military research, the development of instruments of violence," according to Carlsten's recollection.

These themes seem remarkably similar to passages from the Unabomber's manifesto, including a section that explains how children's political views are often shaped by their parents. This does not prove that Kaczynski who wrote the document, but it is fair to conclude that Kaczynski was to some degree influenced by his father's political thoughts, which may help explain his choice of such an obscure dissertation subject. A subject with no readily apparent applicability to human society may have been the safest choice for his father's son, a way that enabled him to live up to both his parents' intellectual and political expectations for him.

David Kaczynski, too, was affected by the parental political influence. When his parents moved back to the Chicago area, he settled nearby and taught high school. It was there that he penned his own argument against technology while he lived a relatively simple life without most amenities. But while he went on camping and canoeing trips, living off the land, he also enjoyed another important staple that was seemingly lacking in his brother's life: an active social life.

It is unclear why David, like his parents, kept up social relationships while Ted turned increasingly reclusive and violent. Like his older brother, David put in his time at menial jobs. After college there was the job as a copper smelter in Great Falls. More than a decade later he worked as a machine operator in Addison, Illinois. But even after David left for Texas and his spate of living alone in his "hole," he was able to emerge and move back into a society in which his once-successful brother never could find comfortable surroundings.

The relationship between the two brothers grew strained after Ted failed to attend their father's funeral. His increasing alienation was difficult for David to deal with. He had a new life, a new wife, and something of a fresh start. Ted took only infrequent trips away from his musty cabin and occasional menial jobs to get through the long Montana winters.

But during this period in Kaczynski's life, an interesting and possibly revealing relationship of sorts had been developing. It was due to David's instigation and was probably a perfect one for Ted: he didn't have to meet the other person face-to-face.

As reported by the *New York Times,* during his time in west Texas, David met an older farmworker from Chihuahua, Mexico, named Juan Sánchez Arreola. David told Ted about Sánchez, and Ted was apparently interested enough in him to begin exchanging letters in Spanish, which he signed "Teodoro." Sánchez later showed some of the letters to a *Times* reporter, and said the two of them had exchanged about fifty over a seven-year period beginning in 1988. In the letters Kaczynski described his life of poverty and self-reliance in the hills of Montana.

Sánchez told the *Times* he had met Kaczynski's parents once when they came to Texas to visit David. He said they were both very disappointed in Ted and he, in turn, was angry at them for their reaction.

In one of the letters, there is a rare and telling insight into Kaczynski's frailties and longings. In May 1994, in response to a letter from Sánchez complaining of a dispute with the Mexican government, the hermit Kaczynski wrote that while he certainly agreed that the government officials were doing Sánchez a severe injustice, at least he had his wife and children to sustain him and make him happy.

In January 1995, Wanda Kaczynski decided to sell the Lombard home and move to the Albany area to be near David and Linda. While cleaning out the house, David found cartons of letters Ted had written to his mother. Over the years, Ted had probably sent their mother hundreds of letters, totaling hundreds of pages, each manually typewritten. And over all those years, she had saved them all. But these were not "Dear Mom, the weather's fine here" sorts of letters. These were political diatribes against technology and the industrial society.

The letters contained turns of phrase that David found strikingly similar to those he'd read in the Unabomber manifesto. Some similarities seemed too odd and too striking to be coincidence. A twisted cliché—"You can't eat your cake and have it too"—appeared in both the manifesto and a letter, turned around exactly the same way in each.

Suspicion began to gnaw at David. Could the unthinkable really be true? Could his brother be a serial killer and terrorist? Actually, this troubling suspicion had begun to surface even before the housecleaning effort when he began to match up the dates of the Unabomber's activities with his knowledge of where his brother had been at those times.

Available evidence indicates that David Kaczynski conducted his own personal investigation into the identity of the Unabomber. He reread the manifesto with the fervent hope that a more careful scrutiny would prove in his own mind that Ted could not have been its author. Instead, he came away with the opposite conviction. Not only that, but publicized aspects of the FBI profile seemed to fit Ted in haunting ways.

According to the profile, the bomber was raised in the Chicago area and spent time in California and Utah: David's brother was born in Chicago, taught at Berkeley, and had odd jobs for a while near Salt Lake City—at times when the Unabomber was active in those areas. David realized that both his brother and the profiled Unabomber practiced constructing explosive devices as children and both had woodworking skills. In a frantic effort to prove themselves wrong, David and Linda compared postmarks on the letters Ted had sent from Montana to see if they would give him an alibi for any of the dates of the attacks. They did not.

David contacted Ted, whom he had not seen for more than six years, and, without saying why, told his brother he'd like to come see him. Ted refused.

Distraught but determined, David and his wife consulted an old school friend of Linda's, Susan Swanson, who was now a private investigator. After conducting an investigation that seemed to confirm David's own, Swanson contacted Clint Van Zandt, a retired FBI special agent who was a specialist in hostage negotiations and had worked in my unit at Quantico. Clint compared the letters with the manifesto and concluded there was at least a 60 percent probability that both were written by the same person. He then very responsibly got a group of experts together to do further analysis to back him up or contradict him. A second expert estimated the probability at 80 percent. Van Zandt made it clear to Swanson that if she wasn't willing to go to the FBI with the information, he felt morally compelled to.

And so David had to make the hardest decision of his life: to turn in his brother or let innocent people continue to die. When he told his mother about his suspicions, Wanda was convinced he was wrong. So convinced was she of Ted's innocence that she agreed to do anything possible, including allowing searches and examinations of the family home in Chicago, to prove that her older son was guiltless. The only thing left for David to decide was whom to call.

Anthony P. Bisceglie, a Washington lawyer who had been a classmate of Swanson's at Antioch Law School in Washington, was enlisted to serve as a liaison between the family and the FBI. Bisceglie, a principal in the firm Bisceglie & Walsh, is no stranger to high-profile cases and is currently handling the federal appeal of Jeffrey MacDonald, the former army physician convicted in 1979 of the murder of his wife and daughters. Bisceglie also specializes in RICO (Racketeering Influenced and Corrupt Organizations) law. His law partner, William C. Walsh, counts the Church of Scientology among current clients. By all accounts, Bisceglie was well equipped to deal with David Kaczynski's revelations. He contacted an FBI agent he knew personally and began negotiations.

Theodore Kaczynski's name was already in the Unabom Task Force's database, along with thousands of others. This is not as startling a fact as it might seem at first. In many cases of murder or other violent crimes, when the offender is finally found, tried, and convicted, it will be learned that the police had seen and interviewed him long before his actual identification as a prime suspect.

There were many reasons why Kaczynski wouldn't have risen instantly to the top of anyone's list. He didn't live in the San Francisco Bay area, which was where the bomber was thought to reside, and there didn't seem to be enough specific information about him to pursue him closely when other leads seemed more promising. Also, to put it plainly, many members of the task force still didn't buy our assertion that the Unabomber was a highly educated guy with a university connection; they doggedly maintained he was a blue-collar type connected with an airline.

The task force began checking out the possible Kaczynski-Unabom connections. Some seemed large, others small but telling. The Unabomber had cited a book on ancient history published in 1963, *The Ancient Engineers,* in his manifesto. Prior to that document's publication, he had checked the book out of the Lincoln library. Pretty soon investigators were checking out the shed behind his mother's home in Illinois, testing it for evidence that it might have been a bomb factory at one time.

Agents began pouring into the Lincoln area, including members of the FBI's elite Hostage Rescue Team who are experienced in survival training and can live for long periods in the wild, if necessary. Montana is cold early in the year, so the agents were prepared to live outdoors in sub-zero temperatures. They employed infrared and satellite surveillance of Kaczynski's meager home. The perimeter area was secured.

One of the reasons agents were able to infiltrate the Lincoln area relatively unremarked upon was that new deposits of platinum and gold had been discovered in the hills north of Lincoln, bringing in a small but steady resurgence of outsiders seeking their fortune. Locals by now were therefore used to seeing new people coming and going, so the agents could easily have passed for modern-day prospectors and no questions would have been asked. In fact, one of the covers they used was that they were conducting research for a book on gold mining.

Around 11:00 A.M. on Wednesday, April 3, FBI Special Agent Donald Sachtleben and a Justice Department lawyer went before a federal judge in Helena with a written request for a search warrant. After obtaining the judge's signature, Sachtleben drove the twenty or so miles back to Lincoln, where he and his team of agents approached Kaczynski's cabin and knocked on the door. When Kaczynski answered, they quickly subdued him and led him outside.

The agents investigating the cabin were reasonably concerned that the premises might have be boobytrapped with explosive devices, so before they went in themselves they sent in an FBI explosives team led by Special Agent Thomas Mohnal.

By the time Mohnal and his colleagues got inside the cabin, dusk was beginning to fall and the place had no electricity. Even so, they could see it was chock full of "interesting" materials, which they immediately began to catalog. According to affidavits later filed in the U.S. District Court in Helena, they included:

- Ten three-ring binders containing writings and sketches of explosive devices, including cross sections of pipes and electrical circuitry of bombs

- Handwritten notes describing chemical compounds that could be used to create explosive charges

- Pipes of galvanized metal, copper, and plastic, four of which appeared to be in the early stages of pipe-bomb construction

- Containers labeled as chemicals that could be used in explosive devices, including zinc, aluminum, lead, silver oxide, potassium chlorate, and sodium chlorate

- Ingots of aluminum that could be used as a fuel and a catalyst in an explosive mixture
- Batteries and electric wires that could be used to power a detonator
- Papers containing what appeared to be logs of experiments to determine the optimum pipe dimension and combination of explosive materials in various weather conditions
- A cylindrical package wrapped in paper and secured with tape, which an X-ray revealed to be a partially completed pipe bomb
- Books on construction of electrical circuitry and chemistry
- Tools, including drills and drill bits, hacksaw blades, wire cutters, and solder

"It is my opinion," Sachtleben wrote, "that these components were designed to be, could be, and were intended to be readily assembled into a destructive device such as a pipe bomb."

Reporters had converged in Lincoln and were trying to draw a parallel: was there anything in Ted Kaczynski's behavior that said Unabomber to the locals the way the components found in his shack seemed to translate into potential Unabombs? Although the "hermit on the hill" was described as everything from smelly to weird, no one seemed ready to proclaim him a mad bomber. In the closest assessment to that effect, one Lincoln local reported that all the dogs hated him and would chase him when he rode his bike to town. Maybe the dogs knew something the people didn't? One neighbor noted that although Kaczynski didn't seem likely to be the Unabomber, it would not have surprised her to learn that he was air pirate D. B. Cooper, who had parachuted out of a commandeered plane with his ransom money and was never heard from again. In a more serious parallel, Kaczynski reportedly asked one of his neighbors not to spray pesticides near his property, especially near the creek that served as his fresh water source. Pesticides are specifically mentioned in the Unabomber's manifesto as a contaminant of modern man's life.

During the perp walk in front of the press in his orange prison jumpsuit, Kaczynski did not try to hide his face or protest his innocence. Rather, he strode past the cameras almost without emotion or concern. I was reminded of George Metesky's perp walk almost forty years earlier.

When Kaczynski was brought before the judge and asked if he was unable to afford a lawyer, he replied, "Quite correct, sir!"

In court, his demeanor was calm and unruffled, but something of the arrogant academic remained. When asked by U.S. District Court Judge Charles C. Lovell if he'd read the complaint against him, Kaczynski said he'd like a few minutes to do so. After thumbing through the complaint and its supporting affidavit, he said he'd seen enough.

He was charged initially with illegally possessing explosive materials to give authorities time to develop more serious charges if they could. He was housed in a special cellblock in the Lewis and Clark County Jail in Helena and placed behind bulletproof glass under a twenty-four-hour suicide watch. I thought this was a good idea. Many control-oriented people, when confronted with the prospect of being out-of-control for the rest of their lives, do attempt to kill themselves. (I have seen a variation of this several times in siege or hostage situations when, rather than giving up to the overwhelming firepower arrayed against him, an offender will make a move that provokes the police to shoot. We call this phenomenon "suicide by cop.")

The investigation into Ted Kaczynski's life revealed several facts which, while they do not prove him to be the mad bomber, do indicate that he is a troubled man, unable to feel comfortable with his identity. Associated Press reports quoted members of the multiagency task force as saying Kaczynski used several different aliases after leaving Berkeley, including Ted Dombek, Ted John Kaczynski, and Walter Teszewski II. As though the name changes weren't enough, Kaczynski reportedly broke his own nose three times in repeated efforts to disguise himself.

Kaczynski's seven-by-ten-foot cell contained a cot, a toilet, a sink, and electric lighting—all the amenities his ten-by-twelve-foot cabin lacked.

Sheriff Chuck O'Reilly described his prisoner as polite but noncommittal: "He's just like any other inmate." Kaczynski gave the guards no trouble and answered when spoken to. He spent his time reading ancient history and exercising and shooting baskets in the prison yard. Despite Sheriff O'Reilly's seeming nonchalance, this was certainly the biggest case these parts had seen since Isaac Gravelle was arrested in 1903 on charges he tried to blow up a Northern Pacific Railroad train as part of an extortion scheme. The infamous Mr. Gravelle was shot to death in 1904 while trying to escape from the old county jailhouse, located across the street from the current jail.

After Kaczynski's arrest, I continued to be interested in the reasoning behind his three-month ultimatum on publishing the Unabomber manifesto. I felt it had to have more to do with the bomber's personal schedule that with giving the media a reasonable amount of time to decide on his demand.

We still can't be sure why he specified three months. It's interesting to note, however, that the timing coincides not only with the academic vacation but also with the most important part of the short Montana growing season. From all reports, Theodore Kaczynski was living at a pretty close to subsistence level. He may have needed three months to tend his parsnips and potatoes and whatever else he could wrest out of the ground. There's also some indication he was able to scrounge a lot of the materials he used and lived on from the surrounding area. The warm summer months would clearly offer the greatest amount of light and be the best time to forage.

In the days following Kaczynski's arrest, agents continued going through all the materials in the small cabin with the meticulous care and precision Howard Carter had used in exploring Tutankhamen's tomb. The agents' haul, in its way, was equally stunning.

In some quarters, the Bureau was criticized for the plodding pace of its search. Some of these people are the same ones who, in past cases, criticized it for moving with too much haste.

"They found a bomb [in the cabin]," one FBI official replied. "That's a good reason to go slow."

As the days wore on, evidence continued to surface linking Kaczynski with the Unabom crimes. On April 12, federal law enforcement officials continuing to search the small cabin reported they had found the original typewritten draft of the Unabomber manifesto. They believed that the document found in the cabin was the one he had used as his master, retyping from it the copies that were then sent to the *New York Times* and *Washington Post*.

Along with the manifesto document, agents found other key pieces of evidence, including the original of a letter the Unabomber had sent the *New York Times* the previous year. They also found the names of about twenty-five professors from the Berkeley math department, about half of whom were there during Kaczynski's time at Berkeley in the late 1960s.

Three typewriters—manual, of course, since the cabin had no electricity—were found. Tests on the first two showed that they didn't match the type in communications sent to the newspapers. But preliminary tests on the third one did indicate a match. If final tests confirmed this, it could be a crucial piece of evidence.

In a frightening development, agents found a completed explosive under Kaczynski's bed. The device was said to be similar to those used by the Unabomber.

All together, agents searched in and around the cabin for thirteen days, compiling a thirty-four-page list of materials entitled "In the Matter of the Search of the Residence of Theodore John Kaczynski and Surrounding 1.4 Acres." In addition to previously enumerated items, this one mentioned a hooded jacket and sunglasses, various guns, thirty-two dollars in cash, a bottle of antidepressants, bus schedules, a map of San Francisco, and a copy of *Growing Up Absurd* by Paul Goodman, a counterculture classic published in 1960s. Printed on the back cover of the book is a testimonial from Sir Herbert Read: "The best analysis I have seen of the spiritual emptiness of our technological paradise."

Justice Department spokesmen announced that Robert J. Cleary, an assistant U.S. Attorney in Newark, New Jersey, had been appointed to lead a six-member team to prosecute the various Unabomber cases. The probable priority would be the two most recent fatal attacks—on Thomas Mosser in New Jersey and on Gilbert Murray in California. Cleary had been the New Jersey U.S. attorney's liaison to the Unabom Task Force since Mosser's murder.

The New Jersey case might be the best one to prosecute first, because the individual claiming to be the Unabomber actually explained and took credit for that incident in his letter to the *New York Times*. Needless to say, I believe a key element in prosecution will be the linkage of the various cases around an identifiable signature.

Investigators are also looking into hotel records and questioning Greyhound ticket agents to see if Kaczynski can be placed in the area from which the bombs were sent at the critical times. Several possible leads have been developed along these lines.

A Greyhound agent in Butte, for example, remembers Kaczynski buying tickets more than a dozen times in the last five years. This would have given him access to larger cities with bus routes heading east and west.

A desk clerk at the Royal Hotel, located next to the bus depot in Sacramento, told the Associated Press that Kaczynski stayed there several times a year, typically in late spring or early summer, during the last five years. One of the visits was in June, the same month two bombs were mailed with Sacramento postmarks to victims in Tiburon, California, and at Yale University.

Kaczynski's family purchased tickets to California for him, reportedly on dates coinciding with Unabomber attacks.

A driver for Rimrock Continental Stages, in the Trailways bus line, reportedly told investigating agents he recognized the suspect as someone who had ridden the bus several times in the past few years.

Two other employees of a bus line reported seeing Kaczynski on his way to places such as Missoula, Montana; Seattle, Washington; and Idaho Falls.

With all of the high-profile and often televised trials of recent years, the pressure will definitely be on for this one. And after eighteen years of gathering evidence, the FBI lab has a separate room for Unabom material.

The *New York Times* quoted an unnamed official as saying, "If we lose this one, we'd better close up and go home."

The psychological injuries inflicted on some of the victims were as hard to live with as the physical ones. One injured victim recalled, "I was looking under my car, checking our doors and windows. I knew it wasn't logical, especially since we knew the so-called Unabomber never struck the same victim twice. But we were never sure."

As soon as Theodore Kaczynski was identified, arrested, and placed in custody, there was a renewed effort, not only on the FBI's part but on the part of everyone who had anything to do with the case, to analyze the victimology and draw connections. It's possible that not all the connections are meaningful, and some may even be coincidental, but the victims' near-encounters with Theodore Kaczynski do tend to be interesting.

Professor Patrick Fischer of Vanderbilt University remembers the day in 1982 when the pipe bomb in the wooden box mailed to him exploded and injured his secretary. His connection? Fischer had visited his father, a professor in the mathematics department at Michigan while Kaczynski was a student there. Coincidentally, Fischer's brother worked at Yale, just down the hall from where David Gelernter was seriously injured by a bomb explosion in 1993. And although there is no evidence, and no recollection on Fischer's part, that they ever met, Fischer spent his time as an undergraduate at MIT in Cambridge, Massachusetts, while Ted Kaczynski was attending Harvard.

Neither Diogenes Angelakos nor John Hauser seems ever to have met Kaczynski, but the bombs that maimed them were left in Cory Hall, not far from Campbell Hall, where Kaczynski taught mathematics from 1967 through 1969; back then, as when the incidents occurred, the building housed the computer science department.

Hugh Scrutton was killed outside his Sacramento computer store in 1985. He studied math at Berkeley when Kaczynski taught there in the 1960s, though he apparently never attended any of Ted's classes. Investigators were also looking into Kaczynski's travels through Montana and Utah.

Professor James McConnell, who was injured by a 1985 package bomb, taught at Michigan while Kaczynski was pursuing his graduate studies there. McConnell was also well known outside the college community, and it is certainly possible, if not provable, that Kaczynski could have become familiar with him from exposure to his work. In 1964, the *Saturday Evening Post* ran an article on McConnell and his work, suggesting that people might someday be able to "learn the piano by taking a pill, or to take calculus by injection." McConnell also appeared on Steve Allen's TV show that year, along with flatworms he used in experiments: he trained worms to navigate a maze, then ground them up and fed them to untrained worms. Once they were so fed, the untrained worms were better able to get through the maze. His theories would have been very distressing to the individual who composed the Unabomber's manifesto, since McConnell taught that people could be changed by modifying their behavior. Kaczynski would have had ample exposure to this frightening theory.

McConnell's book *Understanding Human Behavior,* published in the 1970s, became popular on college campuses nationwide and sold more than a million copies. Kaczynski could certainly have heard of it, if not read it. And McConnell's fame grew with a *People* magazine article published in 1982, which spoke of his earnings from royalties, his Mercedes, and his stunning house.

Given his work and lifestyle, McConnell is one intended victim for which it is not difficult to see the Unabomber's motivation: he embodied all the qualities that aroused the bomber's rage and hostility. He was also powerful—a somebody—in ways that the Unabomber and Kaczynski the hermit were not.

Percy Wood, the president of United Airlines, was on the Bay Area Pollution Control Advisory Board when Kaczynski taught at Berkeley.

David Gelernter had no common area with Kaczynski in his background, but shortly before he was targeted, he was profiled in the *New York Times,* a publication the Unabomber certainly respected. Similarly, although there is no apparent link between

Kaczynski and Charles Epstein, his work with genetic diseases and defects explains why he would have been a target for the Unabomber.

But many of the Unabomber's victims never encountered Kaczynski. And some had no connection to the random university bombings that made up a large part of the Unabomber trail. In the letter he sent to the *New York Times* in June of 1995, the Unabomber addressed some of these victims as he expressed apparent remorse over one of his first attacks, the explosion on the Chicago-Washington 727 flight. "The idea was to kill a lot of business people who we assumed would constitute the majority of passengers," he wrote, but "some passengers would likely have been innocent people—maybe kids or some working stiff going to see his sick grandmother. We're glad now that that attempt failed." While this sentiment is all well and good, in all the time I've spent with violent criminals, it's been my experience that they truly feel remorse in only one instance: when they are captured. I didn't believe that the Unabomber really cared about some ordinary Joe going to visit his grandmother, but I thought it interesting that he would write that, especially after I'd read through the manifesto sections that outlined how important it was to have a strategy for winning over the masses to an ideology instead of alienating them.

Supporting this theory, the Unabomber also expressed regret about the injury to Janet Smith, Patrick Fischer's secretary, but not about the recent killings, noting that she was hurt "when we were young and comparatively reckless." He asserted that "We were much more careless in selecting targets than we are now."

Although the bomber says he chose his later targets carefully, and although we had our theories, remember that no one could find any real connection to Thomas Mosser until the letter came in to the *New York Times* in April 1995.

Investigators have also been looking into Ted Kaczynski's ties to various radical environmentalist groups. One theory popular in the summer of 1995, spurred on by private investigator Barry Clausen and presented by ABC news in August, held that some of the Unabomber's targets appeared on what's known as the "Environmental Hit List." Circulated in a 1990 publication, *Live Wild or Die,* the list included eleven companies and organizations labeled as "enemies of the environment." Exxon Corporation and the Timber Association of California, which later changed its name to the California Forestry Association, were both on that list. In addition, an article in the February 2, 1994, issue of an environmental journal, *Earth First!,* entitled "The International PR Machine" railed against the firm Burson-Marstellar and Exxon for their efforts to underplay the damage done by the *Valdez* oil spill in Alaska. (Although the PR firm confirmed it did work for Exxon, it denied working on anything related to the spill). Spokesmen for *Earth First!* said their group was committed to nonviolent approaches, but that article, or one like it, may have been all the Unabomber needed to provide justification for Thomas Mosser's murder, and the hit list may have helped him indirectly target Gilbert Murray as well.

Just as none of this theory links Kaczynski to the bombings, his arrest does not necessarily provide closure for those close to the victims. Harold Burson, a cofounder of Burson-Marstellar, said of Thomas Mosser, "He was a guy who just symbolized integrity—a very square shooter, a guy who to my knowledge had no known enemies."

Mosser's brother David put it even more plainly: "I'd like to have five minutes alone in a room with this guy to tell him what a great human being my brother was, so he would know the enormity of the mistake he made."

For the victims themselves and their families,

Kaczynski's arrest must be cold compensation for their suffering. But even though peace of mind is hard to find in this world, maybe we'll all sleep a little better now.

Like me, Bill Tafoya had retired from the Bureau by the time Theodore Kaczynski was arrested in Montana. Bill had opened up his own consulting firm, Prometheus Associates, along the coast of central California. The irony of the corporate name was not lost on him. In Greek mythology, Prometheus brought mankind the fire of enlightenment, much to the displeasure of the gods of Olympus. They'd punished him by binding him to a high rock where an eagle would continually eat at his liver.

A reporter called him at home and asked for his reaction to Kaczynski's arrest. He turned on CNN and caught up with the breaking story. Then he called the San Francisco Field Office, only to be told that everyone was up in Montana on the search.

Tafoya says he felt really good, elated that a suspect was in custody and that a member of the media had remembered the profile that had fallen on so many deaf ears for so long. But he says he also felt sad that none of us had been convincing enough and that because of this, the case might have dragged on longer than it should have.

When Tafoya called and couldn't get through to anyone he knew at the field office in San Francisco, he left a message for the associate special agent in charge. But he never got a call back.

Ironically, if Theodore Kaczynski is found in a court of law to be the Unabomber, he will have been felled by two of the evils of society mentioned in his manifesto: technology and weakened family ties. The FBI used highly technological eavesdropping devices in the weeks before they closed in on his cabin and arrested him. The trees truly had ears, as the woods were draped in sensors and microphones. And although he would probably not have appreciated such close scrutiny, the Unabomber himself would have to appreciate the power he held when the U.S. government considered him important enough to use satellites to track his progress by searching for signs of a frustrated man blowing up practice bombs in the wilderness. The modern technologies available in the FBI lab, and even older technologies such as typewriter analysis, may help establish evidence against him. But finally, in perhaps the greatest insult of all, the system will have beaten him because of what the Unabomber might see as the ultimate breakdown of the family—his own brother and mother felt more responsibility, in the end, to society than to him.

A SECOND OPINION

In October 1993, Dr. Robert O'Block happened to be watching television when a report aired about the traces of handwriting, "call Nathan R Wed 7 pm," having been found on wrapping paper around a bomb package. O'Block is a distinguished criminologist and the founder and executive director of the American College of Forensic Examiners, of which I am also a member.

O'Block, I recently discovered, had contacted the Unabom Task Force in San Francisco and spoke with Special Agent Bucky Cox, who sent him a photograph of the note. O'Block had studied the work of our unit in Quantico and read all of our articles and publications, and he approached his work from the same behavioral perspective as I did. Based on the handwriting sample, O'Block wrote and submitted to the FBI the following analysis and proactive suggestions. No one in the FBI responded to him, nor does he have any indication whether anything was done with his submission.

But O'Block's analysis represents the kind of support and strategy I think can be highly effective and should be pursued in future cases. Keep in mind that this material was written in 1993 and perhaps you will find it enlightening and remarkable.

Reference: UNABOM

The following report is a behavioral analysis based on the handwriting examination of the UNABOM suspect and a criminological profile based on the individual's method of operation.

Suspect's handwriting sample reads: **call Nathan R Wed 7 pm**

Forensic Handwriting Analysis: All of the physical characteristics of the handwriting are consistent with the behavior displayed by the suspected bomber. The writer has the ability to be deceptive towards other persons and he is also deceptive towards himself. He is a logical thinker who is very good at keeping other persons from knowing what he is really thinking. His interests are almost totally on the intellectual level. Activities like professional sports are of no interest to him. Among the most striking characteristics is his great depth of emotion. He takes any slight of his abilities as a condemnation of his self worth. However, when given what he feels is an insult, he will almost always hold in his reaction and will get back at the other person only indirectly and not in a direct confrontation. This is consistent with the passive/aggressive personality. Other persons around him will not realize how keen his emotional sensors are because of his ability to protect his inner thoughts. He then is not considered talkative and there is no person that is likely to know about his perceived slights and rejections.

The writer is emotionally immature. Although he is an adult, he has not grown up. Other people do not appreciate his "genius" and they are stupid in his eyes and they have positions that he should have had. He is a loner and does not want to socialize as this would be a waste of time. His present employment position is beneath his true ability. This has left him bitter and preoccupies his thinking. He will be working in a technological position that is on a low level and one that others in the academic world would deem insignificant. He is a very intense person with high energy levels at times. He could work through the day and most of the night on a project that interests him. Because moments of hate and love affect him very greatly long after the experiences have passed, he holds grudges and is not able to forgive or forget. His thinking is systematic and logical (logical for his state of mind) and he takes a step by step approach. When problems cannot be solved logically he invents a creative approach for the solution.

He wants others to think he is totally self-confident and becomes very bitter when anyone questions his competence. He holds an excessive belief in his own significance and intellectual powers. He is an extremely discreet person who is unwilling and unable to reveal personal matters. He denies the uncomfortable truth about himself. The bomber is adaptable and is able to accommodate to changing situations. Actions like losing weight or stopping smoking are easy for him to do. He knows what he wants and can do it but becomes internally outraged when others through their positions prevent him from completing a goal.

He hates social situations because he doesn't like others to crowd him or encroach on his space. He feels uncomfortable when there are too many people around him. His feelings are easily hurt when he is criticized. It is easy for him to keep secrets and he tells other people what they want to hear. He takes great offense when critical remarks are directed towards his abilities or performance. He wants others to look up to him with respect and admiration. In a work setting he wants to take his time and to do it correctly and cannot stand deadlines or being rushed to finish a project. He has a strong desire to become important but because of his sensitivity to criticism he reacts defensively when his performance is questioned.

Criminological Analysis: Because of the nature of his acts the bomber has had a connection with the academic community. It is likely is that he was a graduate student under some of the first victims. He may have completed most of the course work for a Ph.D in computer science or a related field like engineering or technology but may not have completed his dissertation which has left him ABD (all but dissertation). With the Ph.D not completed he would not be able to correctly call himself Doctor and it would close the doors to securing a teaching position at a *highly regarded university* which is where he believes he should be. He may have been able to secure teaching positions at institutions that are not considered prestigious. He will have viewed some of the first victims as being responsible for his current status. At prestigious universities there is tremendous pressures to publish. The expression is "publish or perish". If the bomber was going to perish then he would take those responsible for it with him. His age would be easy to calculate as he would have been a former graduate student at the time of the first bombing. The highest probability is that he was around 28 years of age at that time.

Some of the later victims would have served as editors or reviewers of the journals in which the bomber tried to publish. The anger at them would result from the fact that the bomber has written articles that were rejected for publication. The suspect would be a subscriber to the journals the victims served as editors or reviewers. If because of his financial situation, which he blames them for, he cannot afford to pay the subscription fee, which for some academic journals costs hundreds of dollars, he will be found reading those journals at the nearest library at a prestigious university. These types of journals usually cannot be checked out at all or for only a few hours. He would have a card at the library. He may have signed out for those journals for brief periods in the periodicals section.

It would be almost a certainty that the suspect would be known to the librarian that works in the section of the library that houses the computer related journals. He would be a frequent visitor who kept to himself, who quietly reads his journals and leaves. If he would be frustrated for example by a photocopy machine

that was broken he may act inordinately outraged and may cause a minor scene. He would
be thought of by the library staff as the usual
slightly eccentric type that reads those journals
and keeps to himself. He would almost always
arrive and leave by himself.

Investigative Response:

1. Cross check academic journals that the victims served as editors or reviewers for,
   against the list of subscribers.

2. Ascertain the names of graduate students of
   the *early* victims that did not finish their
   degrees.

3. Ascertain the names of any colleague of
   any of the victims that were denied tenure
   or let go from a teaching or research position.

4. Interview the professional librarians who
   work full time in the computer and technological periodicals section of the *prestigious* university libraries where the victims
   were associated when the bomber was a
   graduate student, or in towns where the
   suspect may now live. For example if you
   believe the suspect lives in the Bay area,
   interview librarians at University of California at Berkeley.

5. Obtain a list of card holders from the library
   and the names of persons who would have
   checked out computer related journals for
   brief periods of time. The bomber may even
   be found at the library.

6. The bomber attacked the later victims because they turned him down for publication.

7. Most journal editors would not keep a list of names of authors who were turned down for publication in their journals but they may remember the submitters if they are questions at length. They may have even received a letter in response to the denial for publication. At the end of the year many journals publish the names of the journals reviewers or referees as they are known in academic circles. This is how the bomber would know their name.

8. Have the Questioned Document lab compare the *call Nathan R* note with the library cards of the library where the bomber was a student and the first victims were associated or where the suspect may now be living if you suspect his location.

9. The bomber may have applied for a position with one of the later victims and was turned down. Obtain lists of persons not hired by the victims.

10. Cross check all of the above information by computer and look for matches which will give you the suspects name.

If no match is found then:

11. Release the photograph of the *call Nathan R* note to the AP, UPI, USA Today and other major papers to publish it and ask if anyone recognizes the handwriting of the bomber. A

similar approach worked in the Rogers case in St. Petersburg, FL.

12. Also release the writing to *The Chronicle of Higher Education,* which is the leading academic newspaper and to *computer and technical* related magazines and journals. Asking their readers if they can identify the handwriting.

Interviewing Protocol:

The bomber has a strong desire to make something of himself and to be thought of as important. Any criticism will make him angry and he will become uncooperative. It would be best to approach him from a tactful position which gives support for his insecurity and builds his ego and self importance and builds up his view of his intellectual superiority. He is not stupid and he will know when the interviewers praise is false. The interviewer should not close in physically on his personal space until the last moments before the confession.

This report was prepared on the examination of the handwriting of the suspect and on news reports. There was no access to official investigative reports. There may be information in the investigative reports that would alter or modify this report.

Prepared by

Dr. Robert L. O'Block

O'Block refers in his analysis to the Rogers case. In June 1989, Joan Rogers and her two teenage daughters, Michelle and Christie, were found murdered, their bodies floating in Florida's Tampa Bay. A note believed to have been written by the killer was recovered. Jana Monroe from my unit, who had been called in to consult on the case, suggested placing a copy of the handwriting on billboards to see if anyone could identify it. Someone did, leading to the arrest, trial, and conviction of Oba Chandler for first degree murder.

NOTES ON THE MANIFESTO

Analyzing the Unabomber's manifesto (see Appendix 3) is a lot like analyzing a crime: to know the artist, you must study his art. And while you have to pay attention to his words and ideas, you can't simply go over it with a fine tooth comb and hope to come away with all the answers. You also have to view it broadly—from three feet away instead of three inches—to uncover the author's true motivations. In reading the manifesto, then, it's not so much the individual points in his argument, or even the anti-technology theme of his essay, that I study, as it is the message behind and interwoven with those words.

On its surface, the document has overtones (though hardly the literary style) of the philosophy of such visionary American thinkers as Henry David Thoreau in the nineteenth century and Lewis Mumford in our own. And while both of those writers protested the problems caused by technology (Thoreau once complained that "We don't ride the railroad; the railroad rides us"), neither of these true philosophers

131

was simplistic by any stretch of the imagination and neither would have offered the ridiculous, nihilistic solutions that are so typical of the Unabomber manifesto.

What does the Unabomber ask for? Simple: "With regard to revolutionary strategy, the only points on which we absolutely insist are that the single overriding goal must be the elimination of modern technology."

Let's be real, here, folks. He knows that ain't gonna happen. Anyone this clearly intelligent who makes such ridiculous demands and has such ridiculous goals isn't interested in reforming society. He's got a personal ax to grind based on his own deep problems and inadequacies.

So let's step back and see what this document really appears to be telling us.

What does the writing *style* tell us about the writer? What can we learn about him from his choice of words, the repetition of key words and phrases, the way he structures his document, and many other considerations? This type of psycholinguistic analysis can sometimes reveal as much or more about the subject as a study of his crime itself.

When we undertake this kind of analysis, we're looking for insights into the author's background, leads on where to conduct the investigation, any clues that could link him with a particular occupation or part of the country. Can we pick up dialect from a particular area, for example?

I didn't see anything new of that nature in the manifesto, but it did confirm many of the profile elements we'd discussed earlier. Reading between the lines in search of behavioral themes, which is what you need to do with a communiqué like this, you see all these personality and profiling-type words. The repetition of negative, depressive words reinforces the fact that the writer is an inadequate nobody who now, for the first time, is becoming a somebody. The profile wouldn't change based on anything I saw in the manifesto.

But in addition to the broad motivations and profile elements that are generally common to bombers, the manifesto can give us insight into this bomber's *personal* motivation. When it was first published, it seemed that everyone who read it came out with his or her own interpretation of the document. In the media, much was made of the antitechnology and anti-industrial themes, and reprints of sections and quotes along those lines appeared everywhere, along with analyses of how environmental concerns fueled the obsession with wood: the bombs were constructed largely of wood, the name of one of his victims was Wood, he used fictional names, streets, and cities in his return addresses that frequently alluded to wood, et cetera, et cetera. A variety of experts speculated about motivations ranging from religious and sociological concerns to the supposition that all his railing against genetic engineering suggested that he must be deformed or diseased in some way.

While all of these theories are interesting, I would advise someone reading the manifesto to consider that the bomber's presentation of these themes is similar to the types of staging we see in other crimes. The writer, a paranoid, inferior type, is attempting to mask his real motivations under an ideology with which some readers may be sympathetic. Instead of the anti–science, industry, and technology themes, therefore, I zeroed in on the document's greater, more personal themes: loss of control over one's life, defeatism, low self-esteem, depression, lack of self-confidence, inferiority, and so on. These themes are repeated over and over throughout the document;

they are so much a part of the author's psyche that he couldn't leave them out.

When analyzing a document like the manifesto, then, we must keep in mind that it is staged and is in many ways a smoke screen meant to disguise the real issues for its author. To get at the true motivation of this person, pay attention to his choice of words. And like an actor or director preparing a scene in a script for performance, we have to understand the *subtext* of those words. What is the meaning underlying them?

Beyond the anti-technology and environmental issues, what personal issues come through? Interestingly, the answers to this question led me to the same personality traits that appeared in the original profile of the bomber: feelings of inferiority, powerlessness, loss of control. An entire section is entitled "Feelings of Inferiority." Another, "Autonomy," explains in detail how important autonomy is to most people and painstakingly lists all the negative feelings that result when they don't have it: "boredom, demoralization, low self-esteem, inferiority feelings, defeatism, depression, anxiety, guilt, frustration, hostility . . ."

Other sections whose subtitles are similarly revealing include "Control of Human Behavior" and "Human Suffering."

Again and again in this document and the other communications we see the writer's ability—let's make that stronger—the *need* to depersonalize everyone other than himself so that he can justify his terrorism and violence. My medical advisers tell me it would be difficult to come up with a specific psychiatric diagnosis without a prolonged face-to-face examination, but I think we can speculate on a possible reason. This guy is so inadequate, and so resentful of everyone who isn't inadequate, that unless he depersonalizes everyone else, he is nothing in comparison to them.

* * *

Before we get deeper into the text of the document, though, another point to note is that this person reveals in his choice of communication how he feels most comfortable—he's a letter writer. Remember that in the original profile we pointed out that a bomber is a cowardly person. Just as he can't walk up to his victim and shoot him face-to-face, he cannot confront these scientists on the street or call them on the phone to argue. He is much more comfortable with the written word, a situation that he can control and that is at least one step removed from direct face-to-face confrontation.

Similarly, I'd suspected from reports of the meticulous nature of the bombs' construction that this guy would be an obsessive-compulsive type. Look at all the evidence of that trait in the manifesto: carefully numbered paragraphs that often refer back to each other; thirty-six footnotes to clarify his ideas and document additional sources; even a diagram to make sure the defeatist themes are presented in clear form for the reader.

The bomber first planted a handmade explosive device in 1978 and now, eighteen years later, this subject is essentially the same person. The manifesto is a written expression of the same obsessive-compulsive nature that was evident in the construction of his bombs. He obviously spent hundreds of hours of tedious, careful work putting those devices together, and he was keeping notes and documenting his ideas all along. Over the years his ideology and rationalizations have evolved, but his signature obsessive-compulsiveness has remained totally consistent.

The individual who wrote this document is also obviously not a blue-collar airline mechanic, as some in the Bureau originally believed. This is an extremely bright, college-educated guy. He writes well: grammatically the manifesto is well constructed; he punctuates correctly and has a consistent, though tedious, style. He is certainly university-connected. He's presented papers before; he knows how to write in the academic style and he's well organized.

The writing itself lacks emotion; it's flat. You might expect more ranting and raving from someone truly dedicated to an ideological cause, but this document is academic. It's similar to a thesis with an introduction, a conclusion, and footnotes. He even states that to win intelligent people over to an argument you have to appeal to them rationally, and he is as capable of putting together complex rational thoughts as he is in meticulously assembling explosive devices. What is missing is true human passion.

In most of the cases I worked on, I saw that what these subjects say in their communications, whether they're letters or audiotapes, is really a type of *projection:* they're projecting characteristics or feelings onto others when they're really talking about themselves. In a sense, they're giving us a profile of themselves. One example of this projection is the writer's lament over the lack of control individuals in today's society have over their lives, the powerlessness.

In fact, if the author felt he had control over his own life, he would not feel so compelled to mail bombs and manifestos. These are his only ways of asserting control.

In the letter accompanying the manifesto, the bomber appears to be using projection to deal with his own anger, turning the question away from himself and projecting it onto society at large: "Why are we so angry? You would do better to ask why there is so much anger and frustration in modern society generally."

He is powerless to do anything other than look away from the mirror.

Variations on the theme of powerlessness are repeated continuously throughout the document. If you evaluate all of these depressive, defeatist themes with an eye toward weighing them in terms of their importance to him, what comes out most strongly—above all the defeatism, low self-esteem, depression, lack of self-confidence, inferiority, anxiety, guilt, frustration, and hostility—is this loss of control. We see this over and over again.

"Our lives depend on decisions made by other people," the Unabomber writes in paragraph 67, "we have no control over these decisions and usually do not even know the people who make them." In other sections of the document, he names a whole host of ways in which modern man is not in control of his own destiny, from the trivial to the critical: from the frustration of traffic jams to government rules and regulations; from the obedience he must show at his job to how much pesticide is allowed in the food he eats; and from the imposition of noise from a neighbor's motorcycle to whether or not safety standards are adequately maintained at nuclear power plants. The people who are in control of the system (and his life) make all these decisions with little or no input from him.

The powerlessness has been with the bomber from the beginning, as we discussed with the original profile. From the very first devices, he has been expressing his anger and hostility, striking out. The rest of it—the antitechnology theme, the disdain for the trappings of modern life—he probably developed later. He may have had some thoughts along those lines earlier in life, but he kept adding to his rationale, defining and refining so as to have some external justification for the inner powerlessness that has been driving him all along.

Projection of this loss of control is also particularly evident when he talks about childhood. In speaking of childhood, he uses two defense mechanisms typical of paranoiacs: denial and projection. Consider this excerpt: "One of the most important means by which our society socializes children is by making them feel ashamed of behavior or speech that is contrary to society's expectations. If this is overdone, or if a particular child is especially susceptible to such feelings, he ends by feeling ashamed of HIMSELF [paragraph 26]."

He appears to be talking about how other people are rearing their children, but look at his emphasis of the word "HIMSELF." He clearly feels strongly about this point. Shame is an important part of his life. He interweaves the theme of powerlessness with that of an unhappy childhood throughout.

The system HAS TO force people to behave in ways that are increasingly remote from the natural pattern of human behavior. For example, the system needs scientists, mathematicians and engineers. It can't function without them. So heavy pressure is put on children to excel in these fields. It isn't natural for an adolescent human being to spend the bulk of his time sitting at a desk absorbed in study. A normal adolescent wants to spend his time in active contact with the real world. Among primitive peoples the things that children are trained to do tend to be in reasonable harmony with natural human impulses. Among the American Indians, for example, boys were trained in active outdoor pursuits—just the sort of thing that boys like. But in our society children are pushed into studying technical subjects, which most do grudgingly [paragraph 115].

If the manifesto's author felt that he was denied a normal, happy childhood while his parents were in control, making decisions about his education and upbringing, then he is also in denial over what he perceives to be their involvement in his unhappiness, and he projects that to society at large: "When parents send their children to Sylvan Learning Centers to have them manipulated into becoming enthusiastic about their studies, they do so from concern for their children's welfare. It may be that some of these parents wish that one didn't have to have specialized training to get a job and that their kid didn't have to be brainwashed into becoming a computer nerd. But what can they do? They can't change society [paragraph 152]."

From my studies of violent criminals, I know that most of them come from an abnormal or dysfunctional family background that usually includes some form of abuse or behavior that the criminal views as abuse. It may not be the parents who are the abusers, and it may not be physical abuse, but their relationships with their parents are at least emotionally conflicted. Although the Unabomber doesn't blame his own parents directly in his writing, his use of projection makes it clear that the relationship between parents and children is a difficult one for him to reconcile.

He writes that "oversocialization is among the more serious cruelties that human beings inflict on one another" (paragraph 24) shortly after discussing how parents contribute to the socialization effort.

In another section, titled "Restriction of Freedom Is Unavoidable in Industrial Society," he writes that "A chorus of voices exhorts kids to study science. No one stops to ask whether it is inhumane to force adolescents to spend the bulk of their time studying subjects most of them hate" (paragraph 119).

Certainly, in his mind, children are subjected to intellectual cruelty, if not physical abuse. In several sections he discusses child abuse and spanking, for example: "Activists have fought gross child abuse, which is reasonable. But now they want to stop all spanking" (paragraph 219). The repetition of these themes throughout the document suggests that he feels he was mistreated at times.

It would also be completely in line with the traditional background of this type of criminal if there were problems between the parents. The writer might not have been beaten or even spanked himself. That would be merely a way of removing the discussion one level from its true focus, since this person quite obviously and clearly has a real problem with any kind of human closeness and intimacy. And again, it doesn't have to be physical abuse he's talking about. He might have witnessed verbal abuse or conflict between his parents. When he refers to social problems such as "spouse or child abuse" (paragraph 44) he may be indicating conflicts he perceives to exist between his mother and father as well as his own perceived mistreatment.

Another common trait of this type of criminal is this overwhelming sense of inferiority. They may not come across this way in their writings, but you can't go by their words; they're telling you they're smart and superior, but deep down they feel very inadequate. The only way they feel they can get some control is by committing some sort of crime, whether it's bombing, product tampering, rape, extortion, or murder.

In addition to the manifesto, other written communiqués from the bomber give us insight into his personality and motivations, and in many cases these also reveal his feeling of inferiority.

The tone of letters sent to various news agencies, for example, reveals both hostility and a tendency to project his emotions onto the authorities who are looking for him. He taunted the FBI in a letter he sent to the *New York Times* in June 1995, saying, "For an organization that pretends to be the world's greatest law-enforcement agency, the FBI seems surprisingly incompetent." He added mockingly, "They can't even get their facts straight."

In the same letter to the *Times* he claimed that his motivation was anger, but the true source of his anger was buried behind antitechnology rhetoric. And he found other ways to get his inferiority-superiority message across, including the use of an invented name as part of the return address on a letter he sent to the *San Francisco Chronicle:* Frederick Benjamin Isaac Wood, 549 Wood Street, Woodlake, California. There is a town named Woodlake, but no F.B.I. Wood is listed as a resident there. By projecting incompetence onto law enforcement, however, he further indicates his unhappiness with himself and his life situation.

Another interesting point that tends to get overlooked is that the Unabomber did not promise to end the bombing once his manifesto was published. In a letter to the *New York Times,* apparently setting ground rules for publication of his article, he drew a distinction between terrorism and sabotage. While terrorism consists of acts where death or injury is the specific intent, sabotage is motivated by the intent to destroy property. In his offer to refrain from terrorism if his manifesto was published, he left the door open for future acts of sabotage.

This is important because it supports a contention that I have held all along: that it would not be satisfying for this subject to stop bombing. As the years went by and his sophistication level rose, so did the lethality of his devices. Since this is his only outlet, the only way he can exercise power over society at large, he could not give it up.

In profiling this subject into the future, if he had remained at large long after the manifesto was published, I would have predicted that this person would continuously write and assemble bombs, driven by his obsessive-compulsiveness. If you could look into his work area, you would expect to find earlier drafts of the manifesto, along with notes and at least the early drafts of "Manifesto II."

He would not stop bombing, he would not stop killing people, despite his promise, and he would need to produce another document to justify his continued violence. This could include a different interpretation of what he was doing or a new slant to his ideology, culled from current events. He'd be going to the library for information, researching new sources, finding ideas and ways for his ideology to evolve.

Readers of the second manifesto would have to study it with the same sort of skepticism that was necessary with the first document. The underlying ideation of powerlessness and inferiority would be evident, but there would be an elaboration of his ideological construct. Consider that over the course of eighteen years these bombs went off all over the country and we still didn't know the true motivation of this person. Then we got the manifesto and we finally began to see where his emphasis lay.

In the manifesto he tries to tell us what his motivation is, tries to convince us that it's this antitechnology theme, but I don't necessarily buy that. He knows a certain element of society will not accept it, so he compulsively attempts to prove it. He's bright, he knows how to conduct research, so he puts together this elaborate document full of footnotes and quotes from outside sources. In the end, despite the words he uses, the underlying feelings of helplessness, hopelessness, and powerlessness would still prevail.

This is why many of us knew the manifesto would be his downfall, because that was something they could show people. This is why the Bureau pushed for its publication. The document should be made public, it was reasoned, because someone may recognize the way it's organized, the compulsive writing style.

And I think it's relevant to note here that the means by which the suspect, Theodore Kaczynski, was identified, was precisely the way those of us in the behavioral field felt it could happen all along. Some commentators have remarked that with all of the FBI's high-tech and state-of-the-art equipment (the very stuff the Unabomber railed against), isn't it ironic that it was a "fluke"—a tip—that brought Kaczynski in?

Excuse me, but it was not a fluke at all. If we had caught him virtually any other way it would have been a fluke, but not by having someone close to him who recognized some aspect of his style or personality turn him in. That is exactly the type of outcome to which all of our work was dedicated.

In using the manifesto as an investigative tool, I would have advised describing the types of behavior associated with the sort of person who would commit this kind of crime—although I would have tried this long before we even had the document. If I knew nothing of Theodore Kaczynski and believed, as many members of the task force did, that the Unabomber lived in California, I would nevertheless have returned to Chicago.

Once I had the manifesto, I'd go back to Chicago with it and describe the physical and behavioral characteristics of this person as I expected he would have exhibited them back in the 1970s. I'd explain that there would have been a precipitating event around the time of the first bombing, although I wouldn't have been able to say what it was. When passing the document around to professors and others who might recognize something in it, I would have explained that we were not looking for somebody to recognize the themes necessarily, but the writing style.

Unfortunately, investigators probably showed it to people and asked if they recognized the content: "Did you have a student who was writing essays like this, or a professor who gave lectures like this?"

But the content could be dynamic. The bomber's ideas and ideological argument could have evolved over the past nearly twenty years whereas his signature thought pattern, patterns of expression, and levels of organization would remain static over time. The problem is that so many years have gone by that memories have waned. Had we taken this approach back then, the images would have been fresh in people's minds, and they very well might have recognized him.

MAD OR BAD?

Mad? Or bad?

This could very well be the key question in any prosecution of the Unabom case.

While it's too early at this writing to know exactly how the trial will unfold, I have been involved in enough criminal prosecutions of violent offenders that I think it's possible to speculate on which issues both the prosecution and the defense will have to emphasize.

In any criminal case in which there is a large amount of evidence against the accused but in which motive may be difficult to explain, there is always a good chance the defense will essentially concede the facts and go for an insanity plea.

If Theodore Kaczynski does come to stand trial for the Unabom crimes, his attorney might offer some of the following in support of an insanity defense.

The defense might start with the biological-organic determinatives. There was the early childhood illness, which close observers might testify changed Kaczynski's personality and left him emotionally flat and unresponsive after he returned home from the hospital. The human brain is so complex that I have seen virtually every organic or possibly organic excuse used to explain away aberrant or antisocial behavior.

Or the defense might stress psychological issues. One such issue is the question of the subject's intelligence. Often an excuse is made that a defendant has such a low IQ that he has no real comprehension of what he's doing. But this argument can work the other way, too. I have seen used as defense the fact that the subject had such a high IQ as a child—Theodore Kaczynski's was reported to be in the 160–170 range—that he was unable to fit in with his schoolmates and peers. He skipped two full grades in school, which put him that much further out of sync with his peers.

Instead of relating in a "normal" fashion, he participated in solitary activities and hobbies such as coin collecting, and also made incendiary explosives and blew them up in the neighborhood. This fact might be brought in to show the early warning signs of his psychopathology, which went unrecognized and untreated.

The defense might then go on to cite the subject's academic record. He graduated from high school at sixteen years of age; won a scholarship to Harvard, from which he graduated at age twenty; received advanced degrees in a highly intellectual field from the University of Michigan; and then secured a hard-to-get teaching job with tenure track at the University of California, Berkeley, arguably the top department in his field in the entire country. Anyone who would walk away from that, after working so hard for so long, to live as a recluse without amenities or conveniences must surely be psychotic. Photographs of the Montana cabin and detailed eyewitness accounts of the subject's appearance would likely be brought in to support this claim and make it vibrant in the jury's minds.

Other likely defense witnesses would be the defendant's mother and brother, who would be asked to testify on the subject's past inappropriate behavior, emphasizing what they perceived to be his loss of touch with reality and his progressive withdrawal from the real world.

When the manifesto was introduced into the trial, the defense would bring in psychiatrists or psychologists and psycholinguistics experts who would attempt to convince the jurors that the author of this document was psychotic, or out of touch with reality. As evidence of this assertion they would cite his irrational demands and illogical reasoning throughout the manifesto, along with the perpetration of the violent acts themselves, arguing that no one in his right mind would do something like that.

There might be testimony that the subject was on a psychotic mission. We see this over and over again in the trials of serial murderers charged with the killing of prostitutes. The defense will claim that the killer believed himself to be on an assignment from God to punish these women for their sins. Using the manifesto as a basis, the defense might claim that the Unabomber thought he was on a mission to punish various carefully chosen elements of society for their sins.

Also, based on the nature of the bombs and on many witnessed aspects of the subject's life, the defense could claim that the accused was suffering from a severe obsessive-compulsive disorder and could not control himself or his actions.

Any one of these factors or a combination of them could and may be used in support of a claim of not guilty by reason of insanity.

Or the defense could take a more direct approach and simply admit that while the subject may possibly be the author of the manifesto published in the *Washington Post,* this fact alone does not tie him to the Unabomber's crimes. He may simply have been fascinated by these crimes when he read about them in the media and merely used them as a way to get his passionately held beliefs before a mass audience.

The fact that bomb-making equipment and partially completed bombs were discovered in his residence merely suggests that he was interested in bombs. The defense would argue that while this might imply something in most rational people's minds, there is still a reasonable doubt that these bombs and those set off by the Unabomber are one and the same.

At least, that's what they might try.

The prosecutors are more likely to accept and propound the "bad" explanation for the subject's actions.

They are likely to state that he is a genius who used his superior intelligence to make bombs requiring technical ability and emotional stability. If he did not possess either of these traits he could have been easily killed while making, planting, or sending the bombs.

They will try to counter the psychotic argument by bringing in their own psychological experts who will testify that the defendant is a psychopath rather than a psychotic. He is not out of his mind; he merely has a severe character disorder that still allows him to comprehend the difference between right and wrong and to mold his actions to fit the standards of society and law. He did what he did, the prosecution will say, because it gave him satisfaction to do so and made him feel better about himself and his own power and status.

The prosecution will point out that the subject was a canny manipulator of the press, of law enforcement,

Over a 16-year period during the '40s and '50s, George Metesky, ''the Mad Bomber,'' planted 32 bombs in public places in New York City. When stymied police brought in New York psychiatrist Dr. James A. Brussel, the modern version of criminal profiling was born. *AP/Wide World*

1958   1958   1959

1962   1994   1996

Theodore J. Kaczynski over the years. Top row from left:
1958 (Evergreen Park, Ill., High School yearbook), 1958
(Evergreen Park High School yearbook), 1959 (Harvard
University), 1962 (Harvard University yearbook), 1994
(Montana driver's license), and 1996 (booking mug photo)
(BPT) *AP/Wide World*

Evergreen Park High School in Evergreen Park, Ill. The suspect graduated in 1958 with a scholarship to Harvard. *AP/Wide World*

Ted Kaczynski, right front, is shown with other National Merit Scholarship finalists in this photo from the 1958 Evergreen Park High School yearbook. *AP/Wide World*

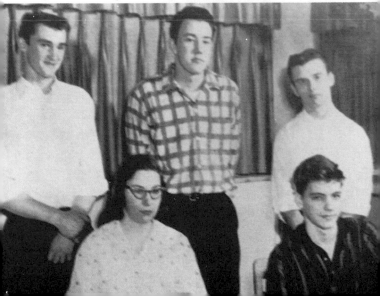

Ted Kaczynski in his senior yearbook photo. *AP/Wide World*

Ted Kaczynski on the campus of the University of California at Berkeley, where he was a professor of mathematics in the late 1960s. *AP/Wide World*

The FBI released this sketch of the Unabomber on Tuesday, April 25, 1995, at the Federal Building in San Francisco. *AP/Wide World*

Advertising executive Thomas J. Mosser is shown in this 1990 file photo. Mosser was a victim of a Unabomber attack in 1994, and was killed when he opened a package bomb at his New Jersey home. *AP/Wide World*

This is an undated photo of Professor Edward J. Smith, reportedly the first professor to receive a bomb from the Unabomber. *AP/Wide World*

Percy Wood, then–president of United Airlines, was injured in an attack linked to the Unabomber at Wood's Chicago-area home in June 1980. *AP/Wide World*

Ted Kaczynski in his booking mug shot at the Lewis and Clark County Jail in Helena, Mont. on Wednesday, April 3, 1996. *AP/Wide World*

The cabin of the suspected Unabomber. The home, on 1.4 acres, is only 10 by 12 feet, with no electricity or plumbing. *AP/Wide World*

The mother of Unabomber suspect Ted Kaczynski sold this Lombard, Ill., house in March. When family members were searching some old boxes, they found some writings from Kaczynski that made them think he might be the Unabomber, according to several federal law enforcement officials. *AP/Wide World*

Ted Kaczynski's 1994 Montana driver's license was released on Wednesday, April 3, 1996, by the Montana Justice Department, after he had been named as a possible suspect in the Unabomber killings. *AP/Wide World*

Materials used by the FBI in its search of Ted Kaczynski's mountain cabin in Lincoln, Mont., sit outside the cabin's door on Saturday, April 6, 1996. *AP/Wide World*

The Royal Hotel in Sacramento, Calif., is shown on Sunday, April 7, 1996. Frank Hensley, a resident and employee of the hotel, said the Unabomber suspect Ted Kaczynski stayed at the hotel several times in the past few years. *AP/Wide World*

Ted Kaczynski was known to have used bicycles for transportation around the Lincoln community. This bicycle sits under cover at the suspect's mountain cabin. *AP/Wide World*

Tony Bisceglie, an attorney for Unabomber suspect Ted Kaczynski's brother, David, meets with reporters in Washington on Monday, April 8, 1996, to discuss the case. *AP/Wide World*

Ted Kaczynski is escorted into the federal courthouse in Helena, Mont., on Thursday, April 4, 1996, to be charged with possessing the components of a bomb found in a search of his mountain cabin. *AP/Wide World*

and the citizenry of the United States. They will claim that he was not interested in social change, but was merely manipulating, dominating, and controlling others, just as rapists and sexual murderers do.

The subject, it will be asserted, was a socially misguided misfit who was angry about the way people treated him and sought only one thing—power.

The defense will point out that offenders who are truly insane are not rational enough to keep their crimes or identities hidden for long. The Unabomber, on the other hand, was able to evade the combined forces of the FBI, ATF, U.S. Postal Service, numerous state and local law enforcement agencies, as well as an army of reporters and amateur sleuths for eighteen years. Anyone who can accomplish this must be criminally sophisticated, orderly, organized, able to think and plan ahead, and highly intelligent.

Of course, the bulk of the prosecution's case can rest on the physical evidence itself, and it appears that in this case there will be a mountain of it, including the documents found on the subject's premises, the equipment he had, the notebooks, the partially completed bombs, and the writings that describe bomb-making. The prosecution will bring in explosives experts to match up the bomb-making signature with the remnants of devices recovered from the crime scenes.

They will point out that the subject created his bombs by handcrafting most of the parts. This also demonstrates criminal sophistication on his part: he knew the authorities would not be able to trace his homemade bomb components to a particular store. In the same vein, the subject removed all fingerprints by wiping down the bombs with an oily rag.

Prosecutors might sum up by reminding the jury that while they are required to prove their case beyond a reasonable doubt, they are not required to prove it beyond a capricious or theoretical doubt.

They must present evidence that a reasonable man or woman would find compelling and convincing.

All of these factors may be used by defense attorneys and prosecutors to help establish their respective cases. The ultimate decision, as it always is in this country, is up to the jury.

WHAT HAVE WE LEARNED?

So what have we learned from this case?

For one thing, I hope we've learned that it's important for investigators to jump in quickly before the offender has an opportunity to develop his modus operandi or expand his operating area of comfort. The authorities have to be on top of things enough to begin linking cases and incidents early in the game.

What do I mean by that? How can we link cases before there's a legitimate link to be made? Part of the answer to this lies in the fact that there are more than seventeen thousand law enforcement agencies across the United States, all trying to do a good and thorough job, but all hampered by the fact that it's a whole lot easier for a criminal to jump from one jurisdiction to another than it is for a law officer to do so.

Far, far too often in this country we'll have a bunch of grisly crimes which appear to be isolated incidents but which will turn out to be the work of a single serial criminal. The problem is that each of the investigating organizations knows only about its own case and has no idea about any of the others. We had a case in Montana several years back in which a serial killer was operating in two adjoining counties and neither police force was aware of the other's situation.

The only way I know of to get around this problem is to employ the modern computer technology the Unabomber found so threatening and unappealing. If a crime that seems unique or isolated is entered into a national computer database by the law enforcement agency that originally investigates it, it can be linked to similar crimes so that a joint, organized, and efficient effort can be mounted quickly to pursue and apprehend the perpetrator.

Throughout this book I've talked about targeting the earliest crimes in our attempt to catch the perpetrator. But I must tell you, we can't always be sure that the earliest crimes have been reported. All we can be sure of is those crimes that have been reported that we can link to one another. Did the Unabomber commit some other criminal acts before the ones at the University of Illinois and Northwestern? Probably not, but if we had more confidence in our crime-reporting system we could be sure. And if there had been earlier crimes, perhaps we could have caught him that much earlier as well.

We already have a reasonably efficient tool known as the National Crime Information Computer, or NCIC, that link most police departments across the country. Many police cars have also been equipped with NCIC terminals. NCIC lists such information as stolen property and fugitive warrants so that if an officer stops a car, he can quickly tell whether it is stolen or if the owner is wanted for anything.

More than a decade ago, under the original leadership of former LAPD homicide detective Pierce Brooks, the FBI instituted VICAP—the Violent Criminal Apprehension Program. VICAP is housed at Quantico and intended to be a national computer database describing individual crimes and thereby allowing linkage between them. The idea was that when a serious crime occurred, the local police agency would enter the information into VICAP, which could then instantly match it to other, similar entries.

This is a very good idea, in my opinion, but the program has languished for lack of funding and our inability to get enough members of enough local law enforcement agencies to participate. When a detective is working up a case, the last thing he wants is more paperwork and more administration. Yet if he could instantly compare his facts with other crimes committed elsewhere in the United States, a lot more crimes would be solved, and much sooner.

Fed up with the lack of federal action, such states as New York, New Jersey, Florida, and Washington are developing their own crime detail computer systems. Of course, even when they get them up and running, there's no guarantee they'll be compatible with each other.

Canada is already setting up a system with people like Ron McKay of the Royal Canadian Mounted Police in Ottawa whom we trained at Quantico. Australia is also working on one, although neither country has anywhere near as much crime as we have in the United States.

Is this the FBI's fault? No. Give the Bureau the money and it'll do the job.

I can't tell you how many times I was asked to give presentations to senators and congressmen visiting Quantico about our funding needs. They always nodded sagely and agreed that crime certainly was a major problem in this country. Then the Bureau PR people would take them to the indoor range and let them shoot real FBI guns. Later, when they were thinking of their visit to the Academy, they would pull out their silhouette targets with the holes in them and remember how cool it was to shoot on the range. That guy in the basement preaching at them would be all but forgotten.

I've often said to anyone who would listen, "Let's buy one or two fewer B-2 bombers and try to get this situation turned around."

Give the computer hardware and software to the local agencies, then do whatever you have to to get them to comply. If the federal government can withhold highway funding from states that don't comply with national requirements, they can certainly do the same thing with law enforcement funds.

Okay, so much for computers and national cooperation and compliance. Now let's talk about cooperation and coordination among the primary federal agencies responsible for handling Unabomber-type crimes.

We've got the FBI, ATF, the Postal Inspector, and others, all with investigative responsibility in a case like this. On some of the incidents, the FAA and other agencies also got involved. Each has its own labs, its own bomb experts, its own street agents. What we really need to do is give serious consideration to a combined resource squad—I call it a "flying squad"—that would be organized in advance rather than reactively and that could immediately swing into action and be anywhere in the country as soon as a serious crime with a potential national character is identified.

After the unfortunate outcomes at Ruby Ridge and Waco, there was some talk about combining the FBI and ATF, or even folding ATF into the Bureau so that there could be unified leadership, unified goals, and unified operational policy. I am very much in favor of this. It would mean being able to approach a serious situation efficiently and uniformly, without turf wars and proprietary notions getting in the way. Of course, the FBI is a creature of the Justice Department and ATF is a creature of Treasury, so someone is going to have to give up some ground. I leave that to the politicians to work out. As a guy much closer to the front lines than any of the politicians, though, I can tell you that it would make our job a lot easier and more effective.

Speaking of making our job more effective, one of the key lessons of Unabom is to use the people you've got who have experience dealing with the challenge. The forensics people and bomb experts all did a fine job of analyzing the crime scenes and the explosive devices. The people who understood what was happening from a behavioral perspective should have been utilized just as effectively.

As I've stated before, to crack a case like this, or virtually any other where you don't have an eyewitness or a confession, the first thing you have to do is establish motive. If you can't do that, then you ought to be prepared to utilize the people who are trained to apply creative proactive techniques.

It appears, as of this writing, that our original profile and behavioral evaluation done almost two decades ago was pretty damn accurate. This is not meant to trumpet the work of my unit or to say we're cleverer than anyone else, because we're not. We are, however, experienced in this avenue of law enforcement in the same way that the bomb experts are experienced in recognizing a particular type of bomb or a bomb-making technique. We've seen enough of this that we do know what makes these guys tick, even if we don't know the specific reasoning that may be going on within their twisted minds.

If all of the ideas I've just talked about had been instituted or available when the search for the Unabomber began, it's possible we might have found him more than a decade earlier.

Next time something like this happens—and there will be a next time—maybe we'll be able to do just that.

APPENDIX 1

AN OVERVIEW AND
CHRONOLOGICAL SUMMARY

I was called in after the fourth Unabomber case, but received information on successive cases as they occurred. What is interesting to me, and very telling in terms of how offender profiling works, is that over eighteen years, my impression of this subject and his behavior remained consistent. To me this bolsters the idea that you do have to look at the first cases as being the most significant, telling you the most about the subject.

This guy changed his M.O. several times, from personally leaving packages lying around to be found, to mailing them to specific individuals, and went back and forth between these two techniques as it suited him. He targeted universities, airlines, computer stores, an advertising executive, seemingly without a connection other than his own rage, alienation, and frustration. Over the years, he moved, involving different jurisdictions across the United States, and he went from leaving us no information about his motivation (besides the bombs, of course), to writing and mailing communiqués to the news media, eventually filling eight newspaper pages with his thoughts, his drives, and potentially his identity, in the process.

But over the past eighteen years, along with other members of the Investigative Support Unit, I have provided numerous written and oral analyses to members of the Unabom Task Force and to other investigators on the case. The profile would change over the years when more information was gleaned through forensic analysis. However, when the written communiqués, including the manifesto, were evaluated, the link between the Unabomber and academe and his having a degree in one of the hard sciences was reinforced.

While the profile was modified over the years, we knew him all along.

What follows is a summary of the public information available on the cases and my retrospective comments.

—— Case 1 ——

Time and Place: May 26, 1978, Northwestern University, Evanston, Illinois.

Crime Scene Details: Package addressed to engineering professor at Rensselaer Polytechnic Institute in Troy, New York, found May 25 at University of Illinois, Chicago, in parking lot of the engineering department. Returned to presumed sender (return address), Buckley Crist, professor at Northwestern University's Technological Institute. Crist turned it in to Northwestern University Police Department when he didn't recognize it. Package exploded when opened, slightly injuring campus police officer Terry Marker.

The package bore ten one-dollar Eugene O'Neill stamps, which may have been a symbolic reference to the playwright's support for anarchists.

No apparent motive for the attack.

Device: Pipe bomb constructed of match heads, wooded initiators, packed in a carved wooden box.

Victimology: Specific target—either professor? Crist was a professor of material sciences.

Kaczynski Connection: Kaczynski was in the general area, applied for Illinois driver's license just six weeks after explosion. He had just moved back to the Chicago area temporarily after living in Montana for years. His license listed his parents' address in Lombard and expired in 1982 without being renewed.

—— Case 2 ——

Time and Place: May 9, 1979, Northwestern University, Technological Institute, Evanston, Illinois.

Crime Scene Details: Explosive device hidden in a cigar box left on a table between study cubicles on second floor in Northwestern University's Technological Institute. Victim opens box, which was taped shut, triggering bomb. Victim is treated for minor cuts and burns. Again, no apparent motive.

Device: After explosion, bomb looks like flashlight batteries with wires sticking out. The floor was covered with match heads.

Victimology: Nonspecific target. John G. Harris, graduate student at Northwestern studying civil engineering.

—— Case 3 ——

Time and Place: November 15, 1979, Dulles International Airport, Virginia, American Airlines flight 444, Chicago to Washington, D.C.

Crime Scene Details: Bomb hidden in package mailed from Chicago sets fire in cargo hold of American Airlines flight from Chicago to Washington, D.C., forces emergency landing at Dulles. Twelve aboard the 727 are treated for smoke inhalation.

Device: Bomb included an altimeter rigged to detonate when pressure in cabin reached critical level.

Victimology: No specific individual targeted. The fire destroyed the exterior of the package so that investigators could not tell to whom it had been mailed. Also, given the care in construction that ensured in-air detonation, the addressee may not have been a target.

------ Case 4 ------

Time and Place: June 10, 1980, Lake Forest, Illinois, residence of United Airlines president.

Crime Scene Details: Victim is injured on his hands, face, and thighs while opening a package sent to his home. The package also included a novel, *Ice Brothers,* published by Arbor House, whose trademark is a leaf. [Note: "FC" is found on device remnants, etched in piece of pipe.]

Device: Package bomb.

Victimology: Victim, Percy A. Wood, was then president of United Airlines.

Kaozynski Connection: Wood served on the Bay Area Air Pollution Control Board while Kaczynski was teaching at Berkeley.

Lessons Learned: I was called in to evaluate all of the first four cases together, from which I developed my original profile. In addition to the basic profile elements—white male, late twenties to early thirties, asocial obsessive-compulsive loner of above-average intelligence, etc.—the evolution in the bombs themselves and the means of delivery indicated a developing degree of technical ability and criminal sophistication. This development was likely to continue, making it important to emphasize the first crime as the place where he would have been most vulnerable to making mistakes. Since people tend to start where they are most comfortable, I felt he would be from the Chicago area and in some way connected with the university setting.

With no apparent motive for any of the crimes, then the switch from nonspecific to specific targets, university to airline settings, the bomber's real motive (anger, frustration) could be linked with universities—first crimes are usually most significant—but perhaps the recent cases were personal-cause crimes directed against airlines. Perhaps in his travels, the subject felt mistreated by someone connected with an airline and so lashed out at them too.

—— Case 5 ——

Time and Place: October 8, 1981, University of Utah, Salt Lake City.

Crime Scene Details: Bomb placed in business classroom is discovered and defused without injuries.

Device: Package bomb.

Victimology: Nonspecific target.

Kaczynski Connection: Kaczynski reportedly resided and held odd jobs in the Salt Lake City area in this time period.

Lessons Learned: This subject is mobile and feels comfortable moving outside his primary zone in the Chicago area. Mobility tends to add years to the profile because he has means to get around and criminal sophistication to feel secure doing so. He's gaining confidence.

He's also back in the university setting, reinforcing that that's where his real motivation lies. His anger is directed toward authority: institutions of higher learning in general, a business classroom and an airline executive in particular.

I am also further convinced this UNSUB has a college background: he's comfortable walking around classrooms while he places these exploding devices; he also blends in there—he's not an airline mechanic in greasy overalls.

The evolution of the bombs shows increased sophistication. Although these are still relatively crude devices that any intelligent person could learn to make, he's compulsively putting in the time to do this. I feel that someone—particularly in his original home base, Chicago—will recognize him if we describe his behavior to the public, including the fact that he has practiced putting bombs together, exploding things, in the past.

There is still no apparent motive for the bomb attacks, though. I believe this is someone who watches the investigation closely, reads newspaper accounts religiously, and may be mixing in different targets in a cat-and-mouse game with investigators. He knows we're frustrated, and probably realizes that involving a third jurisdiction would only pass that frustration around. On the up side for us, if we do circulate information about him, the more specific links we can establish (the more cities he spends time in), the easier it will be for someone to recognize him.

—— Case 6 ——

Time and Place: May 5, 1982, Vanderbilt University, Nashville, Tennessee.

Crime Scene Details: Package addressed to a professor, P. Fischer, explodes when Fischer's secretary opens it, injuring her. Originally addressed incorrectly to Fischer at Pennsylvania State University (he moved from Pennsylvania to Tennessee two years earlier), the package was forwarded from Pennsylvania, although the stamps were already canceled when it was mailed from Provo, Utah, on April 23. Possibly, as in the first bombing, the UNSUB was actually targeting the person named in the return address.

Device: Wooden box containing pipe bomb filled with smokeless powder, match heads.

Victimology: Actual victim, Janet Smith, was not intended target. Intended victim presumed to be Brigham Young University electrical engineering professor LeRoy Bearnson, since package should have been returned to him. Bearnson's middle name is Wood.

Kaczynski Connection: Kaczynski reportedly resided and held odd jobs in the Salt Lake City area in this time period.

Lessons Learned: The bombs are largely made of wood and two victims with "Wood" in their names have been targets. Again he's attacking in a university setting, although he is flexible enough to change M.O., adapt his method of delivery. This case used an M.O. adapted from the very first case to lower his risk of exposure (using the mail instead of leaving it somewhere himself to be found).

His expertise continues to develop, these bombs have to be stable enough to travel through the mail without accidentally detonating.

There is no immediate gratification, although he gets satisfaction from painstakingly assembling the devices. Since he won't be nearby to hear and feel the blast, and it will take time for his bomb to be delivered and opened, he will obsessively read and watch the news for weeks to get word of his accomplishment. He'll need access to regional papers, since a small explosion on campus may not make national news. It is essential to be proactive: the case agents have to get information like this out so people can recognize it.

———— Case 7 ————

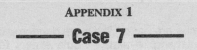

Time and Place: July 2, 1982, Cory Hall, Fourth-Floor Faculty Lounge, University of California–Berkeley.

Crime Scene Details: At approximately 8:00 A.M. victim noticed a can of some type, perhaps left by construction workers or a student. It explodes when he picks it up, causing serious injury.

Device: Small metal pipe bomb.

Victimology: Nonspecific target, a professor of electrical engineering and computer science, Diogenes Angelakos.

Kaczynski Connection: Cory Hall, which housed the computer science department, is not far from Campbell Hall, where Kaczynski taught mathematics from 1967 to 1969.

Lessons Learned: The bomber is increasing his mobility and involving a new area of operations in California, indicating he's comfortable in Berkeley, too. He wouldn't travel far with bombs, that's not feasible or safe; he must be able to stay in these places for as long as it takes to place or mail the bombs, without being missed from work, for example. This information needs to be made public, along with the other behavioral information outlined earlier: his practice with explosives earlier in life, his obsessive news watching, and so forth.

Although it is still not clear what he wants (he's not making extortion-like demands, for example), it is increasingly clear that his focus is the academic world, and he has ties to the locations and schools targeted. The airline targets would be de-emphasized because his first, most revealing crime targeted a university setting; and the airline incidents seemed to be blips on the screen, possibly settling a score that was not part of his overall plan.

The bombs are becoming more dangerous. For this to remain satisfying to him, I would expect to see more experimentation and practice in creating the devices, making the blasts and injuries to victims more serious.

Acquaintances, family members, and neighbors may complain to authorities about the setting off of bombs in their immediate areas.

——— Case 8 ———

Time and Place: May 15, 1985, Cory Hall, Computer Lab, University of California–Berkeley.

Crime Scene Details: Bomb left in computer room in a stack with three-ring binders. Police believe it was there several days before a graduate student noticed it. It exploded when he picked it up, severing two arteries in his right hand, destroying parts of several fingers, causing him to lose partial vision in one eye.

Device: More powerful than previous bombs; contained a mixture of ammonium nitrate and aluminum powder.

Victimology: Nonspecific target. John E. Hauser, graduate student in engineering and air force pilot.

Kaczynski Connection: Cory Hall, which housed the computer science department, is not far from Campbell Hall, where Kaczynski taught mathematics from 1967 to 1969.

On April 29 Kaczynski reportedly stayed at the Parker Hotel in Helena, where he could have caught a bus to California.

Lessons Learned: As expected, the bomber's technical expertise continues to develop and this is the most damaging bomb yet. Still, he has the patience to wait for his results.

This second attack on Berkeley suggests that the UNSUB may have some connection to this school. He is also familiar enough and comfortable enough to walk through the building and personally place his bomb. This guy is an academic: he is invisible in this setting.

—— **Case 9** ——

Time and Place: June 13, 1985, Boeing Company, Fabrication Division, Auburn, Washington.

Crime Scene Details: Mail bomb is sent from Oakland, California, on May 8, 1985, before the last explosion in a Berkeley computer lab, but package is lost in internal mail at Boeing. Employees discover the bomb when the package is opened and does not detonate; they turn it over to the bomb squad, which safely disarms it. No one is injured.

Device: Package bomb in wooden case.

Victimology: Not known if a specific individual was targeted on the address label.

Kaczynski Connection: Kaczynski is reported to have stayed at the Parker Hotel in Helena the night of May 22.

Lessons Learned: This case and the last were set in motion at about the same time. Since bombers in general do follow their own press, this subject probably knows at Berkeley in 1982 we focused our energies on his connection with universities. This time, therefore, he may have sent two at once, thinking that the one at Berkeley would satisfy his need to get that target, while the bomb sent to Boeing would confuse investigators and maybe throw us off the track. In essence, he's using his own proactive technique: just when we think we have a handle on his motivation, he's going to try to shake us off.

The timing of the events could be another clue: Is he in northern California, or could he be just passing through, using it as a base of operations for bomb delivery?

The way to use this would be, again, to reveal all of these behavior patterns to the press, including the press in Chicago.

——— Case 10 ———

Time and Place: November 15, 1985, residence of University of Michigan professor, Ann Arbor.

Crime Scene Details: Explosive device was mailed to University of Michigan psychology professor James V. McConnell's home outside Ann Arbor. A one-page letter postmarked Salt Lake City was taped to the outside, which read, "I'd like you to read this book. . . . Everybody in your position should read this book." McConnell and his young assistant, Nicklaus Suino, were injured when Suino opened the package in the kitchen. He suffered powder burns on his arms and legs, and shrapnel wounds; McConnell lost part of his hearing.

Device: Package bomb.

Victimology: Specific target. A proponent of behavior modification, McConnell was outspoken and well known even outside the collegiate community.

Kaczynski Connection: McConnell was teaching when Kaczynski was a graduate student earning his M.A. and Ph.D. at Michigan, from 1962 to 1967.

Lessons Learned: Another university professor targeted at a new location. The postmark (Salt Lake City, Utah) indicates that the subject is mobile again. He's increasingly confident, moving further outside his earlier sphere of influence. Although this is distracting to officials, I still firmly believe someone in Chicago could recognize this guy if given the chance.

He has also changed his M.O. Although this is another university-related target, this victim is specific. And he targets him at home (placing himself in a position of even greater power and making the victim that much more vulnerable) and by mail, further separating himself from the crime and limiting his exposure. The shift in M.O. shows that as compulsive as he is in design and construction of his bombs, he is flexible enough to adapt, evolve, and stay ahead of the investigation. His proactive techniques could put the task force in a reactive mode. And with months to years between bombings, no one knows where, when, or whom he'll strike next. This UNSUB clearly gets off on the power he has to strike fear in society.

─────── **Case 11** ───────

Time and Place: December 11, 1985, parking lot of computer store, Sacramento, California.

Crime Scene Details: Bomb found in parking lot of computer rental store kills owner of store who attempts to move it. The device is disguised to look like a road hazard and left near the back entrance of the building. Victim is killed by shrapnel that rips through his chest to his heart.

Device: Bomb is filled with pieces of nails to render it more dangerous.

Victimology: Nonspecific target. Businessman Hugh Campbell Scrutton owned the store.

Kaczynski Connection: Scrutton took math courses at Berkeley in the summer of 1967, Kaczynski's first year there, although it is unclear whether he started teaching summer or fall of that year.

Investigators also looked into the victim's travels in Montana and Utah.

Lessons Learned: Subject goes back to earlier method of personal delivery. He probably visited the site ahead of time to get a feel for the landscape, figure out where and how to place the device so it would be found, and become familiar with patterns of activity in the area. Someone at the store may have waited on the bomber, or his picture could have been captured by a surveillance camera.

I did not see the shift to a computer store as unrelated to the university targets, since both represent education of sorts. Also, many of the university targets were connected with engineering or the computer sciences.

This bomb was clearly the most dangerous so far, and the bomber added metal to increase the amount of shrapnel from the blast, indicating that he is ready to kill someone. Subject is growing more confident and more dangerous: anyone could have been his victim. While this bomb was the most dangerous to the victim, the subject felt comfortable enough to transport it and set it up by hand in broad daylight.

——— Case 12 ———

Time and Place: February 20, 1987, computer store, Salt Lake City, Utah.

Crime Scene Details: Victim is injured by bomb left in the parking lot of the Caams Computer Store, disguised as a road hazard. Witness sees man leaving bag of wood in lot approximately one hour before explosion. Police develop composite drawing.

Device: Bomb, disguised to look like wooden two-by-fours with nails sticking out, is left in a parking space.

Victimology: Nonspecific target, Gary Wright, store owner.

Kaczynski Connection: Kaczynski spent time doing odd jobs in Utah around this period.

Lessons Learned: This M.O. worked for the bomber in the last case two years earlier, so he used it again, this time in Salt Lake City. He had established his comfort with the area as a target zone earlier, so it is not entirely a surprise that he would return. It just proves he's still active and mobile.

As predicted, the subject now goes underground for a while, since bombers are cowardly types who are terrified by the prospect of discovery. Although the composite drawing was not specific enough to get him arrested, he was probably driven underground by the threat that the witness represented. I felt he would not hand-deliver the next bomb for this reason.

During that time, we would expect him to continue experimenting with new, probably more powerful, devices—he has already killed once. He would also perfect his rationalization for his actions, to satisfy his obsessive-compulsive nature.

—— **Case 13** ——

Time and Place: June 22, 1993, residence of geneticist-professor, Tiburon, California.

Crime Scene Details: Victim is seriously injured by bomb mailed from Sacramento, California, to his home, postmarked June 18. It explodes as he attempts to open it.

Device: Package bomb.

Victimology: Specific target. Dr. Charles Epstein, a geneticist at the University of California, San Francisco.

Kaczynski Connection: Kaczynski is reported to have spent the night at a hotel in Helena on June 6. From Helena, he could have made bus connections to Sacramento.

Lessons Learned: The more his M.O. evolves, the more it remains the same: another university professor, within his geographic sphere of influence. As predicted, the subject mailed this bomb, having learned from his potentially career-ending mistake during the last event.

We have enough links now that I believe a proactive approach could work. We go public with elements of the profile and the pre- and post-offense behavior of this subject (previously setting off small explosions, following the media on these cases, being a loner, et cetera) in the *Reader's Digest*. The emphasis should be on getting these details out in the Chicago area, indicating that this subject is also comfortable with and active in the Salt Lake City, Sacramento, and Berkeley areas, with at least an interest in the University of Michigan. Especially given his continued involvement with professors, I am fairly certain the other target industries are peripheral, possibly thrown in to thwart the investigation. These types of criminals are known to inject themselves in and/or attempt to manipulate the investigation of their crimes, so this seemed increasingly plausible. This became especially significant when he made contact with the *New York Times* in 1993, establishing his identity (Freedom Club) and a numeric code by which the media would recognize him in future communiqués.

—— Case 14 ——

Time and Place: June 24, 1993, Yale University, New Haven, Connecticut.

Crime Scene Details: Victim is seriously injured when package bomb mailed to his office explodes. The package, postmarked June 18, was mailed from Sacramento, California.

Device: Package bomb.

Victimology: Specific target—Dr. David Gelernter, computer scientist.

Kaczynski Connection: Kaczynski is reported to have spent the night at a hotel in Helena on June 6. From Helena, he could have made bus connections to Sacramento, where which he mailed the bomb that exploded earlier this same week.

Lessons Learned: The fact that this bomb and the previous bomb were both mailed from the same place on the same date seemed significant. Two at a time could indicate that he had only a short time to spend in Sacramento, or it could represent an escalation of emotional significance to him. He may have felt, for example, that he was losing ground to other, stronger terrorist activities and fringe groups such as the bombing of the World Trade Center and the fire at Waco, and he had to do something to get back in the spotlight.

Although the specific link to Yale and/or the victim is unclear, the strength of this explosion, which leaves the victim with permanent damage, indicates that his motivation—anger directed at university and authority figures—is still great.

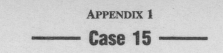

Time and Place: December 10, 1994, residence of advertising executive, Aspen Drive, North Caldwell, New Jersey.

Crime Scene Details: Victim is killed instantly by a bomb he received by mail at his home. The package, about the size of a videocassette, was sent from the San Francisco area and had a fictitious name of a professor at San Francisco State University in the return address. The bomber apparently got some of his information on his victim from an outdated source: he addressed Mosser in his position with Burson-Marsteller, a title he had not held in nearly a year.

Device: Package bomb.

Victimology: Specific target—Thomas Mosser, vice president and general manager of Young & Rubicam, a well-known advertising agency.

Lessons Learned: The motive for this bombing was not apparent until the bomber's explanation was received by the *New York Times* months after the blast. Again, although he emphasized that Mosser's agency was targeted for "manipulating people's attitudes," I saw this blast as a smoke screen, similar to the way other types of criminals stage their crime scenes. The bomber had this elaborate antitechnology ideology, but his true motivation seemed to be rage, the desire to take his frustrations and hurt out on other people. And overwhelmingly, he had directed that rage at people connected with universities.

The shift to a target in New Jersey, adding yet another new jurisdiction to the caseload, seemed another way to deflect the investigation further from him and confuse the issues.

The bomber was articulate in his letters, he had been able to elude investigators for more than a decade, he was mobile, and he was becoming increasingly dangerous. FBI begins to use the media and start really disseminating information about this guy: what he said, what we thought he was like, where he went, and what he did. As smart as he obviously was, his increased activity and communication would be his downfall.

——— Case 16 ———

Time and Place: April 24, 1995, headquarters of California Forestry Association, Sacramento.

Crime Scene Details: Victim is killed in his office when he opens a package addressed to his predecessor. The package was mailed around the same time as letters sent to the *New York Times* and one of the bomber's former victims.

Device: Originally reported as a pipe bomb. In his letter to the *New York Times,* Unabomber provided "correct" details.

Victimology: Specific target, but wrong victim. Gilbert P. Murray, president of the association, seems to have been a victim of opportunity. The package was addressed to William Dennison, his predecessor.

Kaczynski Connection: Dennison graduated from Berkeley in 1959 and lectured there between 1971 and 1988. Murray was a 1975 Berkeley grad.
   Kaczynski is reported to have stayed overnight at a Helena hotel on March 13. From there he could have made bus connections to California.

Lessons Learned: This was the most severe explosion, and that fact, coupled with the timing of this bomb and the various letters he sent in April, indicated he needed to be the center of attention. I had felt all along we were dealing with an insignificant nobody who needed the bombs to gain power and saw this timing as reinforcement of that. He became increasingly active and vociferous after the Oklahoma City blast, no doubt outraged that such an inferior operation could steal his thunder. Although that blast killed far more efficiently and caused much greater damage and more widespread panic, his bombs were so much more carefully and expertly crafted. His response had to be great enough to bring him back in the heart of the public's fear, by act and by deed.

The letters, mailed at the same time as this bomb, also gave me great hope that he would soon be tripped up. His words gave us more insight into his identity, and more to show the public, than all the other evidence from his eighteen-year career.

The crime scene details provide clues we can use to develop proactive techniques to get these guys. They leave themselves behind in everything they do, waiting to be recognized. Over enough time, it happens to all of them.

APPENDIX 2

THE UNABOM LETTERS

Like New York's Mad Bomber before him, the Unabomber is an inveterate letter writer. As investigators and profilers, we came to know him through his bombs and his written communications.

From the bombs themselves we learned he was intelligent, deadly, and willing and able to take lives. From the written communications, we gleaned certain other things about his personality.

As I've stated repeatedly over the years, all bombers are cowards. In their own way, even suicide bombers are cowards, unable to grasp at glory or fulfill themselves in any other way. But bombers who plant or send their devices and then get the hell out of the way—they are definitely physical cowards, unwilling to look their victims in the face at the moment the crime is committed.

The Unabomber's letters show him to be an emotional coward as well, someone who is extremely uncomfortable with human intimacy, and even direct communication. Hence the letters. This is the only way he feels comfortable airing his thoughts and ideas. From the letters alone we can tell that he is severely lacking in human contact and the ability to relate to individuals on a one-to-one level.

Some experts claimed that the sudden flurry of letter writing suggested that the Unabomber was finally cracking up. I didn't feel this way. I thought he was merely basking in the publicity and his ability to control public thought. If we read the letters in chronological order, we see a progression in organization and an apparent increase in confidence which continues right up to the printing of the manifesto itself. (He always uses "we," as if this bolsters his sense of strength.)

Yet in a letter to Tom Tyler, professor of social psychology and head of the department at Berkeley, in the midst of his hectoring, the bomber begins asking him questions, almost asking for advice, as if entreating the professor to verify and authenticate his own positions. Tyler had been quoted in a May 1, 1995, article in the *San Francisco Chronicle* discussing the ideological similarities between the Unabomber and the Oklahoma City bombing.

Now, by the time he responded to Tyler, the Unabomber had already written his lengthy manifesto and had already killed and maimed people, supposedly in support of his cause. Yet after all that, he is still apparently unsure enough in his own mind to ask, "If you think we are wrong, then why do you think so?"

Another interesting psychological mechanism is his deploring the "indiscriminate slaughter" of the Oklahoma City bombing, while still justifying what he is doing. In a perverse way, this reminds me of a murder case I studied in which two subjects, James Russell Odom and James Clayton Lawson, raped and mutilated a convenience store clerk. At their trial Odom took the stand and testified, "All I did was rape her. I didn't kill her."

The jury didn't believe Odom, and I don't believe anything the Unabomber wants us to believe.

Despite his claim to be concerned for the good of society, the only one he really cares about, the only one he can truly focus on, is himself.

Some of the bomber's communications are still obscure, their meaning known only to their author. For instance, the simple first message, "Wu—it works! I told you it would. R.V."

Wu is apparently Hung-Hsi Wu, a professor in the Berkeley math department. After Kaczynski was identified, FBI agents questioned Dr. Wu. Among other questions, they asked him if he could think of anyone who might be envious of his work. Kaczynski's name never came up in the interview.

The R.V. could be fellow professor Robert Vaught, who taught in the same subject area as Kaczynski. Yet when questioned, Dr. Vaught did not recall Kaczynski ever coming to see him or interacting with him in any meaningful way.

The actors in the Unabomber's strange and deadly drama could have been chosen for any number of reasons. At this point, we can only speculate. Perhaps they were people of whom he was specifically envious, whom he felt inadequate in comparison to. Perhaps there was some other reason or a variety of reasons.

Some samples of the Unabomber's communications follow.

Berkeley Bomb Note, June 2, 1982

Description: Note inside bomb; no address, no return address. Placed in bomb at Berkeley; discovered after bomb exploded.

Contents: "Wu—it works! I told you it would. R.V."

New York Times Letter, 1993

Description: Letter addressed to *New York Times;* return address unknown. Mailed from Sacramento; received and opened by *New York Times.*

Contents: On the sheet of paper used to write this 1993 letter to the *Times*, there was a faint impression of a message he may have written to himself on a previous sheet of paper: "call Nathan R Wed 7 pm."

Verification: Authenticated by a nine-digit code the Unabomber included in an earlier letter to the *Times*. Task force members discovered that the nine-digit number was a real Social Security number for a minor criminal in northern California who had been in prison when some of the bombings occurred. He had a tattoo that said "Pure Wood."

Gelernter Letter, April 24, 1995

Description: Letter addressed to Yale University computer science professor and author David Gelernter, who was injured by a Unabom device in 1993; return address, FBI's Washington, D.C., headquarters. Mailed from Oakland, California, April 20; opened by Gelernter the week of April 27.

Contents:

Dr. Gelernter:

People with advanced degrees aren't as smart as they think they are. If you'd had any brains you would have realized that there are a lot of people out there who resent bitterly the way techno-nerds like you are changing the world and you wouldn't have been dumb enough to open an unexpected package from an unknown source.

In the epilog of your book, "Mirror Worlds," you tried to justify your research by claiming that the developments you describe are inevitable, and that any college person can learn enough about computers to compete in a computer-dominated world. Apparently, people without a college degree don't count. In any case, being informed about computers won't enable anyone to prevent invasion of privacy (through computers), genetic engineering (to which computers make an important contribution), environmental degradation through excessive economic growth (computers make an important contribution to economic growth) and so forth.

As for the inevitability argument, if the developments you describe are inevitable, they are not inevitable in the way that old age and bad weather are inevitable. They are inevitable only because techno-nerds like you make them inevitable. If there were no computer scientists there would be no progress in computer science. If you claim you are justified in pursuing your research because the developments involved are inevitable, then you may as well say that theft is inevitable, therefore we shouldn't blame thieves.

But we do not believe that progress and growth are inevitable.

We'll have more to say about that later.

FC

P.S. Warren Hoge of the *New York Times* can confirm that this letter does come from FC.

New York Times Letter, April 24, 1995

Description: Letter addressed to *New York Times;* return address unknown. Mailed in Oakland, California; opened by *New York Times.*

Contents:
(Passage deleted at the request of the FBI.)

This is a message from the terrorist group FC.

We blew up Thomas Mosser last December because he was a Burston-Marsteller [*sic*] executive. Among other misdeeds, Burston-Marsteller helped Exxon clean up its public image after the Exxon Valdez incident. But we attacked Burston-Marsteller less for its specific misdeeds than on general principles. Burston-Marsteller is about the biggest organization in the public relations field. This means that its business is the development of techniques for manipulating people's attitudes. It was for this more than for its actions in specific cases that we sent a bomb to an executive of this company.

Some news reports have made the misleading statement that we have been attacking universities or scholars. We have nothing against universities or scholars as such. All the university people whom we have attacked have been specialists in technical fields. (We consider certain areas of applied psychology, such as behavior modification, to be technical fields.) We would not want anyone to think that we have any desire to hurt professors who study archaeology, history, literature or harmless stuff like that. The people we are out to get are the scientists and engineers, especially in critical fields like computers and genetics. As for the bomb planted in the Business School at the U. of Utah, that was a botched operation. We won't say how or why it was botched because we don't want to give the FBI any clues. No one was hurt by that bomb.

In our previous letter to you we called ourselves anarchists. Since "anarchist" is a vague word that has been applied to a variety of attitudes, further explanation is needed. We call ourselves anarchists because we would like, ideally, to break down all society into very small, completely autonomous units. Regrettably, we don't see any clear road to this goal, so we leave it to the indefinite future. Our more immediate goal, which we think may be attainable at some time during the next several decades, is the destruction of the worldwide industrial system. Through our bombings we hope to promote social instability in industrial society, propagate anti-industrial ideas and give encouragement to those who hate the industrial system.

The FBI has tried to portray these bombings as the work of an isolated nut. We won't waste our time arguing about whether we are nuts, but we certainly are not isolated. For security reasons we won't reveal the number of members of our group, but anyone who will read the anarchist and radical environmentalist journals will see that opposition to the industrial-technological system is widespread and growing.

Why do we announce our goals only now, though we made our first bomb some seventeen years ago? Our early bombs were too ineffectual to attract much public attention or give encouragement to those who hate the system. We found by experience that gunpowder bombs, if small enough to be carried inconspicuously, were too feeble to do much damage, so we took a couple of years off to do some experimenting. We learned how to make pipe bombs that were powerful enough, and we used these in a couple of successful bombings as well as in some unsuccessful ones.

(Passage deleted at the request of the FBI.)

Since we no longer have to confine the explosive in a pipe, we are now free of limitations on the size and shape of our bombs. We are pretty sure we know how to increase the power of our explosives and reduce the number of batteries needed to set them off. And, as we've just indicated, we think we now have more effective fragmentation material. So we expect to be able to pack deadly bombs into ever smaller, lighter and more harmless looking packages. On the other hand, we believe we will be able to make bombs much bigger than any we've made before. With a briefcase-full or a suitcase-full of explosives we should be able to blow out the walls of substantial buildings.

Clearly we are in a position to do a great deal of damage. And it doesn't appear that the FBI is going to catch us any time soon,

The FBI is a joke.

The people who are pushing all this growth and progress garbage deserve to be severely punished. But our goal is less to punish them than to propagate ideas. Anyhow we are getting tired of making bombs. It's no fun having to spend all your evenings and weekends preparing dangerous mixtures, filing trigger mechanisms out of scraps of metal or searching the Sierras for a place isolated enough to test a bomb. So we offer a bargain.

We have a long article, between 29,000 and 37,000 words, that we want to have published. If you can get it published according to our requirements we will permanently desist from terrorist activities. It must be published in the *New York Times, Time* or *Newsweek,* or in some other widely read, nationally distributed periodical. Because of its length we suppose it will have to be serialized. Alternatively, it can be published as a small book, but the book must be well publicized and made available at a moderate price in bookstores nationwide and in at least some places abroad. Whoever agrees to publish the material will have exclusive rights to reproduce it for a period of six months and will be welcome to any profits they may make from it. After six months from the first appearance of the article or book it must become public property, so that anyone can reproduce or publish it. (If material is serialized, first instalment becomes public property six months after appearance of first instalment, second instalment, etc.) We must have the right to publish in the *New York Times, Time* or *Newsweek,* each year for three years after the appearance of our article or book, three thousand words expanding or clarifying our material or rebutting criticisms of it.

The article will not explicitly advocate violence. There will be an unavoidable implication that we favor violence to the extent that it may be necessary, since we advocate eliminating industrial society and we ourselves have been using violence to that end. But the article will not advocate violence explicitly, nor will it propose the overthrow of the United States Government, nor will it contain obscenity or anything else that you would be likely to regard as unacceptable for publication.

How do you know that we will keep our promise to desist from terrorism if our conditions are met? It will be to our advantage to keep our promise. We want to win acceptance for certain ideas. If we break our promise people will lose respect for us and so will be less likely to accept the ideas.

Our offer to desist from terrorism is subject to three qualifications. First: Our promise to desist will not take effect until all parts of our article or book have appeared in print. Second: If the authorities should succeed in tracking us down and an attempt is made to arrest any of us, or even to question us in connection with the bombings, we reserve the right to use violence. Third: We distinguish between terrorism and sabotage. By terrorism we mean actions motivated by a desire to influence the development of a society and intended to cause injury or death to human beings. By sabotage we mean similarly motivated actions intended to destroy property without injuring human beings. The promise we offer is to desist from terrorism. We reserve the right to engage in sabotage.

It may be just as well that failure of our early bombs discouraged us from making any public statements at that time. We were very young then and our thinking was crude. Over the years we have given as much attention to the development of our ideas as to the development of bombs, and we now have something serious to say. And we feel that just now the time is ripe for the presentation of anti-industrial ideas.

Please see to it that the answer to our offer is well publicized in the media so that we won't miss it. Be sure to tell us where and how our material will be published and how long it will take to appear in print once we have sent in the manuscript. If the answer is satisfactory, we will finish typing the manuscript and send it to you. If the answer is unsatisfactory, we will start building our next bomb.

We encourage you to print this letter.

FC

(Passage deleted at the request of the FBI.)

Additional passage reportedly from the same letter: "The idea was to kill a lot of business people who we assumed would constitute the majority of the passengers. . . . But of course some of the passengers likely would have been innocent people—maybe kids, or some working stiff going to see his sick grandmother. We're glad now that that attempt failed."

San Francisco Chronicle **Letter, June 27, 1995**

Description: Letter addressed to editorial page editor Jerry Roberts, *San Francisco Chronicle;* return address, Frederick Benjamin Isaac Wood, 549 Wood Street, Woodlake, Ca 93286. Mailed from San Francisco, June 24, 1995; received Tuesday, June 27, 1995, by the *San Francisco Chronicle.*

Contents: "WARNING. The terrorist group FC, called unabomber by the FBI, is planning to blow up an airliner out of Los Angeles International Airport some time during the next six days. To prove that the writer of this letter knows something about FC, the first two digits of their identifying number are 55."

New York Times Letter, June 28, 1995

Description: Package addressed to *New York Times;* return address, Calgene Inc. of Davis [known for making genetically engineered tomatoes]. Mailed June 24, 1995; opened June 28, 1995, by *New York Times.*

Contents: Manifesto and letter.

Washington Post Letter, June 28, 1995

Description: Package wrapped in brown paper; addressed with cut-out pieces of paper to *Washington Post;* return address, Boon Long Hoe, a San Jose high-tech business executive who is currently the chief financial officer for GSS Array Technology in Singapore. Mailed June 24, 1995; opened at *Washington Post* late on June 28, 1995, after a search was made at the suggestion of the FBI.

Contents: Manifesto, new letter, and copies of earlier letters to the *New York Times* and *Penthouse.*

New York Times Letter No. 2, June 29, 1995

Description: Package addressed to the *New York Times;* no return address. Mailed (date unknown); opened by the *New York Times* on June 29, 1995.

Contents: "Since the public has a short memory, we decided to play one last prank to remind them who we are. . . . But, no, we haven't tried to plant a bomb on an airline (recently). . . . We strongly deplore the kind of indiscriminate slaughter that occurred in the Oklahoma City event."

Tom Tyler Letter, June 30, 1995

Description: A thick 9 × 12-inch manila envelope with hand-canceled stamps, tape, and excessive postage, containing fifty-six pages of typed material, eleven pages of footnotes, and a one-page letter to Professor Tyler from the Unabomber; addressed to Tom Tyler, a University of California–Berkeley social psychology professor and head of the psychology department; return address unknown. Place of origin unknown; received by Tyler at 10:44 A.M. on Friday, June 30, 1995.

Contents:
Dr. Tyler:

This is a message from FC. The FBI calls us "unabom." We read a newspaper article in which you commented on recent bombings, including ours, as an indication of social problems. We are sending you a copy of a manuscript that we hope the *New York Times* will get published for us.

The trouble with psychologists is that in commenting on what people say or do they often concentrate exclusively on the non-rational motivations behind the speech or behavior. But human behavior has a rational as well as an irrational component, and psychologists should not neglect the rational component. So if you take the trouble to read our manuscript and do any further thinking about the "unabom" case, we suggest that you should not only consider our actions as a symptom of social or psychological problems;

189

you should also give attention to the substance of the issues that we raise in the manuscript. You might ask yourself, for example, the following questions:

Do you think we are likely to be right, in a general way, about the kind of future that technology is creating for the human race?

If you think we are wrong, then why do you think so? How would you answer our arguments? Can you sketch a PLAUSABLE [*sic*] scenario for a future technological society that does not have the negative characteristics indicated by our scenario?

If you think we are likely to be right about the future, do you consider that kind of future acceptable? If not, then what, if anything, do you think can be done about it?

Do you think our analysis of PRESENT social problems is approximately correct? If not, why not? How would you answer our arguments?

If you think we have indentified some present social problems correctly, do you think anything can be done about them? Will they get better or worse with continued growth and progress?

We apologize for sending you such a poor carbon copy of our manuscript [copy of manifesto accompanied this letter]. We can't make copies at a public copy machine because people would get suspicious if they saw us handling our copies with gloves.

FC

THE UNABOMBER MANIFESTO

(The following is full text of the Unabomber Manifesto.)

Industrial Society and Its Future

INTRODUCTION

1. The Industrial Revolution and its consequences have been a disaster for the human race. They have greatly increased the life-expectancy of those of us who live in "advanced" countries, but they have destabilized society, have made life unfulfilling, have subjected human beings to indignities, have led to widespread psychological suffering (in the Third World to physical suffering as well) and have inflicted severe damage on the natural world. The continued development of technology will worsen the situation. It will certainly subject human beings to greater indignities and inflict greater damage on the natural world, it will probably lead to greater social disruption and psychological suffering, and it may lead to increased physical suffering even in "advanced" countries.

2. The industrial-technological system may survive or it may break down. If it survives, it MAY eventually achieve a low level of physical and psychological suffering, but only after passing through a long and very painful period of adjustment and only at the cost of permanently reducing human beings and many other living organisms to engineered products and mere cogs in the social machine. Furthermore, if the system survives, the consequences will be inevitable: There is no way of reforming or modifying the system so as to prevent it from depriving people of dignity and autonomy.

3. If the system breaks down the consequences will still be very painful. But the bigger the system grows the more disastrous the results of its breakdown will be, so if it is to break down it had best break down sooner rather than later.

4. We therefore advocate a revolution against the industrial system. This revolution may or may not make use of violence: it may be sudden or it may be a relatively gradual process spanning a few decades. We can't predict any of that. But we do outline in a very general way the measures that those who hate the industrial system should take in order to prepare the way for a revolution against that form of society. This is not to be a POLITICAL revolution. Its object will be to overthrow not governments but the economic and technological basis of the present society.

5. In this article we give attention to only some of the negative developments that have grown out of the industrial-technological system. Other such developments we mention only briefly or ignore altogether. This does not mean that we regard these other developments as unimportant. For practical reasons we have to confine our discussion to areas that have received insufficient public attention or in which we have something new to say. For example, since there are well-developed environmental and wilderness movements, we have written very little about environmental degradation or the destruction of wild nature, even though we consider these to be highly important.

THE PSYCHOLOGY OF MODERN LEFTISM

6. Almost everyone will agree that we live in a deeply troubled society. One of the most widespread manifestations of the craziness of our world is leftism, so a discussion of the psychology of leftism can serve as an introduction to the discussion of the problems of modern society in general.

7. But what is leftism? During the first half of the 20th century leftism could have been practically identified with socialism. Today the movement is fragmented and it is not clear who can properly be called a leftist. When we speak of leftists in this article we have in mind mainly socialists, collectivists, "politically correct" types, feminists, gay and disability activists, animal rights activists and the like. But not everyone who is associated with one of these movements is a leftist. What we are trying to get at in discussing leftism is not so much a movement or an ideology as a psychological type, or rather a collection of related types. Thus, what we mean by "leftism" will emerge more clearly in the course of our discussion of leftist psychology (Also, see paragraphs 227-230.)

8. Even so, our conception of leftism will remain a good deal less clear than we would wish, but there doesn't seem to be any remedy for this. All we are trying to do is indicate in a rough and approximate way the two psychological tendencies that we believe are the main driving force of modern leftism. We by no means claim to be telling the WHOLE truth about leftist psychology. Also, our discussion is meant to apply to modern leftism only. We leave open the question of the extent to which our discussion could be applied to the leftists of the 19th and early 20th centuries.

9. The two psychological tendencies that underlie modern leftism we call "feelings of inferiority" and "oversocialization." Feelings of inferiority are characteristic of modern leftism as a whole, while oversocialization is characteristic only of a certain segment of modern leftism; but this segment is highly influential.

FEELINGS OF INFERIORITY

10. By "feelings of inferiority" we mean not only inferiority feelings in the strictest sense but a whole spectrum of related traits: low self-esteem, feelings of powerlessness, depressive tendencies, defeatism, guilt, self-hatred, etc. We argue that modern leftists tend to have such feelings (possibly more or less repressed) and that these feelings are decisive in determining the direction of modern leftism.

11. When someone interprets as derogatory almost anything that is said about him (or about groups with whom he identifies) we conclude that he has inferiority feelings or low self-esteem. This tendency is pronounced among minority rights advocates, whether or not they belong to the minority groups whose rights they defend. They are hypersensitive about the words used to designate minorities and about anything that is said concerning minorities. The terms "negro," "oriental," "handicapped" or "chick" for an African, an Asian, a disabled person or a woman originally had no derogatory connotation. "Broad" and "chick" were merely the feminine equivalents of "guy," "dude" or "fellow." The negative connotations have been attached to these terms by the activists themselves. Some animal rights advocates have gone so far as to reject the word "pet" and insist on its replacement by "animal companion." Leftish anthropologists go to great lengths to avoid saying anything about primitive peoples that could conceivably be interpreted as negative. They want to replace the word "primitive" by "nonliterate." They seem almost paranoid about anything that might suggest that any primitive culture is inferior to our own. (We do not mean to imply that primitive cultures ARE inferior to ours. We merely point out the hypersensitivity of leftish anthropologists.)

12. Those who are most sensitive about "politically incorrect" terminology are not the average black ghetto-dweller, Asian immigrant, abused woman or disabled person, but a minority of activists, many of whom do not even belong to any "oppressed" group but come from privileged strata of society. Political correctness has its stronghold among university professors, who have secure employment with comfortable salaries, and the majority of whom are heterosexual white males from middle- to upper-middle-class families.

13. Many leftists have an intense identification with the problems of groups that have an image of being weak (women), defeated (American Indians), repellent (homosexuals), or otherwise inferior. The leftists themselves feel that these groups are inferior. They would never admit it to themselves that they have such feelings, but it is precisely because they do see these groups as inferior that they identify with their problems. (We do not mean to suggest that women, Indians, etc., ARE inferior; we are only making a point about leftist psychology.)

14. Feminists are desperately anxious to prove that women are as strong and as capable as men. Clearly they are nagged by a fear that women may NOT be as strong and as capable as men.

15. Leftists tend to hate anything that has an image of being strong, good and successful. They hate America, they hate Western civilization, they hate white males, they hate rationality. The reasons that leftists give for hating the West, etc. clearly do not correspond with their real motives. They SAY they hate the West because it is warlike, imperialistic, sexist, ethnocentric and so forth, but where these same faults appear in socialist countries or in primitive cultures, the leftist finds excuses for them, or at best he GRUDGINGLY admits that they exist; whereas he ENTHUSIASTICALLY points out (and often greatly exaggerates) these faults where they appear in Western civilization. Thus it is clear that these faults are not the leftist's real motive for hating America and the West. He hates America and the West because they are strong and successful.

16. Words like "self-confidence," "self-reliance," "initiative," "enterprise," "optimism," etc. play little role in the liberal and leftist vocabulary. The leftist is anti-individualistic, pro-collectivist. He wants society to solve everyone's problems for them, satisfy everyone's needs for them, take care of them. He is not the sort of person who has an inner sense of confidence in his own ability to solve his own problems and satisfy his own needs. The leftist is antagonistic to the concept of competition because, deep inside, he feels like a loser.

17. Art forms that appeal to modern leftist intellectuals tend to focus on sordidness, defeat and despair, or else they take an orgiastic tone, throwing off rational control as if there were no hope of accomplishing anything through rational calculation and all that was left was to immerse oneself in the sensations of the moment.

18. Modern leftist philosophers tend to dismiss reason, science, objective reality and to insist that everything is culturally relative. It is true that one can ask serious questions about the foundations of scientific knowledge and about how, if at all, the concept of objective reality can be defined. But it is obvious that modern leftish philosophers are not simply cool-headed logicians systematically analyzing the foundations of knowledge. They are deeply involved emotionally in their attack on truth and reality. They attack these concepts because of their own psychological needs. For one thing, their attack is an outlet for hostility, and, to the extent that it is successful, it satisfies the drive for power. More importantly, the leftist hates science and rationality because they classify certain beliefs as true (i.e., successful, superior) and other beliefs as false (i.e. failed, inferior). The leftist's feelings of inferiority run so deep that he cannot tolerate any classification of some things as successful or superior and other things as failed or inferior. This also underlies the rejection by many leftists of the concept of mental illness and of the utility of IQ tests. Leftists are antagonistic to genetic explanations of human abilities or behavior because such explanations tend to make some persons appear superior or inferior to others. Leftists prefer to give society the credit or blame for an individual's ability or lack of it. Thus if a person is "inferior" it is not his fault, but society's, because he has not been brought up properly.

19. The leftist is not typically the kind of person whose feelings of inferiority make him a braggart, an egotist, a bully, a self-promoter, a ruthless competitor. This kind of person has not wholly lost faith in himself. He has a deficit in his sense of power and self-worth, but he can still conceive of himself as having the capacity to be strong, and his efforts to make himself strong produce his unpleasant behavior. [1] But the leftist is too far gone for that. His feelings of inferiority are so ingrained that he cannot conceive of himself as individually strong and valuable. Hence the collectivism of the leftist. He can feel strong only as a member of a large organization or a mass movement with which he identifies himself.

20. Notice the masochistic tendency of leftist tactics. Leftists protest by lying down in front of vehicles, they intentionally provoke police or racists to abuse them, etc.

These tactics may often be effective, but many leftists use them not as a means to an end but because they PREFER masochistic tactics. Self-hatred is a leftist trait.

21. Leftists may claim that their activism is motivated by compassion or by moral principle, and moral principle does play a role for the leftist of the oversocialized type. But compassion and moral principle cannot be the main motives for leftist activism. Hostility is too prominent a component of leftist behavior; so is the drive for power. Moreover, much leftist behavior is not rationally calculated to be of benefit to the people whom the leftists claim to be trying to help. For example, if one believes that affirmative action is good for black people, does it make sense to demand affirmative action in hostile or dogmatic terms? Obviously it would be more productive to take a diplomatic and conciliatory approach that would make at least verbal and symbolic concessions to white people who think that affirmative action discriminates against them. But leftist activists do not take such an approach because it would not satisfy their emotional needs. Helping black people is not their real goal. Instead, race problems serve as an excuse for them to express their own hostility and frustrated need for power. In doing so they actually harm black people, because the activists' hostile attitude toward the white majority tends to intensify race hatred.

22. If our society had no social problems at all, the leftists would have to INVENT problems in order to provide themselves with an excuse for making a fuss.

23. We emphasize that the foregoing does not pretend to be an accurate description of everyone who might be considered a leftist. It is only a rough indication of a general tendency of leftism.

OVERSOCIALIZATION

24. Psychologists use the term "socialization" to designate the process by which children are trained to think and act as society demands. A person is said to be well socialized if he believes in and obeys the moral code of his society and fits in well as a functioning part of that society.

It may seem senseless to say that many leftists are over-socialized, since the leftist is perceived as a rebel. Nevertheless, the position can be defended. Many leftists are not such rebels as they seem.

25. The moral code of our society is so demanding that no one can think, feel and act in a completely moral way. For example, we are not supposed to hate anyone, yet almost everyone hates somebody at some time or other, whether he admits it to himself or not. Some people are so highly socialized that the attempt to think, feel and act morally imposes a severe burden on them. In order to avoid feelings of guilt, they continually have to deceive themselves about their own motives and find moral explanations for feelings and actions that in reality have a non-moral origin. We use the term "oversocialized" to describe such people. [2]

26. Oversocialization can lead to low self-esteem, a sense of powerlessness, defeatism, guilt, etc. One of the most important means by which our society socializes children is by making them feel ashamed of behavior or speech that is contrary to society's expectations. If this is overdone, or if a particular child is especially susceptible to such feelings, he ends by feeling ashamed of HIMSELF. Moreover the thought and the behavior of the oversocialized person are more restricted by society's expectations than are those of the lightly socialized person. The majority of people engage in a significant amount of naughty behavior. They lie, they commit petty thefts, they break traffic laws, they goof off at work, they hate someone, they say spiteful things or they use some underhanded trick to get ahead of the other guy. The oversocialized person cannot do these things, or if he does do them he generates in himself a sense of shame and self-hatred. The oversocialized person cannot even experience, without guilt, thoughts or feelings that are contrary to the accepted morality; he cannot think "unclean" thoughts. And socialization is not just a matter of morality; we are socialized to confirm to many norms of behavior that do not fall under the heading of morality. Thus the oversocialized person is kept on a psychological leash and spends his life running on rails that society has laid down for him. In many oversocialized people this results in a sense of constraint and powerlessness that can be a severe hardship. We suggest that oversocialization is among the more serious cruelties that human beings inflict on one another.

27. We argue that a very important and influential segment of the modern left is oversocialized and that their oversocialization is of great importance in determining the direction of modern leftism. Leftists of the oversocialized type tend to be intellectuals or members of the upper-middle class. Notice that university intellectuals [3] constitute the most highly socialized segment of our society and also the most left-wing segment.

28. The leftist of the oversocialized type tries to get off his psychological leash and assert his autonomy by rebelling. But usually he is not strong enough to rebel against the most basic values of society. Generally speaking, the goals of today's leftists are NOT in conflict with the accepted morality. On the contrary, the left takes an accepted moral principle, adopts it as its own, and then accuses mainstream society of violating that principle. Examples: racial equality, equality of the sexes, helping poor people, peace as opposed to war, nonviolence generally, freedom of expression, kindness to animals. More fundamentally, the duty of the individual to serve society and the duty of society to take care of the individual. All these have been deeply rooted values of our society (or at least of its middle and upper classes [4] for a long time. These values are explicitly or implicitly expressed or presupposed in most of the material presented to us by the mainstream communications media and the educational system. Leftists, especially those of the oversocialized type, usually do not rebel against these principles but justify their hostility to society by claiming (with some degree of truth) that society is not living up to these principles.

29. Here is an illustration of the way in which the oversocialized leftist shows his real attachment to the conventional attitudes of our society while pretending to be in rebellion against it. Many leftists push for affirmative action, for moving black people into high-prestige jobs, for improved education in black schools and more money for such schools; the way of life of the black "underclass" they regard as a social disgrace. They want to integrate the black man into the system, make him a business executive, a lawyer, a scientist just like upper-middle-class white people. The leftists will reply that the last thing they want is to make the black man into a copy of the white man; instead, they want to preserve African American culture. But in what does this preservation of African American culture consist? It can hardly consist in anything more than eating black-style food, listening to black-style music, wearing black-style clothing and going to a black-style church or mosque. In other words, it can express itself only in superficial matters. In all ESSENTIAL respects more leftists of the oversocialized type want to make the black man conform to white, middle-class ideals. They want to make him study technical subjects, become an executive or a scientist, spend his life climbing the status ladder to prove that black people are as good as white. They want to make black fathers "responsible," they want black gangs to become nonviolent, etc. But these are exactly the values of the industrial-technological system. The system couldn't care less what kind of music a man listens to, what kind of clothes he wears or what religion he believes in as long as he studies in school, holds a respectable job, climbs the status ladder, is a "responsible" parent, is nonviolent and so forth. In effect, however much he may deny it, the oversocialized leftist wants to integrate the black man into the system and make him adopt its values.

30. We certainly do not claim that leftists, even of the oversocialized type, NEVER rebel against the fundamental values of our society. Clearly they sometimes do. Some oversocialized leftists have gone so far as to rebel against one of modern society's most important principles by engaging in physical violence. By their own account, violence is for them a form of "liberation." In other words, by committing violence they break through the psychological restraints that have been trained into them. Because they are oversocialized these restraints have been more confining for them than for others; hence their need to break free of them. But they usually justify their rebellion in terms of mainstream values. If they engage in violence they claim to be fighting against racism or the like.

31. We realize that many objections could be raised to the foregoing thumbnail sketch of leftist psychology. The real situation is complex, and anything like a complete description of it would take several volumes even if the necessary data were available. We claim only to have indicated very roughly the two most important tendencies in the psychology of modern leftism.

32. The problems of the leftist are indicative of the problems of our society as a whole. Low self-esteem, depressive tendencies and defeatism are not restricted to the left. Though they are especially noticeable in the left, they are widespread in our society. And today's society tries to socialize us to a greater extent than any previous society. We are even told by experts how to eat, how to exercise, how to make love, how to raise our kids and so forth.

THE POWER PROCESS

33. Human beings have a need (probably based in biology) for something that we will call the "power process." This is closely related to the need for power (which is widely recognized) but is not quite the same thing. The power process has four elements. The three most clear-cut of these we call goal, effort and attainment of goal. (Everyone needs to have goals whose attainment requires effort, and needs to succeed in attaining at least some of his goals.) The fourth element is more difficult to define and may not be necessary for everyone. We call it autonomy and will discuss it later (paragraphs 42-44).

34. Consider the hypothetical case of a man who can have anything he wants just by wishing for it. Such a man has power, but he will develop serious psychological problems. At first he will have a lot of fun, but by and by he will become acutely bored and demoralized. Eventually he may become clinically depressed. History shows that leisured aristocracies tend to become decadent. This is not true of fighting aristocracies that have to struggle to maintain their power. But leisured, secure aristocracies that have no need to exert themselves usually become bored, hedonistic and demoralized, even though they have power. This shows that power is not enough. One must have goals toward which to exercise one's power.

35. Everyone has goals; if nothing else, to obtain the physical necessities of life: food, water and whatever clothing and shelter are made necessary by the climate. But the leisured aristocrat obtains these things without effort. Hence his boredom and demoralization.

36. Nonattainment of important goals results in death if the goals are physical necessities, and in frustration if nonattainment of the goals is compatible with survival. Consistent failure to attain goals throughout life results in defeatism, low self-esteem or depression.

37. Thus, in order to avoid serious psychological problems, a human being needs goals whose attainment requires effort, and he must have a reasonable rate of success in attaining his goals.

SURROGATE ACTIVITIES

38. But not every leisured aristocrat becomes bored and demoralized. For example, the emperor Hirohito, instead of sinking into decadent hedonism, devoted himself to marine biology, a field in which he became distinguished. When people do not have to exert themselves to satisfy their physical needs they often set up artificial goals for themselves. In many cases they then pursue these goals with the same energy and emotional involvement that they otherwise would have put into the search for physical necessities. Thus the aristocrats of the Roman Empire had their literary pretentions; many European aristocrats a few centuries ago invested tremendous time and energy in hunting, though they certainly didn't need the meat; other aristocracies have competed for status through elaborate displays of wealth; and a few aristocrats, like Hirohito, have turned to science.

39. We use the term "surrogate activity" to designate an activity that is directed toward an artificial goal that people set up for themselves merely in order to have some goal to work toward, or let us say, merely for the sake of the "fulfillment" that they get from pursuing the goal. Here is a rule of thumb for the identification of surrogate activities. Given a person who devotes much time and energy to the pursuit of goal X, ask yourself this: If he had to devote most of his time and energy to satisfying his biological needs, and if that effort required him to use his physical and mental facilities in a varied and interesting way, would he feel seriously deprived because he did not attain goal X? If the answer is no, then the person's pursuit of a goal X is a surrogate activity. Hirohito's studies in marine biology clearly constituted a surrogate activity, since it is pretty certain that if Hirohito had had to spend his time working at interesting non-scientific tasks in order to obtain the necessities of life, he would not have felt deprived because he didn't know all about the anatomy and life-cycles of marine animals. On the other hand the pursuit of sex and love (for example) is not a surrogate activity, because most people, even if their existence were otherwise satisfactory, would feel deprived if they passed their lives without ever having a relationship with a member of the opposite sex. (But pursuit of an excessive amount of sex, more than one really needs, can be a surrogate activity.)

40. In modern industrial society only minimal effort is necessary to satisfy one's physical needs. It is enough to go through a training program to acquire some petty technical skill, then come to work on time and exert very modest effort needed to hold a job. The only requirements are a moderate amount of intelligence, and most of all, simple OBEDIENCE. If one has those, society takes care of one from cradle to grave. (Yes, there is an underclass that cannot take physical necessities for granted, but we are speaking here of mainstream society.) Thus it is not surprising that modern society is full of surrogate activities. These include scientific work, athletic achievement, humanitarian work, artistic and literary creation, climbing the corporate ladder, acquisition of money and material goods far beyond the point at which they cease to give any additional physical satisfaction, and social activism when it addresses issues that are not important for the activist personally, as in the case of white activists who work for the rights of nonwhite minorities. These are not always PURE surrogate activities, since for many people they may be motivated in part by needs other than the need to have some goal to pursue. Scientific work may be motivated in part by a drive for prestige, artistic creation by a need to express feelings, militant social activism by hostility. But for most people who pursue them, these activities are in large part surrogate activities. For example, the majority of scientists will probably agree that the "fulfillment" they get from their work is more important than the money and prestige they earn.

41. For many if not most people, surrogate activities are less satisfying than the pursuit of real goals (that is, goals that people would want to attain even if their need for the power process were already fulfilled). One indication of this is the fact that, in many or most cases, people who are deeply involved in surrogate activities are never satisfied, never at rest. Thus the money-maker constantly strives for more and more wealth. The scientist no sooner solves one problem than he moves on to the next. The long-distance runner drives himself to run always farther and faster. Many people who pursue surrogate activities will say that they get far more fulfillment from these activities than they do from the "mundane" business of satisfying their biological needs, but that is because in our society the effort needed to satisfy the biological needs has been reduced to triviality. More importantly, in our society people do not satisfy their biological needs AUTONOMOUSLY but by functioning as parts of an immense social machine. In contrast, people generally have a great deal of autonomy in pursuing their surrogate activities.

AUTONOMY

42. Autonomy as a part of the power process may not be necessary for every individual. But most people need a greater or lesser degree of autonomy in working toward their goals. Their efforts must be undertaken on their own initiative and must be under their own direction and control. Yet most people do not have to exert this initiative, direction and control as single individuals. It is usually enough to act as a member of a SMALL group. Thus if half a dozen people discuss a goal among themselves and make a successful joint effort to attain that goal, their need for the power process will be served. But if they work under rigid orders handed down from above that leave them no room for autonomous decision and initiative, then their need for the power process will not be served. The same is true when decisions are made on a collective basis if the group making the collective decision is so large that the role of each individual is insignificant [5]

43. It is true that some individuals seem to have little need for autonomy. Either their drive for power is weak or they satisfy it by identifying themselves with some powerful organization to which they belong. And then there are unthinking, animal types who seem to be satisfied with a purely physical sense of power (the good combat soldier, who gets his sense of power by developing fighting skills that he is quite content to use in blind obedience to his superiors).

44. But for most people it is through the power process—having a goal, making an AUTONOMOUS effort and attaining the goal—that self-esteem, self-confidence and a sense of power are acquired. When one does not have adequate opportunity to go through the power process the consequences are (depending on the individual and on the way the power process is disrupted) boredom, demoralization, low self-esteem, inferiority feelings, defeatism, depression, anxiety, guilt, frustration, hostility, spouse or child abuse, insatiable hedonism, abnormal sexual behavior, sleep disorders, eating disorders, etc. [6]

SOURCES OF SOCIAL PROBLEMS

45. Any of the foregoing symptoms can occur in any society, but in modern industrial society they are present on a massive scale. We aren't the first to mention that the world today seems to be going crazy. This sort of thing is not normal for human societies. There is good reason to believe that primitive man suffered from less stress and frustration and was better satisfied with his way of life than modern man is. It is true that not all was sweetness and light in primitive societies. Abuse of women was common among the Australian aborigines, transexuality was fairly common among some of the American Indian tribes. But is does appear that GENERALLY SPEAKING the kinds of problems that we have listed in the preceding paragraph were far less common among primitive peoples than they are in modern society.

46. We attribute the social and psychological problems of modern society to the fact that that society requires people to live under conditions radically different from those under which the human race evolved and to behave in ways that conflict with the patterns of behavior that the human race developed while living under the earlier conditions. It is clear from what we have already written that we consider lack of opportunity to properly experience the power process as the most important of the abnormal conditions to which modern society subjects people. But it is not the only one. Before dealing with disruption of the power process as a source of social problems we will discuss some of the other sources.

47. Among the abnormal conditions present in modern industrial society are excessive density of population, isolation of man from nature, excessive rapidity of social change and the breakdown of natural small-scale communities such as the extended family, the village or the tribe.

48. It is well known that crowding increases stress and aggression. The degree of crowding that exists today and the isolation of man from nature are consequences of technological progress. All pre-industrial societies were predominantly rural. The industrial Revolution vastly increased the size of cities and the proportion of the population that lives in them, and modern agricultural technology has made it possible for the Earth to support a far denser population than it ever did before. (Also, technology exacerbates the effects of crowding because it puts increased disruptive powers in people's hands. For example, a variety of noise-making devices: power mowers, radios, motor-cycles, etc. If the use of these devices is unrestricted, people who want peace and quiet are frustrated by the noise. If their use is restricted, people who use the devices are frustrated by the regulations. But if these machines had never been invented there would have been no conflict and no frustration generated by them.)

49. For primitive societies the natural world (which usually changes only slowly) provided a stable framework and therefore a sense of security. In the modern world it is human society that dominates nature rather than the other way around, and modern society changes very rapidly owing to technological change. Thus there is no stable framework.

50. The conservatives are fools: They whine about the decay of traditional values, yet they enthusiastically support technological progress and economic growth. Apparently it never occurs to them that you can't make rapid, drastic changes in the technology and the economy of a society without causing rapid changes in all other aspects of the society as well, and that such rapid changes inevitably break down traditional values.

51. The breakdown of traditional values to some extent implies the breakdown of the bonds that hold together traditional small-scale social groups. The disintegration of small-scale social groups is also promoted by the fact that modern conditions often require or tempt individuals to move to new locations, separating themselves from their communities. Beyond that, a technological society HAS TO weaken family ties and local communities if it is to function efficiently. In modern society an individual's loyalty must be first to the system and only secondarily to a small-scale community, because if the internal loyalties of small-scale communities were stronger than loyalty to the system, such communities would pursue their own advantage at the expense of the system.

52. Suppose that a public official or a corporation executive appoints his cousin, his friend or his co-religionist to a position rather than appointing the person best qualified for the job. He has permitted personal loyalty to supersede his loyalty to the system, and that is "nepotism" or "discrimination," both of which are terrible sins in modern society. Would-be industrial societies that have done a poor job of subordinating personal or local loyalties to loyalty to the system are usually very inefficient. (Look at Latin America.) Thus an advanced industrial society can tolerate only those small-scale communities that are emasculated, tamed and made into tools of the system. [7]

53. Crowding, rapid change and the breakdown of communities have been widely recognized as sources of social problems. but we do not believe they are enough to account for the extent of the problems that are seen today.

54. A few pre-industrial cities were very large and crowded, yet their inhabitants do not seem to have suffered from psychological problems to the same extent as modern man. In America today there still are uncrowded rural areas, and we find there the same problems as in urban areas, though the problems tend to be less acute in the rural areas. Thus crowding does not seem to be the decisive factor.

55. On the growing edge of the American frontier during the 19th century, the mobility of the population probably broke down extended families and small-scale social groups to at least the same extent as these are broken down today. In fact, many nuclear families lived by choice in such isolation, having no neighbors within several miles, that they belonged to no community at all, yet they do not seem to have developed problems as a result.

56. Furthermore, change in American frontier society was very rapid and deep. A man might be born and raised in a log cabin, outside the reach of law and order and fed largely on wild meat; and by the time he arrived at old age he might be working at a regular job and living in an ordered community with effective law enforcement. This was a deeper change that that which typically occurs in the life of a modern individual, yet it does not seem to have led to psychological problems. In fact, 19th century American society had an optimistic and self-confident tone, quite unlike that of today's society. [8]

57. The difference, we argue, is that modern man has the sense (largely justified) that change is IMPOSED on him, whereas the 19th century frontiersman had the sense (also largely justified) that he created change himself, by his own choice. Thus a pioneer settled on a piece of land of his own choosing and made it into a farm through his own effort. In those days an entire county might have only a couple of hundred inhabitants and was a far more isolated and autonomous entity than a modern county is. Hence the pioneer farmer participated as a member of a relatively small group in the creation of a new, ordered community. One may well question whether the creation of this community was an improvement, but at any rate it satisfied the pioneer's need for the power process.

58. It would be possible to give other examples of societies in which there has been rapid change and/or lack of close community ties without he kind of massive behavioral aberration that is seen in today's industrial society. We contend that the most important cause of social and psychological problems in modern society is the fact that people have insufficient opportunity to go through the power process in a normal way. We don't mean to say that modern society is the only one in which the power process has been disrupted. Probably most if not all civilized societies have interfered with the power process to a greater or lesser extent. But in modern industrial society the problem has become particularly acute. Leftism, at least in its recent (mid- to late-20th century) form, is in part a symptom of deprivation with respect to the power process.

DISRUPTION OF THE POWER PROCESS IN MODERN SOCIETY

59. We divide human drives into three groups: (1) those drives that can be satisfied with minimal effort; (2) those that can be satisfied but only at the cost of serious effort; (3) those that cannot be adequately satisfied no matter how much effort one makes. The power process is the process of satisfying the drives of the second group. The more drives there are in the third group, the more there is frustration, anger, eventually defeatism, depression, etc.

60. In modern industrial society natural human drives tend to be pushed into the first and third groups, and the second group tends to consist increasingly of artificially created drives.

61. In primitive societies, physical necessities generally fall into group 2: They can be obtained, but only at the cost of serious effort. But modern society tends to guaranty the physical necessities to everyone [9] in exchange for only minimal effort, hence physical needs are pushed into group 1. (There may be disagreement about whether the effort needed to hold a job is "minimal"; but usually, in lower- to middle-level jobs, whatever effort is required is merely that of OBEDIENCE. You sit or stand where you are told to sit or stand and do what you are told to do in the way you are told to do it. Seldom do you have to exert yourself seriously, and in any case you have hardly any autonomy in work, so that the need for the power process is not well served.)

62. Social needs, such as sex, love and status, often remain in group 2 in modern society, depending on the situation of the individual. [10] But, except for people who have a particularly strong drive for status, the effort required to fulfill the social drives is insufficient to satisfy adequately the need for the power process.

63. So certain artificial needs have been created that fall into group 2, hence serve the need for the power process. Advertising and marketing techniques have been developed that make many people feel they need things that their grandparents never desired or even dreamed of. It requires serious effort to earn enough money to satisfy these artificial needs, hence they fall into group 2. (But see paragraphs 80-82.) Modern man must satisfy his need for the power process largely through pursuit of the artificial needs created by the advertising and marketing industry [11], and through surrogate activities.

64. It seems that for many people, maybe the majority, these artificial forms of the power process are insufficient. A theme that appears repeatedly in the writings of the social critics of the second half of the 20th century is the sense of purposelessness that afflicts many people in modern society. (This purposelessness is often called by other names such as "anomie" or "middle-class vacuity.") We suggest that the so-called "identity crisis" is actually a search for a sense of purpose, often for commitment to a suitable surrogate activity. It may be that existentialism is in large part a response to the purposelessness of modern life. [12] Very widespread in modern society is the search for "fulfillment." But we think that for the majority of people an activity whose main goal is fulfillment (that is, a surrogate activity) does not bring completely satisfactory fulfillment. In other words, it does not fully satisfy the need for the power process. (See paragraph 41.) That need can be fully satisfied only through activities that have some external goal, such as physical necessities, sex, love, status, revenge, etc.

65. Moreover, where goals are pursued through earning money, climbing the status ladder or functioning as part of the system in some other way, most people are not in a position to pursue their goals AUTONOMOUSLY. Most workers are someone else's employee and, as we pointed out in paragraph 61, must spend their days doing what they are told to do in the way they are told to do it. Even most people who are in business for themselves have only limited autonomy. It is a chronic complaint of small-business persons and entrepreneurs that their hands are tied by excessive government regulation. Some of these regulations are doubtless unnecessary, but for the most part government regulations are essential and inevitable parts of our extremely complex society. A large portion of small business today operates on the franchise system. It was reported in the Wall Street Journal a few years ago that many of the franchise-granting companies require applicants for franchises to take a personality test that is designed to EXCLUDE those who have creativity and initiative, because such persons are not sufficiently docile to go along obediently with the franchise system. This excludes from small business many of the people who most need autonomy.

66. Today people live more by virtue of what the system

does FOR them or TO them than by virtue of what they do for themselves. And what they do for themselves is done more and more along channels laid down by the system. Opportunities tend to be those that the system provides, the opportunities must be exploited in accord with the rules and regulations [13], and techniques prescribed by experts must be followed if there is to be a chance of success.

67. Thus the power process is disrupted in our society through a deficiency of real goals and a deficiency of autonomy in pursuit of goals. But it is also disrupted because of those human drives that fall into group 3: the drives that one cannot adequately satisfy no matter how much effort one makes. One of these drives is the need for security. Our lives depend on decisions made by other people; we have no control over these decisions and usually we do not even know the people who make them. ("We live in a world in which relatively few people—maybe 500 or 1,000—make the important decisions" —Philip B. Heymann of Harvard Law School, quoted by Anthony Lewis, New York Times, April 21, 1995.) Our lives depend on whether safety standards at a nuclear power plant are properly maintained; on how much pesticide is allowed to get into our food or how much pollution into our air; on how skillful (or incompetent) our doctor is; whether we lose or get a job may depend on decisions made by government economists or corporation executives; and so forth. Most individuals are not in a position to secure themselves against these threats to more [than] a very limited extent. The individual's search for security is therefore frustrated, which leads to a sense of powerlessness.

68. It may be objected that primitive man is physically less secure than modern man, as is shown by his shorter life expectancy; hence modern man suffers from less, not more than the amount of insecurity that is normal for human beings. but psychological security does not closely correspond with physical security. What makes us FEEL secure is not so much objective security as a sense of confidence in our ability to take care of ourselves. Primitive man, threatened by a fierce animal or by hunger, can fight in self-defense or travel in search of food. He has no certainty of success in these efforts, but he is by no means helpless against the things that threaten him. The modern individual on the other hand is threatened by many things against which he is helpless; nuclear accidents, carcinogens in food, environmental pollution, war, increasing taxes, invasion of his privacy by large organizations, nationwide social or economic phenomena that may disrupt his way of life.

69. It is true that primitive man is powerless against some of the things that threaten him; disease for example. But he can accept the risk of disease stoically. It is part of the nature of things, it is no one's fault, unless is the fault of some imaginary, impersonal demon. But threats to the modern individual tend to be MAN-MADE. They are not the results of chance but are IMPOSED on him by other persons whose decisions he, as an individual, is unable to influence. Consequently he feels frustrated, humiliated and angry.

70. Thus primitive man for the most part has his security in his own hands (either as an individual or as a member of a SMALL group) whereas the security of modern man is in the hands of persons or organizations that are too remote or too large for him to be able personally to influence them. So modern man's drive for security tends to fall into groups 1 and 3; in some areas (food, shelter, etc.) his security is assured at the cost of only trivial effort, whereas in other areas he CANNOT attain security. (The foregoing greatly simplifies the real situation, but it does indicate in a rough, general way how the condition of modern man differs from that of primitive man.)

71. People have many transitory drives or impulses that are necessarily frustrated in modern life, hence fall into group 3. One may become angry, but modern society cannot permit fighting. In many situations it does not even permit verbal aggression. When going somewhere one may be in a hurry, or one may be in a mood to travel slowly, but one generally has no choice but to move with the flow of traffic and obey the traffic signals. One may want to do one's work in a different way, but usually one can work only according to the rules laid down by one's employer. In many other ways as well, modern man is strapped down by a network of rules and regulations (explicit or implicit) that frustrate many of his impulses and thus interfere with the power process. Most of these regulations cannot be dispensed with, because the are necessary for the functioning of industrial society.

72. Modern society is in certain respects extremely permissive. In matters that are irrelevant to the functioning of the system we can generally do what we please. We can believe in any religion we like (as long as it does not encourage behavior that is dangerous to the system). We can go to bed with anyone we like (as long as we practice "safe sex"). We can do anything we like as long as it is UNIMPORTANT. But in all IMPORTANT matters the system tends increasingly to regulate our behavior.

73. Behavior is regulated not only through explicit rules and not only by the government. Control is often exercised through indirect coercion or through psychological pressure or manipulation, and by organizations other than the government, or by the system as a whole. Most large organizations use some form of propaganda [14] to manipulate public attitudes or behavior. Propaganda is not limited to "commercials" and advertisements, and sometimes it is not even consciously intended as propaganda by the people who make it. For instance, the content of entertainment programming is a powerful form of propaganda. An example of indirect coercion: There is no law that says we have to go to work every day and follow our employer's orders. Legally there is nothing to prevent us from going to live in the wild like primitive people or from going into business for ourselves. But in practice there is very little wild country left, and there is room in the economy for only a limited number of small business owners. Hence most of us can survive only as someone else's employee.

74. We suggest that modern man's obsession with longevity, and with maintaining physical vigor and sexual attractiveness to an advanced age, is a symptom of unfulfillment resulting from deprivation with respect to the power process. The "mid-life crisis" also is such a symptom. So is the lack of interest in having children that is fairly common in modern society but almost unheard-of in primitive societies.

75. In primitive societies life is a succession of stages. The needs and purposes of one stage having been fulfilled, there is no particular reluctance about passing on to the next stage. A young man goes through the power process by becoming a hunter, hunting not for sport or for fulfillment but to get meat that is necessary for food. (In young women the process is more complex, with greater emphasis on social power; we won't discuss that here.) This phase having been successfully passed through, the young man has no reluctance about settling down to the responsibilities of raising a family. (In contrast, some modern people indefinitely postpone having children because they are too busy seeking some kind of "fulfillment." We suggest that the fulfillment they need is adequate experience of the power process— with real goals instead of the artificial goals of surrogate activities.) Again, having successfully raised his children, going through the power process by providing them with the physical necessities, the primitive man feels that his work is done and he is prepared to accept old age (if he survives that long) and death. Many modern people, on the other hand, are disturbed by the prospect of physical deterioration and death, as is shown by the amount of effort they expend trying to maintain their physical condition, appearance and health. We argue that this is due to unfulfillment resulting from the fact that they have never put their physical powers to any use, have never gone through the power process using their bodies in a serious way. It is not the primitive man, who has used his body daily for practical purposes, who fears the deterioration of age, but the modern man, who has never had a practical use for his body beyond walking from his car to his house. It is the man whose need for the power process has been satisfied during his life who is best prepared to accept the end of that life.

76. In response to the arguments of this section someone will say, "Society must find a way to give people the opportunity to go through the power process." For such people the value of the opportunity is destroyed by the very fact that society gives it to them. What they need is to find or make their own opportunities. As long as the system GIVES them their opportunities it still has them on a leash. To attain autonomy they must get off that leash.

HOW SOME PEOPLE ADJUST

77. Not everyone in industrial-technological society suffers from psychological problems. Some people even profess to be quite satisfied with society as it is. We now discuss some of the reasons why people differ so greatly in their response to modern society.

78. First, there doubtless are differences in the strength of the drive for power. Individuals with a weak drive for power may have relatively little need to go through the power process, or at least relatively little need for autonomy in the power process. These are docile types who would have been happy as plantation darkies in the Old South. (We don't mean to sneer at "plantation darkies" of the Old South. To their credit, most of the slaves were NOT content with their servitude. We do sneer at people who ARE content with servitude.)

79. Some people may have some exceptional drive, in pursuing which they satisfy their need for the power process. For example, those who have an unusually strong drive for social status may spend their whole lives climbing the status ladder without ever getting bored with that game.

80. People vary in their susceptibility to advertising and marketing techniques. Some people are so susceptible that, even if they make a great deal of money, they cannot satisfy their constant craving for the shiny new toys that the marketing industry dangles before their eyes. So they always feel hard-pressed financially even if their income is large, and their cravings are frustrated.

81. Some people have low susceptibility to advertising and marketing techniques. These are the people who aren't interested in money. Material acquisition does not serve their need for the power process.

82. People who have medium susceptibility to advertising and marketing techniques are able to earn enough money to satisfy their craving for goods and services, but only at the cost of serious effort (putting in overtime, taking a second job, earning promotions, etc.) Thus material acquisition serves their need for the power process. But it does not necessarily follow that their need is fully satisfied. They may have insufficient autonomy in the power process (their work may consist of following orders) and some of their drives may be frustrated (e.g., security, aggression). (We are guilty of oversimplification in paragraphs 80-82 because we have assumed that the desire for material acquisition is entirely a creation of the advertising and marketing industry. Of course it's not that simple. [11]

83. Some people partly satisfy their need for power by identifying themselves with a powerful organization or mass movement. An individual lacking goals or power joins a movement or an organization, adopts its goals as his own, then works toward these goals. When some of the goals are attained, the individual, even though his personal efforts have played only an insignificant part in the attainment of the goals, feels (through his identification with the movement or organization) as if he had gone through the power process. This phenomenon was exploited by the fascists, nazis and communists. Our society uses it too, though less crudely. Example: Manuel Noriega was an irritant to the U.S. (goal: punish Noriega). The U.S. invaded Panama (effort) and punished Noriega (attainment of goal). The U.S. went through the power process and many Americans, because of their identification with the U.S., experienced the power process vicariously. Hence the widespread public approval of the Panama invasion; it gave people a sense of power. [15] We see the same phenomenon in armies, corporations, political parties, humanitarian organizations, religious or ideological movements. In particular, leftist movements tend to attract people who are seeking to satisfy their need for power. But for most people identification with a large organization or a mass movement does not fully satisfy the need for power.

84. Another way in which people satisfy their need for the power process is through surrogate activities. As we explained in paragraphs 38-40, a surrogate activity that is directed toward an artificial goal that the individual pursues for the sake of the "fulfillment" that he gets from pursuing the goal, not because he needs to attain the goal itself. For instance, there is no practical motive for building enormous muscles, hitting a little ball into a hole or acquiring a complete series of postage stamps. Yet many people in our society devote themselves with passion to bodybuilding, golf or stamp-collecting. Some people are more "other-directed" than others, and therefore will more readily attach importance to a surrogate activity simply because the people around them treat it as important or because society tells them it is important. That is why some people get very serious about essentially trivial activities such as sports, or bridge, or chess, or arcane scholarly pursuits, whereas others who are more clear-sighted never see these things as anything but the surrogate activities that they are, and consequently never attach enough importance to them to satisfy their need for the power process in that way. It only remains to point out that in many cases a person's way of earning a living is also a surrogate activity. Not a PURE surrogate activity, since part of the motive for the activity is to gain the physical necessities and (for some people) social status and the luxuries that advertising makes them want. But many people put into their work far more effort than is necessary to earn whatever money and status they require, and this extra effort constitutes a surrogate activity. This extra effort, together with the emotional investment that accompanies it, is one of the most potent forces acting toward the continual development and perfecting of the system, with negative consequences for individual freedom (see paragraph 131). Especially, for the most creative scientists and engineers, work tends to be largely a surrogate activity. This point is so important that it deserves a separate discussion, which we shall give in a moment (paragraphs 87-92).

85. In this section we have explained how many people in modern society do satisfy their need for the power process to a greater or lesser extent. But we think that for the majority of people the need for the power process is not fully satisfied. In the first place, those who have an insatiable drive for status, or who get firmly "hooked" on a surrogate activity, or who identify strongly enough with a movement or organization to satisfy their need for power in that way, are exceptional personalities. Others are not fully satisfied with surrogate activities or by identification with an organization (see paragraphs 41, 64). In the second place, too much control is imposed by the system through explicit regulation or through socialization, which results in a deficiency of autonomy, and in frustration due to the impossibility of attaining certain goals and the necessity of restraining too many impulses.

86. But even if most people in industrial-technological society were well satisfied, we (FC) would still be opposed to that form of society, because (among other reasons) we consider it demeaning to fulfill one's need for the power process through surrogate activities or through identification with an organization, rather then through pursuit of real goals.

THE MOTIVES OF SCIENTISTS

87. Science and technology provide the most important examples of surrogate activities. Some scientists claim that they are motivated by "curiosity" or by a desire to "benefit humanity." But it is easy to see that neither of these can be the principal motive of most scientists. As for "curiosity," that notion is simply absurd. Most scientists work on highly specialized problems that are not the object of any normal curiosity. For example, is an astronomer, a mathematician or an entomologist curious about the properties of isopropyltrimethylmethane? Of course not. Only a chemist is curious about such a thing, and he is curious about it only because chemistry is his surrogate activity. Is the chemist curious about the appropriate classification of a new species of beetle? No. That question is of interest only to the entomologist, and he is interested in it only because entomology is his surrogate activity. If the chemist and the entomologist had to exert themselves seriously to obtain the physical necessities, and if that effort exercised their abilities in an interesting way but in some nonscientific pursuit, then they wouldn't give a damn about isopropyltrimethylmethane or the classification of beetles. Suppose that lack of funds for postgraduate education had led the chemist to become an insurance broker instead of a chemist. In that case he would have been very interested in insurance matters but would have cared nothing about isopropyltrimethylmethane. In any case it is not normal to put into the satisfaction of mere curiosity the amount of time and effort that scientists put into their work. The "curiosity" explanation for the scientists' motive just doesn't stand up.

88. The "benefit of humanity" explanation doesn't work any better. Some scientific work has no conceivable relation to the welfare of the human race—most of archaeology or comparative linguistics for example. Some other areas of science present obviously dangerous possibilities. Yet scientists in these areas are just as enthusiastic about their work as those who develop vaccines or study air pollution. Consider the case of Dr. Edward Teller, who had an obvious emotional involvement in promoting nuclear power plants. Did this involvement stem from a desire to benefit humanity? If so, then why didn't Dr. Teller get emotional about other "humanitarian" causes? If he was such a humanitarian then why did he help to develop the H-bomb? As with many other scientific achievements, it is very much open to question whether nuclear power plants actually do benefit humanity. Does the cheap electricity outweigh the accumulating waste and risk of accidents? Dr. Teller saw only one side of the question. Clearly his emotional involvement with nuclear power arose not from a desire to "benefit humanity" but from a personal fulfillment he got from his work and from seeing it put to practical use.

89. The same is true of scientists generally. With possible rare exceptions, their motive is neither curiosity nor a desire to benefit humanity but the need to go through the power process: to have a goal (a scientific problem to solve), to make an effort (research) and to attain the goal (solution of the problem.) Science is a surrogate activity because scientists work mainly for the fulfillment they get out of the work itself.

90. Of course, it's not that simple. Other motives do play a role for many scientists. Money and status for example. Some scientists may be persons of the type who have an insatiable drive for status (see paragraph 79) and this may provide much of the motivation for their work. No doubt the majority of scientists, like the majority of the general population, are more or less susceptible to advertising and marketing techniques and need money to satisfy their craving for goods and services. Thus science is not a PURE surrogate activity. But it is in large part a surrogate activity.

91. Also, science and technology constitute a mass power movement, and many scientists gratify their need for power through identification with this mass movement (see paragraph 83).

92. Thus science marches on blindly, without regard to the real welfare of the human race or to any other standard, obedient only to the psychological needs of the scientists and of the government officials and corporation executives who provide the funds for research.

THE NATURE OF FREEDOM

93. We are going to argue that industrial-technological society cannot be reformed in such a way as to prevent it from progressively narrowing the sphere of human freedom. But because "freedom" is a word that can be interpreted in many ways, we must first make clear what kind of freedom we are concerned with.

94. By "freedom" we mean the opportunity to go through the power process, with real goals not the artificial goals of surrogate activities, and without interference, manipulation or supervision from anyone, especially from any large organization. Freedom means being in control (either as an individual or as a member of a SMALL group) of the life-and-death issues of one's existence; food, clothing, shelter and defense against whatever threats there may be in one's environment. Freedom means having power; not the power to control other people but the power to control the circumstances of one's own life. One does not have freedom if anyone else (especially a large organization) has power over one, no matter how benevolently, tolerantly and permissively that power may be exercised. It is important not to confuse freedom with mere permissiveness (see paragraph 72).

95. It is said that we live in a free society because we have a certain number of constitutionally guaranteed rights. But these are not as important as they seem. The degree of personal freedom that exists in a society is determined more by the economic and technological structure of the society than by its laws or its form of government. [16] Most of the Indian nations of New England were monarchies, and many of the cities of the Italian Renaissance were controlled by dictators. But in reading about these societies one gets the impression that they allowed far more personal freedom than our society does. In part this was because they lacked efficient mechanisms for enforcing the ruler's will: There were no modern, well-organized police forces, no rapid long-distance communications, no surveillance cameras, no dossiers of information about the lives of average citizens. Hence it was relatively easy to evade control.

96. As for our constitutional rights, consider for example that of freedom of the press. We certainly don't mean to knock that right: it is very important tool for limiting concentration of political power and for keeping those who do have political power in line by publicly exposing any misbehavior on their part. But freedom of the press is of very little use to the average citizen as an individual. The mass media are mostly under the control of large organizations that are integrated into the system. Anyone who has a little money can have something printed, or can distribute it on the Internet or in some such way, but what he has to say will be swamped by the vast volume of material put out by the media, hence it will have no practical effect. To make an impression on society with words is therefore almost impossible for most individuals and small groups. Take us (FC) for example. If we had never done anything violent and had submitted the present writings to a publisher, they probably would not have been accepted. If they had been accepted and published, they probably would not have attracted many readers, because it's more fun to watch the entertainment put out by the media than to read a sober essay. Even if these writings had had many readers, most of these readers would soon have forgotten what they had read as their minds were flooded by the mass of material to which the media expose them. In order to get our message before the public with some chance of making a lasting impression, we've had to kill people.

97. Constitutional rights are useful up to a point, but they do not serve to guarantee much more than what could be called the bourgeois conception of freedom. According to the bourgeois conception, a "free" man is essentially an element of a social machine and has only a certain set of prescribed and delimited freedoms; freedoms that are designed to serve the needs of the social machine more than those of the individual. Thus the bourgeois's "free" man has economic freedom because that promotes growth and progress; he has freedom of the press because public criticism restrains misbehavior by political leaders; he has a right to a fair trial because imprisonment at the whim of the powerful would be bad for the system. This was clearly the attitude of Simon Bolivar. To him, people deserved liberty only if they used it to promote progress (progress as conceived by the bourgeois). Other bourgeois thinkers have taken a similar view of freedom as a mere means to collective ends. Chester C. Tan, "Chinese Political Thought in the Twentieth Century," page 202, explains the philosophy of the Kuomintang leader Hu Han-min: "An individual is granted rights because he is a member of society and his community life requires such rights. By community Hu meant the whole society of the nation." And on page 259 Tan states that according to Carsum Chang (Chang Chun-mai, head of the State Socialist Party in China) freedom had to be used in the interest of the state and of the people as a whole. But what kind of freedom does one have if one can use it only as someone else prescribes? FC's conception of freedom is not that of Bolivar, Hu, Chang or other bourgeois theorists. The trouble with such theorists is that they have made the development and application of social theories their surrogate activity. Consequently the theories are designed to serve the needs of the theorists more than the needs of any people who may be unlucky enough to live in a society on which the theories are imposed.

98. One more point to be made in this section: It should not be assumed that a person has enough freedom just because he SAYS he has enough. Freedom is restricted in part by psychological control of which people are unconscious, and moreover many people's ideas of what constitutes freedom are governed more by social convention than by their real needs. For example, it's likely that many leftists of the oversocialized type would say that most people, including themselves, are socialized too little rather than too much, yet the oversocialized leftist pays a heavy psychological price for his high level of socialization.

SOME PRINCIPLES OF HISTORY

99. Think of history as being the sum of two components: an erratic component that consists of unpredictable events that follow no discernible pattern, and a regular component that consists of long-term historical trends. Here we are concerned with the long-term trends.

100. FIRST PRINCIPLE. If a SMALL change is made that affects a long-term historical trend, then the effect of that change will almost always be transitory—the trend will soon revert to its original state. (Example: A reform movement designed to clean up political corruption in a society rarely has more than a short-term effect; sooner or later the reformers relax and corruption creeps back in. The level of political corruption in a given society tends to remain constant, or to change only slowly with the evolution of the society. Normally, a political cleanup will be permanent only if accompanied by widespread social changes; a SMALL change in the society won't be enough.) If a small change in a long-term historical trend appears to be permanent, it is only because the change acts in the direction in which the trend is already moving, so that the trend is not altered but only pushed a step ahead.

101. The first principle is almost a tautology. If a trend were not stable with respect to small changes, it would wander at random rather than following a definite direction; in other words it would not be a long-term trend at all.

102. SECOND PRINCIPLE. If a change is made that is sufficiently large to alter permanently a long-term historical trend, than it will alter the society as a whole. In other words, a society is a system in which all parts are interrelated, and you can't permanently change any important part without changing all the other parts as well.

103. THIRD PRINCIPLE. If a change is made that is large enough to alter permanently a long-term trend, then the consequences for the society as a whole cannot be predicted in advance. (Unless various other societies have passed through the same change and have all experienced the same consequences, in which case one can predict on empirical grounds that another society that passes through the same change will be like to experience similar consequences.)

104. FOURTH PRINCIPLE. A new kind of society cannot be designed on paper. That is, you cannot plan out a new form of society in advance, then set it up and expect it to function as it was designed to.

105. The third and fourth principles result from the complexity of human societies. A change in human behavior will affect the economy of a society and its physical environment; the economy will affect the environment and vice versa, and the changes in the economy and the environment will affect human behavior in complex, unpredictable ways; and so forth. The network of causes and effects is far too complex to be untangled and understood.

106. FIFTH PRINCIPLE. People do not consciously and rationally choose the form of their society. Societies develop through processes of social evolution that are not under rational human control.

107. The fifth principle is a consequence of the other four.

108. To illustrate: By the first principle, generally speaking an attempt at social reform either acts in the direction in which the society is developing anyway (so that it merely accelerates a change that would have occurred in any case) or else it has only a transitory effect, so that the society soon slips back into its old groove. To make a lasting change in the direction of development of any important aspect of a society, reform is insufficient and revolution is required. (A revolution does not necessarily involve an armed uprising or the overthrow of a government.) By the second principle, a revolution never changes only one aspect of a society; and by the third principle changes occur that were never expected or desired by the revolutionaries. By the fourth principle, when revolutionaries or utopians set up a new kind of society, it never works out as planned.

109. The American Revolution does not provide a counterexample. The American "Revolution" was not a revolution in our sense of the word, but a war of independence followed by a rather far-reaching political reform. The Founding Fathers did not change the direction of development of American society, nor did they aspire to do so. They only freed the development of American society from the retarding effect of British rule. Their political reform did not change any basic trend, but only pushed American political culture along its natural direction of development. British society, of which American society was an offshoot, had been moving for a long time in the direction of representative democracy. And prior to the War of Independence the Americans were already practicing a significant degree of representative democracy in the colonial assemblies. The political system established by the Constitution was modeled on the British system and on the colonial assemblies. With major alteration, to be sure—there is no doubt that the Founding Fathers took a very important step. But it was a step along the road the English-speaking world was already traveling. The proof is that Britain and all of its colonies that were populated predominantly by people of British descent ended up with systems of representative democracy essentially similar to that of the United States. If the Founding Fathers had lost their nerve and declined to sign the Declaration of Independence, our way of life today would not have been significantly different. Maybe we would have had somewhat closer ties to Britain, and would have had a Parliament and Prime Minister instead of a Congress and President. No big deal. Thus the American Revolution provides not a counterexample to our principles but a good illustration of them.

110. Still, one has to use common sense in applying the principles. They are expressed in imprecise language that allows latitude for interpretation, and exceptions to them can be found. So we present these principles not as inviolable laws but as rules of thumb, or guides to thinking, that may provide a partial antidote to naive ideas about the future of society. The principles should be borne constantly in mind, and whenever one reaches a conclusion that conflicts with them one should carefully reexamine one's thinking and retain the conclusion only if one has good, solid reasons for doing so.

INDUSTRIAL-TECHNOLOGICAL SOCIETY CANNOT BE REFORMED

111. The foregoing principles help to show how hopelessly difficult it would be to reform the industrial system in such a way as to prevent it from progressively narrowing our sphere of freedom. There has been a consistent tendency, going back at least to the Industrial Revolution for technology to strengthen the system at a high cost in individual freedom and local autonomy. Hence any change designed to protect freedom from technology would be contrary to a fundamental trend in the development of our society. Consequently, such a change either would be a transitory one—soon swamped by the tide of history—or, if large enough to be permanent would alter the nature of our whole society. This by the first and second principles. Moreover, since society would be altered in a way that could not be predicted in advance (third principle) there would be great risk. Changes large enough to make a lasting difference in favor of freedom would not be initiated because it would realized that they would gravely disrupt the system. So any attempts at reform would be too timid to be effective. Even if changes large enough to make a lasting difference were initiated, they would be retracted when their disruptive effects became apparent. Thus, permanent changes in favor of freedom could be brought about only by persons prepared to accept radical, dangerous and unpredictable alteration of the entire system. In other words, by revolutionaries, not reformers.

112. People anxious to rescue freedom without sacrificing the supposed benefits of technology will suggest naive schemes for some new form of society that would reconcile freedom with technology. Apart from the fact that people who make suggestions seldom propose any practical means by which the new form of society could be set up in the first place, it follows from the fourth principle that even if the new form of society could be once established, it either would collapse or would give results very different from those expected.

113. So even on very general grounds it seems highly improbable that any way of changing society could be found that would reconcile freedom with modern technology. In the next few sections we will give more specific reasons for concluding that freedom and technological progress are incompatible.

RESTRICTION OF FREEDOM IS UNAVOIDABLE IN INDUSTRIAL SOCIETY

114. As explained in paragraphs 65-67, 70-73, modern man is strapped down by a network of rules and regulations, and his fate depends on the actions of persons remote from him whose decisions he cannot influence. This is not accidental or a result of the arbitrariness of arrogant bureaucrats. It is necessary and inevitable in any technologically advanced society. The system HAS TO regulate human behavior closely in order to function. At work, people have to do what they are told to do, otherwise production would be thrown into chaos. Bureaucracies HAVE TO be run according to rigid rules. To allow any substantial personal discretion to lower-level bureaucrats would disrupt the system and lead to charges of unfairness due to differences in the way individual bureaucrats exercised their discretion. It is true that some restrictions on our freedom could be eliminated, but GENERALLY SPEAKING the regulation of our lives by large organizations is necessary for the functioning of industrial-technological society. The result is a sense of powerlessness on the part of the average person. It may be, however, that formal regulations will tend increasingly to be replaced by psychological tools that make us want to do what the system requires of us. (Propaganda [14], educational techniques, "mental health" programs, etc.)

115. The system HAS TO force people to behave in ways that are increasingly remote from the natural pattern of human behavior. For example, the system needs scientists, mathematicians and engineers. It can't function without them. So heavy pressure is put on children to excel in these fields. It isn't natural for an adolescent human being to spend the bulk of his time sitting at a desk absorbed in study. A normal adolescent wants to spend his time in active contact with the real world. Among primitive peoples the things that children are trained to do tend to be in reasonable harmony with natural human impulses. Among the American Indians, for example, boys were trained in active outdoor pursuits—just the sort of things that boys like. But in our society children are pushed into studying technical subjects, which most do grudgingly.

116. Because of the constant pressure that the system exerts to modify human behavior, there is a gradual increase in the number of people who cannot or will not adjust to society's requirements: welfare leeches, youth-gang members, cultists, anti-government rebels, radical environmentalist saboteurs, dropouts and resisters of various kinds.

117. In any technologically advanced society the individual's fate MUST depend on decisions that he personally cannot influence to any great extent. A technological society cannot be broken down into small, autonomous communities, because production depends on the cooperation of very large numbers of people and machines. Such a society MUST be highly organized and decisions HAVE TO be made that affect very large numbers of people. When a decision affects, say, a million people, then each of the affected individuals has, on the average, only a one-millionth share in making the decision. What usually happens in practice is that decisions are made by public officials or corporation executives, or by technical specialists, but even when the public votes on a decision the number of voters ordinarily is too large for the vote of any one individual to be significant. [17] Thus most individuals are unable to influence measurably the major decisions that affect their lives. Their is no conceivable way to remedy this in a technologically advanced society. The system tries to "solve" this problem by using propaganda to make people WANT the decisions that have been made for them, but even if this "solution" were completely successful in making people feel better, it would be demeaning.

118. Conservatives and some others advocate more "local autonomy." Local communities once did have autonomy; but such autonomy becomes less and less possible as local communities become more enmeshed with and dependent on large-scale systems like public utilities, computer networks, highway systems, the mass communications media, the modern health care system. Also operating against autonomy is the fact that technology applied in one location often affects people at other locations far away. Thus pesticide or chemical use near a creek may contaminate the water supply hundreds of miles downstream, and the greenhouse effect affects the whole world.

119. The system does not and cannot exist to satisfy human needs. Instead, it is human behavior that has to be modified to fit the needs of the system. This has nothing to do with the political or social ideology that may pretend to guide the technological system. It is the fault of technology, because the system is guided not by ideology but by technical necessity. [18] Of course the system does satisfy many human needs, but generally speaking it does this only to the extent that it is to the advantage of the system to do it. It is the needs of the system that are paramount, not those of the human being. For example, the system provides people with food because the system couldn't function if everyone starved; it attends to people's psychological needs whenever it can CONVENIENTLY do so, because it couldn't function if too many people became depressed or rebellious. But the system, for good, solid, practical reasons, must exert constant pressure on people to mold their behavior to the needs of the system. Too much waste accumulating? The government, the media, the educational system, environmentalists, everyone inundates us with a mass of propaganda about recycling. Need more technical personnel? A chorus of voices exhorts kids to study science. No one stops to ask whether it is inhumane to force adolescents to spend the bulk of their time studying subjects most of them hate. When skilled workers are put out of a job by technical advances and have to undergo "retraining," no one asks whether it is humiliating for them to be pushed around in this way. It is simply taken for granted that everyone must bow to technical necessity and for good reason: If human needs were put before technical necessity there would be economic problems, unemployment, shortages or worse. The concept of "mental health" in our society is defined largely by the extent to which an individual behaves in accord with the needs of the system and does so without showing signs of stress.

120. Efforts to make room for a sense of purpose and for autonomy within the system are no better than a joke. For example, one company, instead of having each of its employees assemble only one section of a catalogue, had each assemble a whole catalogue, and this was supposed to give them a sense of purpose and achievement. Some companies have tried to give their employees more autonomy in their work, but for practical reasons this usually can be done only to a very limited extent, and in any case employees are never given autonomy as to ultimate goals—their "autonomous" efforts can never be directed toward goals that they select personally, but only toward their employer's goals, such as the survival and growth of the company. Any company would soon go out of business if it permitted its employees to act otherwise. Similarly, in any enterprise within a socialist system, workers must direct their efforts toward the goals of the enterprise, otherwise the enterprise will not serve its purpose as part of the system. Once again, for purely technical reasons it is not possible for most individuals or small groups to have much autonomy in industrial society. Even the small-business owner commonly has only limited autonomy. Apart from the necessity of government regulation, he is restricted by the fact that he must fit into the economic system and conform to its requirements. For instance, when someone develops a new technology, the small-business person often has to use that technology whether he wants to or not, in order to remain competitive.

THE 'BAD' PARTS OF TECHNOLOGY CANNOT BE SEPARATED FROM THE 'GOOD' PARTS

121. A further reason why industrial society cannot be reformed in favor of freedom is that modern technology is a unified system in which all parts are dependent on one another. You can't get rid of the "bad" parts of technology and retain only the "good" parts. Take modern medicine, for example. Progress in medical science depends on progress in chemistry, physics, biology, computer science and other fields. Advanced medical treatments require expensive, high-tech equipment that can be made available only by a technologically progressive, economically rich society. Clearly you can't have much progress in medicine without the whole technological system and everything that goes with it.

122. Even if medical progress could be maintained without the rest of the technological system, it would by itself bring certain evils. Suppose for example that a cure for diabetes is discovered. People with a genetic tendency to diabetes will then be able to survive and reproduce as well as anyone else. Natural selection against genes for diabetes will cease and such genes will spread throughout the population. (This may be occurring to some extent already, since diabetes, while not curable, can be controlled through the use of insulin.) The same thing will happen with many other diseases susceptibility to which is affected by genetic degradation of the population. The only solution will be some sort of eugenics program or extensive genetic engineering of human beings, so that man in the future will no longer be a creation of nature, or of chance, or of God (depending on your religious or philosophical opinions), but a manufactured product.

123. If you think that big government interferes in your life too much NOW, just wait till the government starts regulating the genetic constitution of your children. Such regulation will inevitably follow the introduction of genetic engineering of human beings, because the consequences of unregulated genetic engineering would be disastrous. [19]

124. The usual response to such concerns is to talk about "medical ethics." But a code of ethics would not serve to protect freedom in the face of medical progress; it would only make matters worse. A code of ethics applicable to genetic engineering would be in effect a means of regulating the genetic constitution of human beings. Somebody (probably the upper-middle class, mostly) would decide that such and such applications of genetic engineering were "ethical" and others were not, so that in effect they would be imposing their own values on the genetic constitution of the population at large. Even if a code of ethics were chosen on a completely democratic basis, the majority would be imposing their own values on any minorities who might have a different idea of what constituted an "ethical" use of genetic engineering. The only code of ethics that would truly protect freedom would be one that prohibited ANY genetic engineering of human beings, and you can be sure that no such code will ever be applied in a technological society. No code that reduced genetic engineering to a minor role could stand up for long, because the temptation presented by the immense power of biotechnology would be irresistible, especially since to the majority of people many of its applications will seem obviously and unequivocally good (eliminating physical and mental diseases, giving people the abilities they need to get along in today's world). Inevitably, genetic engineering will be used extensively, but only in ways consistent with the needs of the industrial-technological system. [20]

TECHNOLOGY IS A MORE POWERFUL SOCIAL FORCE THAN THE ASPIRATION FOR FREEDOM

125. It is not possible to make a LASTING compromise between technology and freedom, because technology is by far the more powerful social force and continually encroaches on freedom through REPEATED compromises. Imagine the case of two neighbors, each of whom at the outset owns the same amount of land, but one of whom is more powerful than the other. The powerful one demands a piece of the other's land. The weak one refuses. The powerful one says, "OK, let's compromise. Give me half of what I asked." The weak one has little choice but to give in. Some time later the powerful neighbor demands another piece of land, again there is a compromise, and so forth. By forcing a long series of compromises on the weaker man, the powerful one eventually gets all of his land. So it goes in the conflict between technology and freedom.

126. Let us explain why technology is a more powerful social force than the aspiration for freedom.

127. A technological advance that appears not to threaten freedom often turns out to threaten it very seriously later on. For example, consider motorized transport. A walking man formerly could go where he pleased, go at his own pace without observing any traffic regulations, and was independent of technological support-systems. When motor vehicles were introduced they appeared to increase man's freedom. They took no freedom away from the walking man, no one had to have an automobile if he didn't want one, and anyone who did choose to buy an automobile could travel much faster than the walking man. But the introduction of motorized transport soon changed society in such a way as to restrict greatly man's freedom of locomotion. When automobiles became numerous, it became necessary to regulate their use extensively. In a car, especially in densely populated areas, one cannot just go where one likes at one's own pace one's movement is governed by the flow of traffic and by various traffic laws. One is tied down by various obligations: license requirements, driver test, renewing registration, insurance, maintenance required for safety, monthly payments on purchase price. Moreover, the use of motorized transport is no longer optional. Since the introduction of motorized transport the arrangement of our cities has changed in such a way that the majority of people no longer live within walking distance of their place of employment, shopping areas and recreational opportunities, so that they HAVE

TO depend on the automobile for transportation. Or else they must use public transportation, in which case they have even less control over their own movement than when driving a car. Even the walker's freedom is now greatly restricted. In the city he continually has to stop and wait for traffic lights that are designed mainly to serve auto traffic. In the country, motor traffic makes it dangerous and unpleasant to walk along the highway. (Note the important point we have illustrated with the case of motorized transport: When a new item of technology is introduced as an option that an individual can accept or not as he chooses, it does not necessarily REMAIN optional. In many cases the new technology changes society in such a way that people eventually find themselves FORCED to use it.)

128. While technological progress AS A WHOLE continually narrows our sphere of freedom, each new technical advance CONSIDERED BY ITSELF appears to be desirable. Electricity, indoor plumbing, rapid long-distance communications . . . how could one argue against any of these things, or against any other of the innumerable technical advances that have made modern society? It would have been absurd to resist the introduction of the telephone, for example. It offered many advantages and no disadvantages. Yet as we explained in paragraphs 59-76, all these technical advances taken together have created world in which the average man's fate is no longer in his own hands or in the hands of his neighbors and friends, but in those of politicians, corporation executives and remote, anonymous technicians and bureaucrats whom he as an individual has no power to influence. [21] The same process will continue in the future. Take genetic engineering, for example. Few people will resist the introduction of a genetic technique that eliminates a hereditary disease It does no apparent harm and prevents much suffering. Yet a large number of genetic improvements taken together will make the human being into an engineered product rather than a free creation of chance (or of God, or whatever, depending on your religious beliefs).

129. Another reason why technology is such a powerful social force is that, within the context of a given society, technological progress marches in only one direction; it can never be reversed. Once a technical innovation has been introduced, people usually become dependent on it, so that they can never again do without it, unless it is replaced by some still more advanced innovation. Not only do people become dependent as individuals on a new item of technology, but, even more, the system as a whole becomes dependent on it. (Imagine what would happen to the system today if computers, for example, were eliminated.) Thus the system can move in only one direction, toward greater technologization. Technology repeatedly forces freedom to take a step back, but technology can never take a step back—short of the overthrow of the whole technological system.

130. Technology advances with great rapidity and threatens freedom at many different points at the same time (crowding, rules and regulations, increasing dependence of individuals on large organizations, propaganda and other psychological techniques, genetic engineering, invasion of privacy through surveillance devices and computers, etc.) To hold back any ONE of the threats to freedom would require a long and different social struggle. Those who want to protect freedom are overwhelmed by the sheer number of new attacks and the rapidity with which they develop, hence they become pathetic and no longer resist. To fight each of the threats separately would be futile. Success can be hoped for only by fighting the technological system as a whole; but that is revolution, not reform.

131. Technicians (we use this term in its broad sense to describe all those who perform a specialized task that requires training) tend to be so involved in their work (their surrogate activity) that when a conflict arises between their technical work and freedom, they almost always decide in favor of their technical work. This is obvious in the case of scientists, but it also appears elsewhere: Educators, humanitarian groups, conservation organizations do not hesitate to use propaganda or other psychological techniques to help them achieve their laudable ends. Corporations and government agencies, when they find it useful, do not hesitate to collect information about individuals without regard to their privacy. Law enforcement agencies are frequently inconvenienced by the constitutional rights of suspects and often of completely innocent persons, and they do whatever they can do legally (or sometimes illegally) to restrict or circumvent those rights. Most of these educators, government officials and law officers believe in freedom, privacy and constitutional rights, but when these conflict with their work, they usually feel that their work is more important.

132. It is well known that people generally work better and more persistently when striving for a reward than when attempting to avoid a punishment or negative outcome. Scientists and other technicians are motivated mainly by the rewards they get through their work. But those who oppose technological invasions of freedom are working to avoid a negative outcome, consequently there are a few who work persistently and well at this discouraging task. If reformers ever achieved a signal victory that seemed to set up a solid barrier against further erosion of freedom through technological progress, most would tend to relax and turn their attention to more agreeable pursuits. But the scientists would remain busy in their laboratories, and technology as it progresses would find ways, in spite of any barriers, to exert more and more control over individuals and make them always more dependent on the system.

133. No social arrangements, whether laws, institutions, customs or ethical codes, can provide permanent protection against technology. History shows that all social arrangements are transitory; they all change or break down eventually. But technological advances are permanent within the context of a given civilization. Suppose for example that it were possible to arrive at some social arrangements that would prevent genetic engineering from being applied to human beings, or prevent it from being applied in such a ways as to threaten freedom and dignity. Still, the technology would remain waiting. Sooner or later the social arrangement would break down. Probably sooner, given the pace of change in our society. Then genetic engineering would begin to invade our sphere of freedom, and this invasion would be irreversible (short of a breakdown of technological civilization itself). Any illusions about achieving anything permanent through social arrangements should be dispelled by what is currently happening with environmental legislation. A few years ago it seemed that there were secure legal barriers preventing at least SOME of the worst forms of environmental degradation. A change in the political wind, and those barriers begin to crumble.

134. For all of the foregoing reasons, technology is a more powerful social force than the aspiration for freedom. But this statement requires an important qualification. It appears that during the next several decades the industrial-technological system will be undergoing severe stresses due to economic and environmental problems, and especially due to problems of human behavior (alienation, rebellion, hostility, a variety of social and psychological difficulties). We hope that the stresses through which the system is likely to pass will cause it to break down, or at least weaken it sufficiently so that a revolution against it becomes possible. If such a revolution occurs and is successful, then at that particular moment the aspiration for freedom will have proved more powerful than technology.

135. In paragraph 125 we used an analogy of a weak neighbor who is left destitute by a strong neighbor who takes all his land by forcing on him a series of compromises. But suppose now that the strong neighbor gets sick, so that he is unable to defend himself. The weak neighbor can force the strong one to give him his land back, or he can kill him. If he lets the strong man survive and only forces him to give his land back, he is a fool, because when the strong man gets well he will again take all the land for himself. The only sensible alternative for the weaker man is to kill the strong one while he has the chance. In the same way, while the industrial system is sick we must destroy it. If we compromise with it and let it recover from its sickness, it will eventually wipe out all of our freedom.

SIMPLER SOCIAL PROBLEMS HAVE PROVED INTRACTABLE

136. If anyone still imagines that it would be possible to reform the system in such a way as to protect freedom from technology, let him consider how clumsily and for the most part unsuccessfully our society has dealt with other social problems that are far more simple and straightforward. Among other things, the system has failed to stop environmental degradation, political corruption, drug trafficking or domestic abuse.

137. Take our environmental problems, for example. Here the conflict of values is straightforward: economic expedience now versus saving some of our natural resources for our grandchildren. [22] But on this subject we get only a lot of blather and obfuscation from the people who have power, and nothing like a clear, consistent line of action, and we keep on piling up environmental problems that our grandchildren will have to live with. Attempts to resolve the environmental issue consist of struggles and compromises between different factions, some of which are ascendant at one moment, others at another moment. The line of struggle changes with the shifting currents of public opinion. This is not a rational process, or is it one that is likely to lead to a timely and successful solution to the problem. Major social problems, if they get "solved" at all, are rarely or never solved through any rational, comprehensive plan. They just work themselves out through a process in which various competing groups pursing their own (usually short-term) self-interest [23] arrive (mainly by luck) at some more or less stable modus vivendi. In fact, the principles we formulated in paragraphs 100-106 make it seem doubtful that rational, long-term social planning can EVER be successful.

138. Thus it is clear that the human race has at best a very limited capacity for solving even relatively straightforward social problems. How then is it going to solve the far more difficult and subtle problem of reconciling freedom with technology? Technology presents clear-cut material advantages, whereas freedom is an abstraction that means different things to different people, and its loss is easily obscured by propaganda and fancy talk.

139. And note this important difference: It is conceivable that our environmental problems (for example) may some day be settled through a rational, comprehensive plan, but if this happens it will be only because it is in the long-term interest of the system to solve these problems. But it is NOT in the interest of the system to preserve freedom or small-group autonomy. On the contrary, it is in the interest of the system to bring human behavior under control to the greatest possible extent. [24] Thus, while practical considerations may eventually force the system to take a rational, prudent approach to environmental problems, equally practical considerations will force the system to regulate human behavior ever more closely (preferably by indirect means that will disguise the encroachment on freedom.) This isn't just our opinion. Eminent social scientists (e.g. James Q. Wilson) have stressed the importance of "socializing" people more effectively.

REVOLUTION IS EASIER THAN REFORM

140. We hope we have convinced the reader that the system cannot be reformed in a such a way as to reconcile freedom with technology. The only way out is to dispense with the industrial-technological system altogether. This implies revolution, not necessarily an armed uprising, but certainly a radical and fundamental change in the nature of society.

141. People tend to assume that because a revolution involves a much greater change than reform does, it is more difficult to bring about than reform is. Actually, under certain circumstances revolution is much easier than reform. The reason is that a revolutionary movement can inspire an intensity of commitment that a reform movement cannot inspire. A reform movement merely offers to solve a particular social problem A revolutionary movement offers to solve all problems at one stroke and create a whole new world; it provides the kind of ideal for which people will take great risks and make great sacrifices. For this reasons it would be much easier to overthrow the whole technological system than to put effective, permanent restraints on the development of application of any one segment of technology, such as genetic engineering, for example. Not many people will devote themselves with single-minded passion to imposing and maintaining restraints on genetic engineering, but under suitable conditions large numbers of people may devote themselves passionately to a revolution against the industrial-technological system. As we noted in paragraph 132, reformers seeking to limit certain aspects of technology would be working to avoid a negative outcome. But revolutionaries work to gain a powerful reward—fulfillment of their revolutionary vision—and therefore work harder and more persistently than reformers do.

142. Reform is always restrained by the fear of painful consequences if changes go too far. But once a revolutionary fever has taken hold of a society, people are willing to undergo unlimited hardships for the sake of their revolution. This was clearly shown in the French and Russian Revolutions. It may be that in such cases only a minority of the population is really committed to the revolution, but this minority is sufficiently large and active so that it becomes the dominant force in society. We will have more to say about revolution in paragraphs 180-205.

CONTROL OF HUMAN BEHAVIOR

143. Since the beginning of civilization, organized societies have had to put pressures on human beings of the sake of the functioning of the social organism. The kinds of pressures vary greatly from one society to another. Some of the pressures are physical (poor diet, excessive labor, environmental pollution), some are psychological (noise, crowding, forcing human behavior into the mold that society requires). In the past, human nature has been approximately constant, or at any rate has varied only within certain bounds. Consequently, societies have been able to push people only up to certain limits. When the limit of human endurance has been passed, things start going wrong: rebellion, or crime, or corruption, or evasion of work, or depression and other mental problems, or an elevated death rate, or a declining birth rate or something else, so that either the society breaks down, or its functioning becomes too inefficient and it is (quickly or gradually, through conquest, attrition or evolution) replaced by some more efficient form of society. [25]

144. Thus human nature has in the past put certain limits on the development of societies. People coud be pushed only so far and no farther. But today this may be changing, because modern technology is developing ways of modifying human beings.

145. Imagine a society that subjects people to conditions that make them terribly unhappy, then gives them drugs to take away their unhappiness. Science fiction? It is already happening to some extent in our own society. It is well known that the rate of clinical depression has been greatly increasing in recent decades. We believe that this is due to disruption of the power process, as explained in paragraphs 59-76. But even if we are wrong, the increasing rate of depression is certainly the result of SOME conditions that exist in today's society. Instead of removing the conditions that make people depressed, modern society gives them antidepressant drugs. In effect, antidepressants are a means of modifying an individual's internal state in such a way as to enable him to tolerate social conditions that he would otherwise find intolerable. (Yes, we know that depression is often of purely genetic origin. We are referring here to those cases in which environment plays the predominant role.)

146. Drugs that affect the mind are only one example of the methods of controlling human behavior that modern society is developing. Let us look at some of the other methods.

147. To start with, there are the techniques of surveillance. Hidden video cameras are now used in most stores and in many other places, computers are used to collect and process vast amounts of information about individuals. Information so obtained greatly increases the effectiveness of physical coercion (i.e., law enforcement). [26] Then there are the methods of propaganda, for which the mass communication media provide effective vehicles. Efficient techniques have been developed for winning elections, selling products, influencing public opinion. The entertainment industry serves as an important psychological tool of the system, possibly even when it is dishing out large amounts of sex and violence. Entertainment provides modern man with an essential means of escape. While absorbed in television, videos, etc., he can forget stress, anxiety, frustration, dissatisfaction. Many primitive peoples, when they don't have work to do, are quite content to sit for hours at a time doing nothing at all, because they are at peace with themselves and their world. But most modern people must be contantly occupied or entertained, otherwise the get "bored," i.e., they get fidgety, uneasy, irritable.

148. Other techniques strike deeper that the foregoing. Education is no longer a simple affair of paddling a kid's behind when he doesn't know his lessons and patting him on the head when he does know them. It is becoming a scientific technique for controlling the child's development. Sylvan Learning Centers, for example, have had great success in motivating children to study, and psychological techniques are also used with more or less success in many conventional schools. "Parenting" techniques that are taught to parents are designed to make children accept fundamental values of the system and behave in ways that the system finds desirable. "Mental health" programs, "intervention" techniques, psychotherapy and so forth are ostensibly designed to benefit individuals, but in practice they usually serve as methods for inducing individuals to think and behave as the system requires. (There is no contradiction here; an individual whose attitudes or behavior bring him into conflict with the system is up against a force that is too powerful for him to conquer or escape from, hence he is likely to suffer from stress, frustration, defeat. His path will be much easier if he thinks and behaves as the system requires. In that sense the system is acting for the benefit of the individual when it brainwashes him into conformity.) Child abuse in its gross and obvious forms is disapproved in most if not all cultures. Tormenting a child for a trivial reason or no reason at all is something that appalls almost everyone. But many psychologists interpret the concept of abuse much more broadly. Is spanking, when used as part of a rational and consistent system of discipline, a form of abuse? The question will ultimately be decided by whether or not spanking tends to produce behavior that makes a person fit in well with the existing system of society. In practice, the word "abuse" tends to be interpreted to include any method of child-rearing that produces behavior inconvenient for the system. Thus, when they go beyond the prevention of obvious, senseless cruelty, programs for preventing "child abuse" are directed toward the control of human behavior on behalf of the system.

149. Presumably, research will continue to increase the effectiveness of psychological techniques for controlling human behavior. But we think it is unlikely that psychological techniques alone will be sufficient to adjust human beings to the kind of society that technology is creating. Biological methods probably will have to be used. We have already mentiond the use of drugs in this connection. Neurology may provide other avenues of modifying the human mind. Genetic engineering of human beings is already beginning to occur in the form of "gene therapy," and there is no reason to assume the such methods will not eventually be used to modify those aspects of the body that affect mental funtioning.

150. As we mentioned in paragraph 134, industrial society seems likely to be entering a period of severe stress, due in part to problems of human behavior and in part to economic and environmental problems. And a considerable proportion of the system's economic and environmental problems result from the way human beings behave. Alienation, low self-esteem, depression, hostility, rebellion; children who won't study, youth gangs, illegal drug use, rape, child abuse, other crimes, unsafe sex, teen pregnancy, population growth, political corruption, race hatred, ethnic rivalry, bitter ideological conflict (i.e., pro-choice vs. pro-life), political extremism, terrorism, sabotage, anti-government groups, hate groups. All these threaten the very survival of the system. The system will be FORCED to use every practical means of controlling human behavior.

151. The social disruption that we see today is certainly not the result of mere chance. It can only be a result of the conditions of life that the system imposes on people. (We have argued that the most important of these conditions is disruption of the power process.) If the systems succeeds in imposing sufficient control over human behavior to assure its own survival, a new watershed in human history will have been passed. Whereas formerly the limits of human endurance have imposed limits on the development of societies (as we explained in paragraphs 143, 144), industrial-technological society will be able to pass those limits by modifying human beings, whether by psychological methods or biological methods or both. In the future, social systems will not be adjusted to suit the needs of human beings. Instead, human being will be adjusted to suit the needs of the system. [27]

152. Generally speaking, technological control over human behavior will probably not be introduced with a totalitarian intention or even through a conscious desire to restrict human freedom. [28] Each new step in the assertion of control over the human mind will be taken as a rational response to a problem that faces society, such as curing alcoholism, reducing the crime rate or inducing young people to study science and engineering. In many cases, there will be humanitarian justification. For example, when a psychiatrist prescribes an anti-depressant for a depressed patient, he is clearly doing that individual a favor. It would be inhumane to withhold the drug from someone who needs it. When parents send their children to Sylvan Learning Centers to have them manipulated into becoming enthusiastic about their studies, they do so from concern for their children's welfare. It may be that some of these parents wish that one didn't have to have specialized training to get a job and that their kid didn't have to be brainwashed into becoming a computer nerd. But what can they do? They can't change society, and their child may be unemployable if he doesn't have certain skills. So they send him to Sylvan.

153. Thus control over human behavior will be introduced not by a calculated decision of the authorities but through a process of social evolution (RAPID evolution, however). The process will be impossible to resist, because each advance, considered by itself, will appear to be beneficial, or at least the evil involved in making the advance will appear to be beneficial, or at least the evil involved in making the advance will seem to be less than that which would result from not making it (see paragraph 127). Propaganda for example is used for many good purposes, such as discouraging child abuse or race hatred. [14] Sex education is obviously useful, yet the effect of sex education (to the extent that it is successful) is to take the shaping of sexual attitudes away from the family and put it into the hands of the state as represented by the public school system.

154. Suppose a biological trait is discovered that increases the likelihood that a child will grow up to be a criminal and suppose some sort of gene therapy can remove this trait. [29] Of course most parents whose children possess the trait will have them undergo the therapy. It would be inhumane to do otherwise, since the child would probably have a miserable life if he grew up to be a criminal. But many or most primitive societies have a low crime rate in comparison with that of our society, even though they have neither high-tech methods of child-rearing nor harsh systems of punishment. Since there is no reason to suppose that more modern men than primitive men have innate predatory tendencies, the high crime rate of our society must be due to the pressures that modern conditions put on people, to which many cannot or will not adjust. Thus a treatment designed to remove potential criminal tendencies is at least in part a way of re-engineering people so that they suit the requirements of the system.

155. Our society tends to regard as a "sickness" any mode of thought or behavior that is inconvenient for the system, and this is plausible because when an individual doesn't fit into the system it causes pain to the individual as well as problems for the system. Thus the manipulation of an individual to adjust him to the system is seen as a "cure" for a "sickness" and therefore as good.

156. In paragraph 127 we pointed out that if the use of a new item of technology is INITIALLY optional, it does not necessarily REMAIN optional, because the new technology tends to change society in such a way that it becomes difficult or impossible for an individual to function without using that technology. This applies also to the technology of human behavior. In a world in which most children are put through a program to make them enthusiastic about studying, a parent will almost be forced to put his kid through such a program, because if he does not, then the kid will grow up to be, comparatively speaking, an ignoramus and therefore unemployable. Or suppose a biological treatment is discovered that, without undesirable side-effects, will greatly reduce the psychological stress from which so many people suffer in our society. If large numbers of people choose to undergo the treatment, then the general level of stress in society will be reduced, so that it will be possible for the system to increase the stress-producing pressures. In fact, something like this seems to have happened already with one of our society's most important psychological tools for enabling people to reduce (or at least temporarily escape from) stress, namely, mass entertainment (see paragraph 147). Our use of mass entertainment is "optional": No law requires us to watch television, listen to the radio, read magazines. Yet mass entertainment is a means of escape and stress-reduction on which most of us have become dependent. Everyone complains about the trashiness of television, but almost everyone watches it. A few have kicked the TV habit, but it would be a rare person who could get along today without using ANY form of mass entertainment. (Yet until quite recently in human history most people got along very nicely with no other entertainment than that which each local community created for itself.) Without the entertainment industry the system probably would not have been able to get away with putting as much stress-producing pressure on us as it does.

157. Assuming that industrial society survives, it is likely that technology will eventually acquire something approaching complete control over human behavior. It has been established beyond any rational doubt that human thought and behavior have a largely biological basis. As experimenters have demonstrated, feelings such as hunger, pleasure, anger and fear can be turned on and off by electrical stimulation of appropriate parts of the brain. Memories can be destroyed by damaging parts of the brain or they can be brought to the surface by electrical stimulation. Hallucinations can be induced or moods changed by drugs. There may or may not be an immaterial human soul, but if there is one it clearly is less powerful that the biological mechanisms of human behavior. For if that were not the case then researchers would not be able so easily to manipulate human feelings and behavior with drugs and electrical currents.

158. It presumably would be impractical for all people to have electrodes inserted in their heads so that they could be controlled by the authorities. But the fact that human thoughts and feelings are so open to biological intervention shows that the problem of controlling human behavior is mainly a technical problem; a problem of neurons, hormones and complex molecules; the kind of problem that is accessible to scientific attack. Given the outstanding record of our society in solving technical problems, it is overwhelmingly probable that great advances will be made in the control of human behavior.

159. Will public resistance prevent the introduction of technological control of human behavior? It certainly would if an attempt were made to introduce such control all at once. But since technological control will be introduced through a long sequence of small advances, there will be no rational and effective public resistance. (See paragraphs 127, 132, 153.)

160. To those who think that all this sounds like science fiction, we point out that yesterday's science fiction is today's fact. The Industrial Revolution has radically altered man's environment and way of life, and it is only to be expected that as technology is increasingly applied to the human body and mind, man himself will be altered as radically as his environment and way of life have been.

HUMAN RACE AT A CROSSROADS

161. But we have gotten ahead of our story. It is one thing to develop in the laboratory a series of psychological or biological techniques for manipulating human behavior and quite another to integrate these techniques into a functioning social system. The latter problem is the more difficult of the two. For example, while the techniques of educational psychology doubtless work quite well in the "lab schools" where they are developed, it is not necessarily easy to apply them effectively throughout our educational system. We all know what many of our schools are like. The teachers are too busy taking knives and guns away from the kids to subject them to the latest techniques for making them into computer nerds. Thus, in spite of all its technical advances relating to human behavior, the system to date has not been impressively successful in controlling human beings. The people whose behavior is fairly well under the control of the system are those of the type that might be called "bourgeois." But there are growing numbers of people who in one way or another are rebels against the system: welfare leaches, youth gangs, cultists, satanists, nazis, radical environmentalists, militiamen, etc..

162. The system is currently engaged in a desperate struggle to overcome certain problems that threaten its survival, among which the problems of human behavior are the most important. If the system succeeds in acquiring sufficient control over human behavior quickly enough, it will probably survive. Otherwise it will break down. We think the issue will most likely be resolved within the next several decades, say 40 to 100 years.

163. Suppose the system survives the crisis of the next several decades. By that time it will have to have solved, or at least brought under control, the principal problems that confront it, in particular that of "socializing" human beings; that is, making people sufficiently docile so that their behavior no longer threatens the system. That being accomplished, it does not appear that there would be any further obstacle to the development of technology, and it would presumably advance toward its logical conclusion, which is complete control over everything on Earth, including human beings and all other important organisms. The system may become a unitary, monolithic organization, or it may be more or less fragmented and consist of a number of organizations coexisting in a relationship that includes elements of both cooperation and competition, just as today the government, the corporations and other large organizations both cooperate and compete with one another. Human freedom mostly will have vanished, because individuals and small groups will be impotent vis-a-vis large organizations armed with supertechnology and an arsenal of advanced psychological and biological tools for manipulating human beings, besides instruments of surveillance and physical coercion. Only a small number of people will have any real power, and even these probably will have only very limited freedom, because their behavior too will be regulated; just as today our politicians and corporation executives can retain their positions of power only as long as their behavior remains within certain fairly narrow limits.

164. Don't imagine that the systems will stop developing further techniques for controlling human beings and nature once the crisis of the next few decades is over and increasing control is no longer necessary for the system's survival. On the contrary, once the hard times are over the system will increase its control over people and nature more rapidly, because it will no longer be hampered by difficulties of the kind that it is currently experiencing. Survival is not the principal motive for extending control. As we explained in paragraphs 87-90, technicians and scientists carry on their work largely as a surrogate activity; that is, they satisfy their need for power by solving technical problems. They will continue to do this with unabated enthusiasm, and among the most interesting and challenging problems for them to solve will be those of understanding the human body and mind and intervening in their development. For the "good of humanity," of course.

165. But suppose on the other hand that the stresses of the coming decades prove to be too much for the system. If the system breaks down there may be a period of chaos, a "time of troubles" such as those that history has recorded: at various epochs in the past. It is impossible to predict what would emerge from such a time of troubles, but at any rate the human race would be given a new chance. The greatest danger is that industrial society may begin to reconstitute itself within the first few years after the breakdown. Certainly there will be many people (power-hungry types especially) who will be anxious to get the factories running again.

166. Therefore two tasks confront those who hate the

servitude to which the industrial system is reducing the human race. First, we must work to heighten the social stresses within the system so as to increase the likelihood that it will break down or be weakened sufficiently so that a revolution against it becomes possible. Second, it is necessary to develop and propagate an ideology that opposes technology and the industrial society if and when the system becomes sufficiently weakened. And such an ideology will help to assure that, if and when industrial society breaks down, its remnants will be smashed beyond repair, so that the system cannot be reconstituted. The factories should be destroyed, technical books burned, etc.

HUMAN SUFFERING

167. The industrial system will not break down purely as a result of revolutionary action. It will not be vulnerable to revolutionary attack unless its own internal problems of development lead it into very serious difficulties. So if the system breaks down it will do so either spontaneously, or through a process that is in part spontaneous but helped along by revolutionaries. If the breakdown is sudden, many people will die, since the world's population has become so overblown that it cannot even feed itself any longer without advanced technology. Even if the breakdown is gradual enough so that reduction of the population can occur more through lowering of the birth rate than through elevation of the death rate, the process of deindustrialization probably will be very chaotic and involve much suffering. It is naive to think it likely that technology can be phased out in a smoothly managed orderly way, especially since the technophiles will fight stubbornly at every step. Is it therefore cruel to work for the breakdown of the system? Maybe, but maybe not. In the first place, revolutionaries will not be able to break the system down unless it is already in deep trouble so that there would be a good chance of its eventually breaking down by itself anyway; and the bigger the system grows, the more disastrous the consequences of its breakdown will be; so it may be that revolutionaries, by hastening the onset of the breakdown will be reducing the extent of the disaster.

168. In the second place, one has to balance struggle and death against the loss of freedom and dignity. To many of us, freedom and dignity are more important than a long life or avoidance of physical pain. Besides, we all have to die some time, and it may be better to die fighting for survival, or for a cause, than to live a long but empty and purposeless life.

169. In the third place, it is not all certain that the survival of the system will lead to less suffering than the breakdown of the system would. The system has already caused, and is continuing to cause, immense suffering all over the world. Ancient cultures, that for hundreds of years gave people a satisfactory relationship with each other and with their environment, have been shattered by contact with industrial society, and the result has been a whole catalogue of economic, environmental, social and psychological problems. One of the effects of the intrusion of industrial society has been that over much of the world traditional controls on population have been thrown out of balance. Hence the population explosion, with all that that implies. Then there is the psychological suffering that is widespread throughout the supposedly fortunate countries of the West (see paragraphs 44, 45). No one knows what will happen as a result of ozone depletion, the greenhouse effect and other environmental problems that cannot yet be foreseen. And, as nuclear proliferation has shown, new technology cannot be kept out of the hands of dictators and irresponsible Third World nations. Would you like to speculate abut what Iraq or North Korea will do with genetic engineering?

170. "Oh!" say the technophiles, "Science is going to fix all that! We will conquer famine, eliminate psychological suffering, make everybody healthy and happy!" Yeah, sure. That's what they said 200 years ago. The Industrial Revolution was supposed to eliminate poverty, make everybody happy, etc. The actual result has been quite different. The technophiles are hopelessly naive (or self-deceiving) in their understanding of social problems. They are unaware of (or choose to ignore) the fact that when large changes, even seemingly beneficial ones, are introduced into a society, they lead to a long sequence of other changes, most of which are impossible to predict (paragraph 103). The result is disruption of the society. So it is very probable that in their attempts to end poverty and disease, engineer docile, happy personalities and so forth, the technophiles will create social systems that are terribly troubled, even more so that the present one. For example, the scientists boast that they will end famine by creating new, genetically engineered food plants. But this will allow the human population to keep expanding indefinitely, and it is well known that crowding leads to increased stress and aggression. This is merely one example of the PREDICTABLE problems that will arise. We emphasize that, as past experience has shown, technical progress will lead to other new problems that CANNOT be predicted in advance (paragraph 103). In fact, ever since the Industrial Revolution, technology has been creating new problems for society far more rapidly than it has been solving old ones. Thus it will take a long and difficult period of trial and error for the technophiles to work the bugs out of their Brave New World (if they ever do). In the meantime there will be great suffering. So it is not at all clear that the survival of industrial society would involve less suffering than the breakdown of that society would. Technology has gotten the human race into a fix from which there is not likely to be any easy escape.

THE FUTURE

171. But suppose now that industrial society does survive the next several decades and that the bugs do eventually get worked out of the system, so that it functions smoothly. What kind of system will it be? We will consider several possibilities.

172. First let us postulate that the computer scientists succeed in developing intelligent machines that can do all things better that human beings can do them. In that case presumably all work will be done by vast, highly organized systems of machines and no human effort will be necessary. Either of two cases might occur. The machines might be permitted to make all of their own decisions without human oversight, or else human control over the machines might be retained.

173. If the machines are permitted to make all their own decisions, we can't make any conjectures as to the results, because it is impossible to guess how such machines might behave. We only point out that the fate of the human race would be at the mercy of the machines. It might be argued that the human race would never be foolish enough to hand over all the power to the machines. But we are suggesting neither that the human race would voluntarily turn power over to the machines nor that the machines would willfully seize power. What we do suggest is that the human race might easily permit itself to drift into a position of such dependence on the machines that it would have no practical choice but to accept all of the machines decisions. As society and the problems that face it become more and more complex and as machines become more and more intelligent, people will let machines make more of their decisions for them, simply because machine-made decisions will bring better result than man-made ones. Eventually a stage may be reached at which the decisions necessary to keep the system running will be so complex that human beings will be incapable of making them intelligently. At that stage the machines will be in effective control. People won't be able to just turn the machines off, because they will be so dependent on them that turning them off would amount to suicide.

174. On the other hand it is possible that human control over the machines may be retained. In that case the average man may have control over certain private machines of his own, such as his car or his personal computer, but control over large systems of machines will be in the hands of a tiny elite—just as it is today, but with two differences. Due to improved techniques the elite will have greater control over the masses; and because human work will no longer be necessary the masses will be superfluous, a useless burden on the system. If the elite is ruthless they may simply decide to exterminate the mass of humanity. If they are humane they may use propaganda or other psychological or biological techniques to reduce the birth rate until the mass of humanity becomes extinct, leaving the world to the elite. Or, if the elite consist of soft-hearted liberals, they may decide to play the role of good shepherds to the rest of the human race. They will see to it that everyone's physical needs are satisfied, that all children are raised under psychologically hygienic conditions, that everyone has a wholesome hobby to keep him busy, and that anyone who may become dissatisfied undergoes "treatment" to cure his "problem." Of course, life will be so purposeless that people will have to be biologically or psychologically engineered either to remove their need for the power process or to make them "sublimate" their drive for power into some harmless hobby. These engineered human beings may be happy in such a society, but they most certainly will not be free. They will have been reduced to the status of domestic animals.

175. But suppose now that the computer scientists do not succeed in developing artificial intelligence, so that human work remains necessary. Even so, machines will take care of more and more of the simpler tasks so that there will be an increasing surplus of human workers at the lower levels of ability. (We see this happening already. There are many people who find it difficult or impossible to get work, because for intellectual or psychological reasons they cannot acquire the level of training necessary to make themselves useful in the present system.) On those who are employed, ever-increasing demands will be placed; They will need more and more training, more and more ability, and will have to be ever more reliable, conforming and docile, because they will be more and more like cells of a giant organism. Their tasks will be increasingly specialized so that their work will be, in a sense, out of touch with the real world, being concentrated on one tiny slice of reality. The system will have to use any means that it can, whether psychological or biological, to engineer people to be docile, to have the abilities that the system requires and to "sublimate" their drive for power into some specialized task. But the statement that the people of such a society will have to be docile may require qualification. The society may find competitiveness useful, provided that ways are found of directing competitiveness into channels that serve the needs of the system. We can imagine a future society in which there is endless competition for positions of prestige and power. But no more than a very few people will ever reach the top, where the only real power is (see end of paragraph 163). Very repellent is a society in which a person can satisfy his needs for power only by pushing large numbers of other people out of the way and depriving them of THEIR opportunity for power.

176. One can envision scenarios that incorporate aspects of more than one of the possibilities that we have just discussed. For instance, it may be that machines will take over most of the work that is of real, practical importance, but that human beings will be kept busy by being given relatively unimportant work. It has been suggested, for example, that a great development of the service industries might provide work for human beings. Thus people would spend their time shining each other's shoes, driving each other around in taxicabs making handicrafts for one another, waiting on each other's tables, etc. This seems to us a thoroughly contemptible way for the human race to end up, and we doubt that many people would find fulfilling lives in such pointless busy-work. They would seek other, dangerous outlets (drugs, crime, "cults," hate groups) unless they were biologically or psychologically engineered to adapt them to such a way of life.

177. Needless to day, the scenarios outlined above do not exhaust all the possibilities. They only indicate the kinds of outcomes that seem to us most likely. But we can envision no plausible scenarios that are any more palatable than the ones we've just described. It is overwhelmingly probable that if the industrial-technological system survives the next 40 to 100 years, it will by that time have developed certain general characteristics: Individuals (at least those of the "bourgeois" type, who are integrated into the system and make it run, and who therefore have all the power) will be more dependent than ever on large organizations; they will be more "socialized" than ever and their physical and mental qualities to a significant extent (possibly to a very great extent) will be those that are engineered into them rather than being the results of chance (or of God's will, or whatever); and whatever may be left of wild nature will be reduced to remnants preserved for scientific study and kept under the supervision and management of scientists (hence it will no longer be truly wild). In the long run (say a few centuries from now) it is likely that neither the human race nor any other important organisms will exist as we know them today, because once you start modifying organisms through genetic engineering there is no reason to stop at any particular point, so that the modifications will probably continue until man and other organisms have been utterly transformed.

178. Whatever else may be the case, it is certain that technology is creating for human begins a new physical and social environment radically different from the spectrum of environments to which natural selection has adapted the human race physically and psychologically. If man is not adjusted to this new environment by being artificially re-engineered, then he will be adapted to it through a long and painful process of natural selection. The former is far more likely than the latter.

179. It would be better to dump the whole stinking system and take the consequences.

STRATEGY

180. The technophiles are taking us all on an utterly reckless ride into the unknown. Many people understand something of what technological progress is doing to us yet take a passive attitude toward it because they think it is inevitable. But we (FC) don't think it is inevitable. We think it can be stopped, and we will give here some indications of how to go about stopping it.

181. As we stated in paragraph 166, the two main tasks for the present are to promote social stress and instability in industrial society and to develop and propagate an ideology that opposes technology and the industrial system. When the system becomes sufficiently stressed and unstable, a revolution against technology may be possible. The pattern would be similar to that of the French and Russian Revolutions. French society and Russian society, for several decades prior to their respective revolutions, showed increasing signs of stress and weakness. Meanwhile, ideologies were being developed that offered a new world view that was quite different from the old one. In the Russian case, revolutionaries were actively working to undermine the old order. Then, when the old system was put under sufficient additional stress (by financial crisis in France, by military defeat in Russia) it was swept away by revolution. What we propose in something along the same lines.

182. It will be objected that the French and Russian Revolutions were failures. But most revolutions have two goals. One is to destroy an old form of society and the other is to set up the new form of society envisioned by the revolutionaries. The French and Russian revolutionaries failed (fortunately!) to create the new kind of society of which they dreamed, but they were quite successful in destroying the old society. We have no illusions about the feasibility of creating a new, ideal form of society. Our goal is only to destroy the existing form of society.

183. But an ideology, in order to gain enthusiastic support, must have a positive ideal as well as a negative one; it must be FOR something as well as AGAINST something. The positive ideal that we propose is Nature. That is, WILD nature; those aspects of the functioning of the Earth and its living things that are independent of human management and free of human interference and control. And with wild nature we include human nature, by which we mean those aspects of the functioning of the human individual that are not subject to regulation by organized society but are products of chance, or free will, or God (depending on your religious or philosophical opinions).

184. Nature makes a perfect counter-ideal to technology for several reasons. Nature (that which is outside the power of the system) is the opposite of technology (which seeks to expand indefinitely the power of the system). Most people will agree that nature is beautiful; certainly it has tremendous popular appeal. The radical environmentalists ALREADY hold an ideology that exalts nature and opposes technology. [30] It is not necessary for the sake of nature to set up some chimerical utopia or any new kind of social order. Nature takes care of itself: It was a spontaneous creation that existed long before any human society, and for countless centuries many different kinds of human societies coexisted with nature without doing it an excessive amount of damage. Only with the Industrial Revolution did the effect of human society on nature become really devastating. To relieve the pressure on nature it is not necessary to create a special kind of social system, it is only necessary to get rid of industrial society. Granted, this will not solve all problems. Industrial society has already done tremendous damage to nature and it will take a very long time for the scars to heal. Besides, even pre-industrial societies can do significant damage to nature. Nevertheless, getting rid of industrial society will accomplish a great deal. It will relieve the worst of the pressure on nature so that the scars can begin to heal. It will remove the capacity of organized society to keep increasing its control over nature (including human nature). Whatever kind of society may exist after the demise of the industrial system, it is certain that most people will live close to nature, because in the absence of advanced technology there is no other way that people CAN live. To feed themselves they must be peasants or herdsmen or fishermen or hunters, etc., And, generally speaking, local autonomy should tend to increase, because lack of advanced technology and rapid communications will limit the capacity of governments or other large organizations to control local communities.

185. As for the negative consequences of eliminating industrial society—well, you can't eat your cake and have it too. To gain one thing you have to sacrifice another.

186. Most people hate psychological conflict. For this reason they avoid doing any serious thinking about difficult social issues, and they like to have such issues presented to them in simple, black-and-white terms: THIS is all good and THAT is all bad. The revolutionary ideology should therefore be developed on two levels.

187. On the more sophisticated level the ideology should address itself to people who are intelligent, thoughtful and rational. The object should be to create a core of people who will be opposed to the industrial system on a rational, thought-out basis, with full appreciation of the problems and ambiguities involved, and of the price that has to be paid for getting rid of the system. It is particularly important to attract people of this type, as they are capable people and will be instrumental in influencing others. These people should be addressed on as rational a level as possible. Facts should never intentionally be distorted and intemperate language should be avoided. This does not mean that no appeal can be made to the emotions, but in making

259

such appeal care should be taken to avoid misrepresenting the truth or doing anything else that would destroy the intellectual respectability of the ideology.

188. On a second level, the ideology should be propagated in a simplified form that will enable the unthinking majority to see the conflict of technology vs. nature in unambiguous terms. But even on this second level the ideology should not be expressed in language that is so cheap, intemperate or irrational that it alienates people of the thoughtful and rational type. Cheap, intemperate propaganda sometimes achieves impressive short-term gains, but it will be more advantageous in the long run to keep the loyalty of a small number of intelligently committed people than to arouse the passions of an unthinking, fickle mob who will change their attitude as soon as someone comes along with a better propaganda gimmick. However, propaganda of the rabble-rousing type may be necessary when the system is nearing the point of collapse and there is a final struggle between rival ideologies to determine which will become dominant when the old world-view goes under.

189. Prior to that final struggle, the revolutionaries should not expect to have a majority of people on their side. History is made by active, determined minorities, not by the majority, which seldom has a clear and consistent idea of what it really wants. Until the time comes for the final push toward revolution [31], the task of revolutionaries will be less to win the shallow support of the majority than to build a small core of deeply committed people. As for the majority, it will be enough to make them aware of the existence of the new ideology and remind them of it frequently; though of course it will be desirable to get majority support to the extent that this can be done without weakening the core of seriously committed people.

190. Any kind of social conflict helps to destabilize the system, but one should be careful about what kind of conflict one encourages. The line of conflict should be drawn between the mass of the people and the power-holding elite of industrial society (politicians, scientists, upper-level business executives, government officials, etc.). It should NOT be drawn between the revolutionaries and the mass of the people. For example, it would be bad strategy for the revolutionaries to condemn Americans for their habits of consumption. Instead, the average American should be portrayed as a victim of the advertising and marketing industry, which has suckered him into buying a lot of junk that he doesn't need and that is very poor compensation for his lost freedom. Either approach is consistent with the facts. It is merely a matter of attitude whether you blame the advertising industry for manipulating the public or blame the public for allowing itself to be manipulated. As a matter of strategy one should generally avoid blaming the public.

191. One should think twice before encouraging any other social conflict than that between the power-holding elite (which wields technology) and the general public (over which technology exerts its power). For one thing, other conflicts tend to distract attention from the important conflicts (between power-elite and ordinary people, between technology and nature); for another thing, other conflicts may actually tend to encourage technologization, because each side in such a conflict wants to use technological power to gain advantages over its adversary. This is clearly seen in rivalries between nations. It also appears in ethnic conflicts within nations. For example, in America many black leaders are anxious to gain power for African Americans by placing back individuals in the technological power-elite. They want there to be many black government officials, scientists, corporation executives and so forth. In this way they are helping to absorb the African American subculture into the technological system. Generally speaking, one should encourage only those social conflicts that can be fitted into the framework of the conflicts of power—elite vs. ordinary people, technology vs nature.

192. But the way to discourage ethnic conflict is NOT through militant advocacy of minority rights (see paragraphs 21, 29). Instead, the revolutionaries should emphasize that although minorities do suffer more or less disadvantage, this disadvantage is of peripheral significance. Our real enemy is the industrial-technological system, and in the struggle against the system, ethnic distinctions are of no importance.

193. The kind of revolution we have in mind will not

necessarily involve an armed uprising against any government. It may or may not involve physical violence, but it will not be a POLITICAL revolution. Its focus will be on technology and economics, not politics. [32]

194. Probably the revolutionaries should even AVOID assuming political power, whether by legal or illegal means, until the industrial system is stressed to the danger point and has proved itself to be a failure in the eyes of most people. Suppose for example that some "green" party should win control of the United States Congress in an election. In order to avoid betraying or watering down their own ideology they would have to take vigorous measures to turn economic growth into economic shrinkage. To the average man the results would appear disastrous: There would be massive unemployment, shortages of commodities, etc. Even if the grosser ill effects could be avoided through superhumanly skillful management, still people would have to begin giving up the luxuries to which they have become addicted. Dissatisfaction would grow, the "green" party would be voted out of office and the revolutionaries would have suffered a severe setback. For this reason the revolutionaries should not try to acquire political power until the system has gotten itself into such a mess that any hardships will be seen as resulting from the failures of the industrial system itself and not from the policies of the revolutionaries. The revolution against technology will probably have to be a revolution by outsiders, a revolution from below and not from above.

195. The revolution must be international and worldwide. It cannot be carried out on a nation-by-nation basis. Whenever it is suggested that the United States, for example, should cut back on technological progress or economic growth, people get hysterical and start screaming that if we fall behind in technology the Japanese will get ahead of us. Holy robots! The world will fly off its orbit if the Japanese ever sell more cars than we do! (Nationalism is a great promoter of technology.) More reasonably, it is argued that if the relatively democratic nations of the world fall behind in technology while nasty, dictatorial nations like China, Vietnam and North Korea continue to progress, eventually the dictators may come to dominate the world.

That is why the industrial system should be attacked in all nations simultaneously, to the extent that this may be possible. True, there is no assurance that the industrial system can be destroyed at approximately the same time all over the world, and it is even conceivable that the attempt to overthrow the system could lead instead to the domination of the system by dictators. That is a risk that has to be taken. And it is worth taking, since the difference between a "democratic" industrial system and one controlled by dictators is small compared with the difference between an industrial system and a non-industrial one. [33] It might even be argued that an industrial system controlled by dictators would be preferable, because dictator-controlled systems usually have proved inefficient, hence they are presumably more likely to break down. Look at Cuba.

196. Revolutionaries might consider favoring measures that tend to bind the world economy into a unified whole. Free trade agreements like NAFTA and GATT are probably harmful to the environment in the short run, but in the long run they may perhaps be advantageous because they foster economic interdependence between nations. It will be easier to destroy the industrial system on a worldwide basis if the world economy is so unified that its breakdown in any one major nation will lead to its breakdown in all industrialized nations.

197. Some people take the line that modern man has too much power, too much control over nature; they argue for a more passive attitude on the part of the human race. At best these people are expressing themselves unclearly, because they fail to distinguish between power for LARGE ORGANIZATIONS and power for INDIVIDUALS and SMALL GROUPS. It is a mistake to argue for power-lessness and passivity, because people NEED power. Modern man as a collective entity—that is, the industrial system—has immense power over nature, and we (FC) regard this as evil. But modern INDIVIDUALS and SMALL GROUPS OF INDIVIDUALS have far less power than primitive man ever did. Generally speaking, the vast power of "modern man" over nature is exercised not by individuals or small groups but by large organizations. To the extent that the average modern INDIVIDUAL can wield the power of technology, he is permitted to do so only within narrow limits and only under the supervision and control of the system. (You need a license for everything and with the license come rules and regulations). The individual has only those technological powers with which the system chooses to provide him. His PERSONAL power over nature is slight.

198. Primitive INDIVIDUALS and SMALL GROUPS actually had considerable power over nature; or maybe it would be better to say power WITHIN nature. When primitive man needed food he knew how to find and prepare edible roots, how to track game and take it with homemade weapons. He knew how to protect himself from heat, cold, rain, dangerous animals, etc. But primitive man did relatively little damage to nature because the COLLECTIVE power of primitive society was negligible compared to the COLLECTIVE power of industrial society.

199. Instead of arguing for powerlessness and passivity, one should argue that the power of the INDUSTRIAL SYSTEM should be broken, and that this will greatly INCREASE the power and freedom of INDIVIDUALS and SMALL GROUPS.

200. Until the industrial system has been thoroughly wrecked, the destruction of that system must be the revolutionaries' ONLY goal. Other goals would distract attention and energy from the main goal. More importantly, if the revolutionaries permit themselves to have any other goal than the destruction of technology, they will be tempted to use technology as a tool for reaching that other goal. If they give in to that temptation, they will fall right back into the technological trap, because modern technology is a unified, tightly organized system, so that, in order to retain SOME technology, one finds oneself obliged to retain MOST technology, hence one ends up sacrificing only token amounts of technology.

201. Suppose for example that the revolutionaries took "social justice" as a goal. Human nature being what it is, social justice would not come about spontaneously; it would have to be enforced. In order to enforce it the revolutionaries would have to retain central organization and control. For that they would need rapid long-distance transportation and communication, and therefore all the technology needed to support the transportation and communication systems. To feed and clothe poor people they would have to use agricultural and manufacturing technology. And so forth. So that the attempt to insure social justice would force them to retain most parts of the technological system. Not that we have anything against social justice, but it must not be allowed to interfere with the effort to get rid of the technological system.

202. It would be hopeless for revolutionaries to try to attack the system without using SOME modern technology. If nothing else they must use the communications media to spread their message. But they should use modern technology for only ONE purpose: to attack the technological system.

203. Imagine an alcoholic sitting with a barrel of wine in front of him. Suppose he starts saying to himself, "Wine isn't bad for you if used in moderation. Why, they say small amounts of wine are even good for you! It won't do me any harm if I take just one little drink . . . ." Well you know what is going to happen. Never forget that the human race with technology is just like an alcoholic with a barrel of wine.

204. Revolutionaries should have as many children as they can. There is strong scientific evidence that social attitudes are to a significant extent inherited. No one suggests that a social attitude is a direct outcome of a person's genetic constitution, but it appears that personality traits are partly inherited and that certain personality traits tend, within the context of our society, to make a person more likely to hold this or that social attitude. Objections to these findings have been raised, but the objections are feeble and seem to be ideologically motivated. In any event, no one denies that children tend on the average to hold social attitudes similar to those of their parents. From our point of view it doesn't matter all that much whether the attitudes are passed on genetically or through childhood training. In either case they ARE passed on.

205. The trouble is that many of the people who are inclined to rebel against the industrial system are also concerned about the population problems, hence they are apt to have few or no children. In this way they may be handing the world over to the sort of people who support or at least accept the industrial system. To insure the strength of the next generation of revolutionaries the present generation must reproduce itself abundantly. In doing so they will be worsening the population problem only slightly. And the most important problem is to get rid of the industrial system, because once the industrial system is gone the world's population necessarily will decrease (see paragraph 167); whereas, if the industrial system survives, it will continue developing new techniques of food production that may enable the world's population to keep increasing almost indefinitely.

206. With regard to revolutionary strategy, the only points on which we absolutely insist are that the single overriding goal must be the elimination of modern technology, and that no other goal can be allowed to compete with this one. For the rest, revolutionaries should take an empirical approach. If experience indicates that some of the recommendations made in the foregoing paragraphs are not going to give good results, then those recommendations should be discarded.

TWO KINDS OF TECHNOLOGY

207. An argument likely to be raised against our proposed revolution is that it is bound to fail, because (it is claimed) throughout history technology has always progressed, never regressed, hence technological regression is impossible. But this claim is false.

208. We distinguish between two kinds of technology, which we will call small-scale technology and organization-dependent technology. Small-scale technology is technology that can be used by small-scale communities without outside assistance. Organization-dependent technology is technology that depends on large-scale social organization. We are aware of no significant cases of regression in small-scale technology. But organization-dependent technology DOES regress when the social organization on which it depends breaks down. Example: When the Roman

Empire fell apart the Romans' small-scale technology survived because any clever village craftsman could build, for instance, a water wheel, any skilled smith could make steel by Roman methods, and so forth. But the Romans' organization-dependent technology DID regress. Their aqueducts fell into disrepair and were never rebuilt. Their techniques of road construction were lost. The Roman system of urban sanitation was forgotten, so that not until rather recent times did the sanitation of European cities equal that of Ancient Rome.

209. The reason why technology has seemed always to progress is that, until perhaps a century or two before the Industrial Revolution, most technology was small-scale technology. But most of the technology developed since the Industrial Revolution is organization-dependent technology. Take the refrigerator for example. Without factory-made parts or the facilities of a post-industrial machine shop it would be virtually impossible for a handful of local craftsmen to build a refrigerator. If by some miracle they did succeed in building one it would be useless to them without a reliable source of electric power. So they would have to dam a stream and build a generator. Generators require large amounts of copper wire. Imagine trying to make that wire without modern machinery. And where would they get a gas suitable for refrigeration? It would be much easier to build an icehouse or preserve food by drying or picking, as was done before the invention of the refrigerator.

210. So it is clear that if the industrial system were once thoroughly broken down, refrigeration technology would quickly be lost. The same is true of other organization-dependent technology. And once this technology had been lost for a generation or so it would take centuries to rebuild it, just as it took centuries to build it the first time around. Surviving technical books would be few and scattered. An industrial society, if built from scratch without outside help, can only be built in a series of stages: You need tools to make tools to make tools to make tools . . . . A long process of economic development and progress in social organization is required. And, even in the absence of an ideology opposed to technology, there is no reason to believe that anyone would be interested in rebuilding industrial society. The enthusiasm for "progress" is a phenomenon particular to the modern form of society, and it seems not to have existed prior to the 17th century or thereabouts.

211. In the late Middle Ages there were four main civilizations that were about equally "advanced": Europe, the Islamic world, India, and the Far East (China, Japan, Korea). Three of those civilizations remained more or less stable, and only Europe became dynamic. No one knows why Europe became dynamic at that time; historians have their theories but these are only speculation. At any rate, it is clear that rapid development toward a technological form of society occurs only under special conditions. So there is no reason to assume that long-lasting technological regression cannot be brought about.

212. Would society EVENTUALLY develop again toward an industrial-technological form? Maybe, but there is no use in worrying about it, since we can't predict or control events 500 or 1,000 years in the future. Those problems must be dealt with by the people who will live at that time.

THE DANGER OF LEFTISM

213. Because of their need for rebellion and for membership in a movement, leftists or persons of similar psychological type are often unattracted to a rebellious or activist movement whose goals and membership are not initially leftist. The resulting influx of leftish types can easily turn a non-leftist movement into a leftist one, so that leftist goals replace or distort the original goals of the movement.

214. To avoid this, a movement that exalts nature and opposes technology must take a resolutely anti-leftist stance and must avoid all collaboration with leftists. Leftism is in the long run inconsistent with wild nature, with human freedom and with the elimination of modern technology. Leftism is collectivist; it seeks to bind together the entire world (both nature and the human race) into a unified whole. But this implies management of nature and of human life by organized society, and it requires advanced technology. You can't have a united world without rapid transportation and communication, you can't make all people love one another without sophisticated psychological techniques, you can't have a "planned society" without the necessary technological base. Above all, leftism is driven by the need for power, and the leftist seeks power on a collective basis, through identification with a mass movement or an organization. Leftism is unlikely ever to give up technology, because technology is too valuable a source of collective power.

215. The anarchist [34] too seeks power, but he seeks it on an individual or small-group basis; he wants individuals and small groups to be able to control the circumstances of their own lives. He opposes technology because it makes small groups dependent on large organizations.

216. Some leftists may seem to oppose technology, but they will oppose it only so long as they are outsiders and the technological system is controlled by non-leftists. If leftism ever becomes dominant in society, so that the technological system becomes a tool in the hands of leftists, they will enthusiastically use it and promote its growth. In doing this they will be repeating a pattern that leftism has shown again and again in the past. When the Bolsheviks in Russia were outsiders, they vigorously opposed censorship and the secret police, they advocated self-determination for ethnic minorities, and so forth; but as soon as they came into power themselves, they imposed a tighter censorship and created a more ruthless secret police than any that had existed under the tsars, and they oppressed ethnic minorities at least as much as the tsars had done. In the United States, a couple of decades ago when leftists were a minority in our universities, leftist professors were vigorous proponents of academic freedom, but today, in those universities where leftists have become dominant, they have shown themselves ready to take away from everyone else's academic freedom. (This is "political correctness.") The same will happen with leftists and technology: They will use it to oppress everyone else if they ever get it under their own control.

217. In earlier revolutions, leftists of the most power-hungry type, repeatedly, have first cooperated with non-leftist revolutionaries, as well as with leftists of a more libertarian inclination, and later have double-crossed them to seize power for themselves. Robespierre did this in the French Revolution, the Bolsheviks did it in the Russian Revolution, the communists did it in Spain in 1938 and Castro and his followers did it in Cuba. Given the past history of leftism, it would be utterly foolish for non-leftist revolutionaries today to collaborate with leftists.

218. Various thinkers have pointed out that leftism is a kind of religion. Leftism is not a religion in the strict sense because leftist doctrine does not postulate the existence of any supernatural being. But for the leftist, leftism plays a psychological role much like that which religion plays for some people. The leftist NEEDS to believe in leftism; it plays a vital role in his psychological economy. His beliefs are not easily modified by logic or facts. He has a deep conviction that leftism is morally Right with a capital R, and that he has not only a right but a duty to impose leftist morality on everyone. (However, many of the people we are referring to as "leftists" do not think of themselves as leftists and would not describe their system of beliefs as leftism. We use the term "leftism" because we don't know of any better words to designate the spectrum of related creeds that includes the feminist, gay rights, political correctness, etc., movements, and because these movements have a strong affinity with the old left. See paragraphs 227-230.)

219. Leftism is a totalitarian force. Wherever leftism is in a position of power it tends to invade every private corner and force every thought into a leftist mold. In part this is because of the quasi-religious character of leftism; everything contrary to leftists beliefs represents Sin. More importantly, leftism is a totalitarian force because of the leftists' drive for power. The leftist seeks to satisfy his need for power through identification with a social movement and he tries to go through the power process by helping to pursue and attain the goals of the movement (see paragraph 83). But no matter how far the movement has gone in attaining its goals the leftist is never satisfied, because his activism is a surrogate activity (see paragraph 41). That is, the leftist's real motive is not to attain the ostensible goals of leftism; in reality he is motivated by the sense of power he gets from struggling for and then reaching a social goal. [35] Consequently the leftist is never satisfied with the goals he has already attained; his need for the power process leads him always to pursue some new goal. The leftist wants equal opportunities for minorities. When that is attained he insists on statistical equality of achievement by minorities. And as long as anyone harbors in some corner of his mind a negative attitude toward some minority, the leftist has to re-educated him. And ethnic minorities are not enough; no one can be allowed to have a negative attitude toward homosexuals, disabled people, fat people, old people, ugly people, and on and on and on. It's not enough that the public should be informed about the hazards of smoking; a warning has to be stamped on every package of cigarettes. Then cigarette advertising has to be restricted if not banned. The activists will never be satisfied until tobacco is outlawed, and after that it will be alcohol, then junk food, etc. Activists have fought gross child abuse, which is reasonable. But now they want to stop all spanking. When they have done that they will want to ban something else they consider unwholesome, then another thing and then another. They will never be satisfied until they have complete control over all child rearing practices. And then they will move on to another cause.

220. Suppose you asked leftists to make a list of ALL the things that were wrong with society, and then suppose you instituted EVERY social change that they demanded. It is safe to say that within a couple of years the majority of leftists would find something new to complain about, some new social "evil" to correct because, once again, the leftist is motivated less by distress at society's ills than by the need to satisfy his drive for power by imposing his solutions on society.

221. Because of the restrictions placed on their thoughts and behavior by their high level of socialization, many leftists of the over-socialized type cannot pursue power in the ways that other people do. For them the drive for power has only one morally acceptable outlet, and that is in the struggle to impose their morality on everyone.

222. Leftists, especially those of the oversocialized type, are True Believers in the sense of Eric Hoffer's book, "The True Believer." But not all True Believers are of the same psychological type as leftists. Presumably a true-believing nazi, for instance, is very different psychologically from a true-believing leftist. Because of their capacity for single-minded devotion to a cause, True Believers are a useful, perhaps a necessary, ingredient of any revolutionary movement. This presents a problem with which we must admit we don't know how to deal. We aren't sure how to harness the energies of the True Believer to a revolution against technology. At present all we can say is that no True Believer will make a safe recruit to the revolution unless his commitment is exclusively to the destruction of technology. If he is committed also to another ideal, he may want to use technology as a tool for pursuing that other ideal (see paragraphs 220, 221).

223. Some readers may say, "This stuff about leftism is a lot of crap. I know John and Jane who are leftish types and they don't have all these totalitarian tendencies." It's quite true that many leftists, possibly even a numerical majority, are decent people who sincerely believe in tolerating others' values (up to a point) and wouldn't want to use high-handed methods to reach their social goals. Our remarks about leftism are not meant to apply to every individual leftist but to describe the general character of leftism as a movement. And the general character of a movement is not necessarily determined by the numerical proportions of the various kinds of people involved in the movement.

224. The people who rise to positions of power in leftist movements tend to be leftists of the most power-hungry type because power-hungry people are those who strive hardest to get into positions of power. Once the power-hungry types have captured control of the movement, there are many leftists of a gentler breed who inwardly disapprove of many of the actions of the leaders, but cannot bring themselves to oppose them. They NEED their faith in the movement, and because they cannot give up this faith they go along with the leaders. True, SOME leftists do have the guts to oppose the totalitarian tendencies that emerge, but they generally lose, because the power-hungry types are better organized, are more ruthless and Machiavellian and have taken care to build themselves a strong power base.

225. These phenomena appeared clearly in Russia and other countries that were taken over by leftists. Similarly, before the breakdown of communism in the USSR, leftish types in the West would seldom criticize that country. If prodded they would admit that the USSR did many wrong things, but then they would try to find excuses for the communists and begin talking about the faults of the West. They always opposed Western military resistance to communist aggression. Leftish types all over the world vigorously protested the U.S. military action in Vietnam, but when the USSR invaded Afghanistan they did nothing. Not that they approved of the Soviet actions; but because of their leftist faith, they just couldn't bear to put themselves in opposition to communism. Today, in those of our universities where "political correctness" has become dominant, there are probably many leftish types who privately disapprove of the suppression of academic freedom, but they go along with it anyway.

226. Thus the fact that many individual leftists are personally mild and fairly tolerant people by no means prevents leftism as a whole form having a totalitarian tendency.

227. Our discussion of leftism has a serious weakness. It is still far from clear what we mean by the word "leftist." There doesn't seem to be much we can do about this. Today leftism is fragmented into a whole spectrum of activist movements. Yet not all activist movements are leftist, and some activist movements (e.g., radical environmentalism) seem to include both personalities of the leftist type and personalities of thoroughly un-leftist types who ought to know better than to collaborate with leftists. Varieties of leftists fade out gradually into varieties of non-leftists and we ourselves would often be hard-pressed to decide whether a given individual is or is not a leftist. To the extent that it is defined at all, our conception of leftism is defined by the discussion of it that we have given in this article, and we can only advise the reader to use his own judgment in deciding who is a leftist.

228. But it will be helpful to list some criteria for diagnosing leftism. These criteria cannot be applied in a cut and dried manner. Some individuals may meet some of the criteria without being leftists, some leftists may not meet any of the criteria. Again, you just have to use your judgment.

229. The leftist is oriented toward large-scale collectivism. He emphasizes the duty of the individual to serve society and the duty of society to take care of the individual. He has a negative attitude toward individualism. He often takes a moralistic tone. He tends to be for gun control, for sex education and other psychologically "enlightened" educational methods, for social planning, for affirmative action, for multiculturalism. He tends to identify with victims. He tends to be against competition and against violence, but he often finds excuses for those leftists who do commit violence. He is fond of using the common catch-phrases of the left like "racism," "sexism," "homophobia," "capitalism," "imperialism," "neocolonialism," "genocide," "social change," "social justice," "social responsibility." Maybe the best diagnostic trait of the leftist is his tendency to sympathize with the following movements: feminism, gay rights, ethnic rights, disability rights, animal rights, political correctness. Anyone who strongly sympathizes with ALL of these movements is almost certainly a leftist. [36]

230. The more dangerous leftists, that is, those who are most power-hungry, are often characterized by arrogance or by a dogmatic approach to ideology. However, the most dangerous leftists of all may be certain oversocialized types who avoid irritating displays of aggressiveness and refrain from advertising their leftism, but work quietly and unobtrusively to promote collectivist values, "enlightened" psychological techniques for socializing children, dependence of the individual on the system, and so forth. These crypto-leftists (as we may call them) approximate certain bourgeois types as far as practical action is concerned, but differ from them in psychology, ideology and motivation. The ordinary bourgeois tries to bring people under control of the system in order to protect his way of life, or he does so simply because his attitudes are conventional. The crypto-leftist tries to bring people under control of the system because he is a True Believer in a collectivistic ideology. The crypto-leftist is differentiated from the average leftist of the oversocialized type by the fact that his rebellious impulse is weaker and he is more securely socialized. He is differentiated from the ordinary well-socialized bourgeois by the fact that there is some deep lack within him that makes it necessary for him to devote himself to a cause and immerse himself in a collectivity. And maybe his (well-sublimated) drive for power is stronger than that of the average bourgeois.

FINAL NOTE

231. Throughout this article we've made imprecise statements and statements that ought to have had all sorts of qualifications and reservations attached to them; and some of our statements may be flatly false. Lack of sufficient information and the need for brevity made it impossible for us to fomulate our assertions more precisely or add all the necessary qualifications. And of course in a discussion of this kind one must rely heavily on intuitive judgment, and that can sometimes be wrong. So we don't claim that this article expresses more than a crude approximation to the truth.

232. All the same, we are reasonably confident that the general outlines of the picture we have painted here are roughly correct. We have portrayed leftism in its modern form as a phenomenon peculiar to our time and as a symptom of the disruption of the power process. But we might possibly be wrong about this. Oversocialized types who try to satisfy their drive for power by imposing their morality on everyone have certainly been around for a long time. But we THINK that the decisive role played by feelings of inferiority, low self-esteem, powerlessness, identification with victims by people who are not themselves victims, is a peculiarity of modern leftism. Identification with victims by people not themselves victims can be seen to some extent in 19th century leftism and early Christianity but as far as we can make out, symptoms of low self-esteem, etc., were not nearly so evident in these movements, or in any other movements, as they are in modern leftism. But we are not in a position to assert confidently that no such movements have existed prior to modern leftism. This is a significant question to which historians ought to give their attention.

NOTES

1. (Paragraph 19) We are asserting that ALL, or even most, bullies and ruthless competitors suffer from feelings of inferiority.

2. (Paragraph 25) During the Victorian period many over-socialized people suffered from serious psychological problems as a result of repressing or trying to repress their sexual feelings. Freud apparently based his theories on people of this type. Today the focus of socialization has shifted from sex to aggression.

3. (Paragraph 27) Not necessarily including specialists in engineering "hard" sciences.

4. (Paragraph 28) There are many individuals of the middle and upper classes who resist some of these values, but usually their resistance is more or less covert. Such resistance appears in the mass media only to a very limited extent. The main thrust of propaganda in our society is in favor of the stated values.

The main reasons why these values have become, so to speak, the official values of our society is that they are useful to the industrial system. Violence is discouraged because it disrupts the functioning of the system. Racism is discouraged because ethnic conflicts also disrupt the system, and discrimination wastes the talent of minority-group members who could be useful to the system. Poverty must be "cured" because the underclass causes problems for the system and contact with the underclass lowers the moral of the other classes. Women are encouraged to have careers because their talents are useful to the system and, more importantly because by having regular jobs women become better integrated into the system and tied directly to it rather than to their families. This helps to weaken family solidarity. (The leaders of the system say they want to strengthen the family, but they really mean is that they want the family to serve as an effective tool for socializing children in accord with the needs of the system. We argue in paragraphs 51, 52 that the system cannot afford to let the family or other small-scale social groups be strong or autonomous.)

5. (Paragraph 42) It may be argued that the majority of people don't want to make their own decisions but want leaders to do their thinking for them. There is an element of truth in this. People like to make their own decisions in small matters, but making decisions on difficult, fundamental questions requires facing up to psychological conflict, and most people hate psychological conflict. Hence they tend to lean on others in making difficult decisions. But it does not follow that they like to have decisions imposed upon them without having any opportunity to influence those decisions. The majority of people are natural followers, not leaders, but they like to have direct personal access to their leaders, they want to be able to influence the leaders and participate to some extent in making difficult decisions. At least to that degree they need autonomy.

6. (Paragraph 44) Some of the symptoms listed are similar to those shown by caged animals.

To explain how these symptoms arise from deprivation with respect to the power process:

Common-sense understanding of human nature tells one that lack of goals whose attainment requires effort leads to boredom and that boredom, long continued, often leads eventually to depression. Failure to obtain goals leads to frustration and lowering of self-esteem. Frustration leads to anger, anger to aggression, often in the form of spouse or child abuse. It has been shown that long-continued frustration commonly leads to depression and that depression tends to cause guilt, sleep disorders, eating disorders and bad feelings about oneself. Those who are tending toward depression seek pleasure as an antidote; hence insatiable hedonism and excessive sex, with perversions as a means of getting new kicks. Boredom too tends to cause excessive pleasure-seeking since, lacking other goals, people often use pleasure as a goal. See accompanying diagram.

The foregoing is a simplification. Reality is more complex, and of course deprivation with respect to the power process is not the ONLY cause of the symptoms described.

By the way, when we mention depression we do not

necessarily mean depression that is severe enough to be treated by a psychiatrist. Often only mild forms of depression are involved. And when we speak of goals we do not necessarily mean long-term, thought-out goals. For many or most people through much of human history, the goals of a hand-to-mouth existence (merely providing oneself and one's family with food from day to day) have been quite sufficient.

7. (Paragraph 52) A partial exception may be made for a few passive, inward-looking groups, such as the Amish, which have little effect on the wider society. Apart from these, some genuine small-scale communities do exist in America today. For instance, youth gangs and "cults." Everyone regards them as dangerous, and so they are, because the members of these groups are loyal primarily to one another rather than to the system, hence the system cannot control them.

Or take the gypsies. The gypsies commonly get away with theft and fraud because their loyalties are such that they can always get other gypsies to give testimony that "proves" their innocence. Obviously the system would be in serious trouble if too many people belonged to such groups.

Some of the early-20th century Chinese thinkers who were concerned with modernizing China recognized the necessity of breaking down small-scale social groups such as the family: "(According to Sun Yat-sen) the Chinese people needed a new surge of patriotism, which would lead to a transfer of loyalty from the family to the state. . . . (According to Li Huang) traditional attachments, particularly to the family had to be abandoned if nationalism were to develop in China." (Chester C. Tan, "Chinese Political Thought in the Twentieth Century," page 125, page 297.)

8. (Paragraph 56) Yes, we know that 19th century America had its problems, and serious ones, but for the sake of breviety we have to express ourselves in simplified terms.

9. (Paragraph 61) We leave aside the "underclass." We are speaking of the mainstream.

10. (Paragraph 62) Some social scientists, educators, "mental health" professionals and the like are doing their best to push the social drives into group 1 by trying to see to it that everyone has a satisfactory social life.

11. (Paragraphs 63, 82) Is the drive for endless material acquisition really an artificial creation of the advertising and marketing industry? Certainly there is no innate human drive for material acquisition. There have been many cultures in which people have desired little material wealth beyond what was necessary to satisfy their basic physical needs (Australian aborigines, traditional Mexican peasant culture, some African cultures). On the other hand there have also been many pre-industrial cultures in which material acquisition has played an important role. So we can't claim that today's acquisition-oriented culture is exclusively a creation of the advertising and marketing industry. But it is clear that the advertising and marketing industry has had an important part in creating that culture. The big corporations that spend millions on advertising wouldn't be spending that kind of money without solid proof that they were getting it back in increased sales. One member of FC met a sales manager a couple of years ago who was frank enough to tell him, "Our job is to make people buy things they don't want and don't need." He then described how an untrained novice could present people with the facts about a product, and make no sales at all, while a trained and experienced professional salesman would make lots of sales to the same people. This shows that people are manipulated into buying things they don't really want.

12. (Paragraph 64) The problem of purposelessness seems to have become less serious during the last 15 years or so, because people now feel less secure physically and economically than they did earlier, and the need for security provides them with a goal. But purposelessness has been replaced by frustration over the difficulty of attaining security. We emphasize the problem of purposelessness because the liberals and leftists would wish to solve our social problems by having society guarantee everyone's security; but if that could be done it would only bring back the problem of purposelessness. The real issue is not whether society provides well or poorly for people's security; the trouble is that people are dependent on the system for their security rather than having it in their own hands. This, by the way, is part of the reason why some people get worked up about the right to bear arms; possession of a gun puts that aspect of their security in their own hands.

13. (Paragraph 66) Conservatives' efforts to decrease the amount of government regulation are of little benefit to the average man. For one thing, only a fraction of the regulations can be eliminated because most regulations are necessary. For another thing, most of the deregulation affects business rather than the average individual, so that its main effect is to take power from the government and give it to private corporations. What this means for the average man is that government interference in his life is replaced by interference from big corporations, which may be permitted, for example, to dump more chemicals that get into his water supply and give him cancer. The conservatives are just taking the average man for a sucker, exploiting his resentment of Big Government to promote the power of Big Business.

14. (Paragraph 73) When someone approves of the purpose for which propaganda is being used in a given case, he generally calls it "education" or applies to it some similar euphemism. But propaganda is propaganda regardless of the purpose for which it is used.

15. (Paragraph 83) We are not expressing approval or disapproval of the Panama invasion. We only use it to illustrate a point.

16. (Paragraph 95) When the American colonies were under British rule there were fewer and less effective legal guarantees of freedom than there were after the American Constitution went into effect, yet there was more personal freedom in pre-industrial America, both before and after the War of Independence, than there was after the Industrial Revolution took hold in this country. We quote from "Violence in America: Historical and Comparative Perspectives," edited by Hugh Davis Graham and Ted Robert Gurr, Chapter 12 by Roger Lane, pages 476-478: "The progressive heightening of standards of propriety, and with it the increasing reliance on official law enforcement (in 19th century America) . . . were common to the whole society. . . . [T]he change in social behavior is so long term and so widespread as to suggest a connection with the most fundamental of contemporary social processes; that of industrial urbanization itself. . . . "Massachusetts in 1835 had a population of some 660,940, 81 percent rural, overwhelmingly preindustrial and native born. It's citizens were used to considerable personal freedom. Whether teamsters, farmers or artisans, they were all accustomed to setting their own schedules, and the nature of their work made them physically dependent on each other. . . . Individual problems, sins or even crimes, were not generally cause for wider social concern . . ." But the impact of the twin movements to the city and to the factory, both just gathering force in 1835, had a progressive effect on personal behavior throughout the 19th century and into the 20th. The factory demanded regularity of behavior, a life governed by obedience to the rhythms of clock and calendar, the demands of foreman and supervisor. In the city or town, the needs of living in closely packed neighborhoods inhibited many actions previously unobjectionable. Both blue- and white-collar employees in larger establishments were mutually dependent on their fellows. as one man's work fit into another's, so one man's business was no longer his own. "The results of the new organization of life and work were apparent by 1900, when some 76 percent of the 2,805,346 inhabitants of Massachusetts were classified as urbanites. Much violent or irregular behavior which had been tolerable in a casual, independent society was no longer acceptable in the more formalized, cooperative atmosphere of the later period. . . . The move to the cities had, in short, produced a more tractable, more socialized, more 'civilized' generation than its predecessors."

17. (Paragraph 117) Apologists for the system are fond of citing cases in which elections have been decided by one or two votes, but such cases are rare.

18. (Paragraph 119) "Today, in technologically advanced lands, men live very similar lives in spite of geographical, religious, and political differences. The daily lives of a Christian bank clerk in Chicago, a Buddhist bank clerk in Tokyo, a Communist bank clerk in Moscow are far more alike than the life any one of them is like that of any single man who lived a thousand years ago. These similarities are the result of a common technology. . . ." L. Sprague de

Camp, "The Ancient Engineers," Ballantine edition, page 17.

The lives of the three bank clerks are not IDENTICAL. Ideology does have SOME effect. But all technological societies, in order to survive, must evolve along APPROXIMATELY the same trajectory.

19. (Paragraph 123) Just think an irresponsible genetic engineer might create a lot of terrorists.

20. (Paragraph 124) For a further example of undesirable consequences of medical progress, suppose a reliable cure for cancer is discovered. Even if the treatment is too expensive to be available to any but the elite, it will greatly reduce their incentive to stop the escape of carcinogens into the environment.

21. (Paragraph 128) Since many people may find paradoxical the notion that a large number of good things can add up to a bad thing, we will illustrate with an analogy. Suppose Mr. A is playing chess with Mr. B. Mr. C, a Grand Master, is looking over Mr. A's shoulder. Mr. A of course wants to win his game, so if Mr. C points out a good move for him to make, he is doing Mr. A a favor. But suppose now that Mr. C tells Mr. A how to make ALL of his moves. In each particular instance he does Mr. A a favor by showing him his best move, but by making ALL of his moves for him he spoils the game, since there is not point in Mr. A's playing the game at all if someone else makes all his moves.

The situation of modern man is analogous to that of Mr. A. The system makes an individual's life easier for him in innumerable ways, but in doing so it deprives him of control over his own fate.

22. (Paragraph 137) Here we are considering only the conflict of values within the mainstream. For the sake of simplicity we leave out of the picture "outsider" values like the idea that wild nature is more important than human economic welfare.

23. (Paragraph 137) Self-interest is not necessarily MATERIAL self-interest. It can consist in fulfillment of some psychological need, for example, by promoting one's own ideology or religion.

24. (Paragraph 139) A qualification: It is in the interest of the system to permit a certain prescribed degree of freedom in some areas. For example, economic freedom (with suitable limitations and restraints) has proved effective in promoting economic growth. But only planned, circumscribed, limited freedom is in the interest of the system. The individual must always be kept on a leash, even if the leash is sometimes long (see paragraphs 94, 97).

25. (Paragraph 143) We don't mean to suggest that the efficiency or the potential for survival of a society has always been inversely proportional to the amount of pressure or discomfort to which the society subjects people. That is certainly not the case. There is good reason to believe that many primitive societies subjected people to less pressure than the European society did, but European society proved far more efficient than any primitive society and always won out in conflicts with such societies because of the advantages conferred by technology.

26. (Paragraph 147) If you think that more effective law enforcement is unequivocally good because it suppresses crime, then remember that crime as defined by the system is not necessarily what YOU would call crime. Today, smoking marijuana is a "crime," and, in some places in the U.S., so is possession of an unregistered handgun. Tomorrow, possession of ANY firearm, registered or not, may be made a crime, and the same thing may happen with disapproved methods of child-rearing, such as spanking. In some countries, expression of dissident political opinions is a crime, and there is no certainty that this will never happen in the U.S., since no constitution or political system lasts forever.

If a society needs a large, powerful law enforcement establishment, then there is something gravely wrong with that society; it must be subjecting people to severe pressures if so many refuse to follow the rules, or follow them only because forced. Many societies in the past have gotten by with little or no formal law-enforcement.

27. (Paragraph 151) To be sure, past societies have had means of influencing behavior, but these have been primitive and of low effectiveness compared with the technological means that are now being developed.

28. (Paragraph 152) However, some psychologists have publicly expressed opinions indicating their contempt for human freedom. And the mathematician Claude Shannon was quoted in Omni (August 1987) as saying, "I visualize a time when we will be to robots what dogs are to humans, and I'm rooting for the machines."

29. (Paragraph 154) This is no science fiction! After writing paragraph 154 we came across an article in Scientific American according to which scientists are actively developing techniques for identifying possible future criminals and for treating them by a combination of biological and psychological means. Some scientists advocate compulsory application of the treatment, which may be available in the near future. (See "Seeking the Criminal Element", by W. Wayt Gibbs, Scientific American, March 1995.) Maybe you think this is OK because the treatment would be applied to those who might become violent criminals. But of course it won't stop there. Next, a treatment will be applied to those who might become drunk drivers (they endanger human life too), then perhaps to peel who spank their children, then to environmentalists who sabotage logging equipment, eventually to anyone whose behavior is inconvenient for the system.

30. (Paragraph 184) A further advantage of nature as a counter-ideal to technology is that, in many people, nature inspires the kind of reverence that is associated with religion, so that nature could perhaps be idealized on a religious basis. It is true that in many societies religion has served as a support and justification for the established order, but it is also true that religion has often provided a basis for rebellion. Thus it may be useful to introduce a religious element into the rebellion against technology, the more so because Western society today has no strong religious foundation. Religion, nowadays either is used as cheap and transparent support for narrow, short-sighted selfishness (some conservatives use it this way), or even is cynically exploited to make easy money (by many evangelists), or has degenerated into crude irrationalism (fundamentalist Protestant sects, "cults"), or is simply stagnant (Catholicism, main-line Protestantism). The nearest thing to a strong, widespread, dynamic religion that the West has seen in recent times has been the quasi-religion of leftism, but leftism today is fragmented and has no clear, unified inspiring goal.

Thus there is a religious vaccuum in our society that could perhaps be filled by a religion focused on nature in opposition to technology. But it would be a mistake to try to concoct artificially a religion to fill this role. Such an invented religion would probably be a failure. Take the "Gaia" religion for example. Do its adherents REALLY believe in it or are they just play-acting? If they are just play-acting their religion will be a flop in the end.

It is probably best not to try to introduce religion into the conflict of nature vs. technology unless you REALLY believe in that religion yourself and find that it arouses a deep, strong, genuine response in many other people.

31. (Paragraph 189) Assuming that such a final push occurs. Conceivably the industrial system might be eliminated in a somewhat gradual or piecemeal fashion. (see paragraphs 4, 167 and Note 4).

32. (Paragraph 193) It is even conceivable (remotely) that the revolution might consist only of a massive change of attitudes toward technology resulting in a relatively gradual and painless disintegration of the industrial system. But if this happens we'll be very lucky. It's far more probably that the transition to a nontechnological society will be very difficult and full of conflicts and disasters.

33. (Paragraph 195) The economic and technological structure of a society are far more important than its political structure in determining the way the average man lives (see paragraphs 95, 119 and Notes 16, 18).

34. (Paragraph 215) This statement refers to our particular brand of anarchism. A wide variety of social attitudes have been called "anarchist," and it may be that many who consider themselves anarchists would not accept our statement of paragraph 215. It should be noted, by the way, that there is a nonviolent anarchist movement whose members probably would not accept FC as anarchist and certainly would not approve of FC's violent methods.

35. (Paragraph 219) Many leftists are motivated also by hostility, but the hostility probably results in part from a frustrated need for power.

36. (Paragraph 229) It is important to understand that we mean someone who sympathizes with these MOVEMENTS as they exist today in our society. One who believes that women, homosexuals, etc., should have equal rights is not necessarily a leftist. The feminist, gay rights, etc., movements that exist in our society have the particular ideological tone that characterizes leftism, and if one believes, for example, that women should have equal rights it does not necessarily follow that one must sympathize with the feminist movement as it exists today.

If copyright problems make it impossible for this long quotation to be printed, then please change Note 16 to read as follows:

16. (Paragraph 95) When the American colonies were under British rule there were fewer and less effective legal guarantees of freedom than there were after the American Constitution went into effect, yet there was more personal freedom in pre-industrial America, both before and after the War of Independence, than there was after the Industrial Revolution took hold in this country. In "Violence In America: Historical and Comparative Perspectives," edited by Hugh Davis Graham and Ted Robert Gurr, Chapter 12 by Roger Lane, it is explained how in pre-industrial America the average person had greater independence and autonomy than he does today, and how the process of industrialization necessarily led to the restriction of personal freedom.

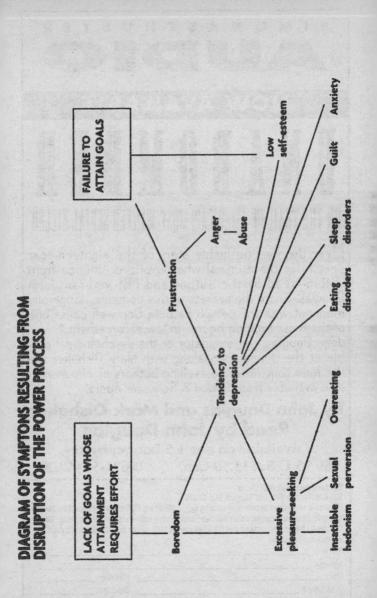

DIAGRAM OF SYMPTONS RESULTING FROM DISRUPTION OF THE POWER PROCESS

FAILURE TO ATTAIN GOALS

LACK OF GOALS WHOSE ATTAINMENT REQUIRES EFFORT

Frustration

Anger

Abuse

Low self-esteem

Anxiety

Guilt

Sleep disorders

Eating disorders

Tendency to depression

Boredom

Overeating

Excessive pleasure-seeking

Sexual perversion

Insatiable hedonism

POCKET STAR BOOKS
PROUDLY PRESENTS

MINDHUNTER:
INSIDE THE FBI'S
ELITE SERIAL CRIME UNIT

JOHN DOUGLAS
AND
MARK OLSHAKER

Coming Mid-July from
Pocket Star Books

The following is a preview of
Mindhunter . . .

Put yourself in the position of the hunter.

That's what I have to do. Think of one of those nature films: a lion on the Serengeti plain in Africa. He sees this huge herd of antelope at a watering hole. But somehow— we can see it in his eyes—the lion locks on a single one out of those thousands of animals. He's trained himself to sense weakness, vulnerability, something different in one antelope out of the herd that makes it the most likely victim.

It's the same with certain people. If I'm one of them, then I'm on the hunt daily, looking for my victim, looking for my victim of opportunity. Let's say I'm at a shopping mall where there are thousands of people. So I go into the video arcade, and as I look over the fifty or so children playing there, I've got to be a hunter, I've got to be a profiler, I've got to be able to profile that potential prey. I've got to figure out which of those fifty children is the vulnerable one, which one is the likely victim. I have to look at the way the child is dressed. I have to train myself to pick up the nonverbal clues the child is putting out. And I have to do this all in a split second, so I have to be very, very good at it. Then, once I decide, once I make my move, I've got to know how

I am going to get this child out of the mall quietly and without creating any fuss or suspicion when his or her parents are probably two stores down. I can't afford to make any mistakes.

It's the thrill of the hunt that gets these guys going. If you could get a galvanic skin response reading on one of them as he focuses in on his potential victim, I think you'd get the same reaction as from that lion in the wilderness. And it doesn't matter whether we're talking about the ones who hunt children, who hunt young women or the elderly or prostitutes or any other definable group—or the ones who don't seem to have any particular preferred victim. In some ways, they're all the same.

But it is the ways they are different, and the clues that they leave to their individual personalities, that have led us to a new weapon in the interpretation of certain types of violent crimes, and the hunting, apprehension, and prosecution of their perpetrators. I've spent most of my professional career as an FBI special agent trying to develop that weapon, and that's what this book is about. In the case of every horrible crime since the beginning of civilization, there is always that searing, fundamental question: what kind of person could have done such a thing? The type of profiling and crime-scene analysis we do at the FBI's Investigative Support Unit attempts to answer that question.

Behavior reflects personality.

It isn't always easy, and it's never pleasant, putting yourself in these guys' shoes—or inside their minds. But that's what my people and I have to do. We have to try to feel what it was like for each one.

Everything we see at a crime scene tells us something about the unknown subject—or UNSUB, in police jargon—who committed the crime. By studying as many crimes as we could, and through talking to the experts—the perpetrators themselves—we have learned to interpret those clues in much the same way a doctor evaluates various symptoms to diagnose a particular disease or condition. And just as a doctor can begin forming a diagnosis after recognizing several aspects of a disease presentation he or she has seen before, we can make various conclusions when we see patterns start to emerge.

One time in the early 1980s when I was actively interviewing incarcerated killers for our in-depth study, I was sitting in a circle of violent offenders in the ancient, stone, gothic Maryland State Penitentiary in Baltimore. Each man was an interesting case in his own right—a cop killer, a child killer, drug dealers, and enforcers—but I was most concerned with interviewing a rapist-murderer about his modus operandi, so I asked the other prisoners if they knew of one at the prison I might be able to talk to.

"Yeah, there's Charlie Davis," one of the inmates says, but the rest agree it's unlikely he'll talk to a fed. Someone goes to find him in the prison yard. To everyone's surprise, Davis does come over and join the circle, probably as much out of curiosity or boredom as any other reason. One thing we had going for us in the study is that prisoners have a lot of time on their hands and not much to do with it.

Normally, when we conduct prison interviews—and this has been true right from the beginning—we try to know as much as we can about the subject in advance. We go over the police files and crime-scene photos, autopsy protocols, trial transcripts; anything that might shed light on motives or personality. It's also the surest way to make certain the subject isn't playing self-serving or self-amusing games with you and is giving it to you straight. But in this case, obviously, I hadn't done any preparation, so I admit it and try to use it to my advantage.

Davis was a huge, hulking guy, about six foot five, in his early thirties, clean-shaven, and well groomed. I start out by saying, "You have me at a disadvantage, Charlie. I don't know what you did."

"I killed five people," he replies.

I ask him to describe the crime scenes and what he did with his victims. Now, it turns out, Davis had been a part-time ambulance driver. So what he'd do was strangle the woman, place her body by the side of a highway in his driving territory, make an anonymous call, then respond to the call and pick up the body. No one knew, when he was putting the victim on the stretcher, that the killer was right there among them. This degree of control and orchestration was what really turned him on and gave him his biggest thrill. Anything like this that I could learn about technique would always prove extremely valuable.

The strangling told me he was a spur-of-the-moment killer, that the primary thing on his mind had been rape.

I say to him, "You're a real police buff. You'd love to be a cop yourself, to be in a position of power instead of some menial job far below your abilities." He laughs, says his father had been a police lieutenant.

I ask him to describe his MO: he would follow a good-looking young woman, see her pull into the parking lot of a restaurant, let's say. Through his father's police contacts, he'd be able to run a license-plate check on the car. Then, when he had the owner's name, he'd call the restaurant and have her paged and told she'd left her lights on. When she came outside, he'd abduct her—push her into his car or hers, handcuff her, then drive off.

He describes each of the five kills in order, almost as if he's reminiscing. When he gets to the last one, he mentions that he covered her over in the front seat of the car, a detail he remembers for the first time.

At that point in the conversation, I turn things further around. I say, "Charlie, let me tell you something about yourself: You had relationship problems with women. You were having financial problems when you did your first kill. You were in your late twenties and you knew your abilities were way above your job, so everything in your life was frustrating and out of control."

He just sort of nods. So far, so good. I haven't said anything terribly hard to predict or guess at.

"You were drinking heavily," I continue. "You owed money. You were having fights with the woman you lived with. [He hadn't told me he lived with anyone, but I felt pretty certain he did.] And on the nights when things were the worst, you'd go out on the hunt. You wouldn't go after your old lady, so you had to dish it out to someone else."

I can see Davis's body language gradually changing, opening up. So, going with the scant information I have, I go on, "But this last victim was a much more gentle kill. She was different from the others. You let her get dressed again after you raped her. You covered up her head. You didn't do that with the previous four. Unlike the others, you didn't feel good about this one."

When they start listening closely, you know you're onto something. I learned this from the prison interviews and was able to use it over and over in interrogation situations. I see I have his complete attention here. "She told you something that made you feel bad about killing her, but you killed her anyway.

Suddenly, he becomes red as a beet. He seems in a trance-like state, and I can see that in his mind, he's back at the scene. Hesitantly, he tells me the woman had said her husband was having serious health problems and that she was worried about him; he was sick and maybe dying. This may have been a ruse on her part, it may not have been—I don't have any way of knowing. But clearly, it had affected Davis.

"But I hadn't disguised myself. She knew who I was, so I had to kill her."

I pause a few moments, then say, "You took something from her, didn't you?"

He nods again, then admits he went into her wallet. He took out a photograph of her with her husband and child at Christmas and kept it.

I'd never met this guy before, but I'm starting to get a firm image of him, so I say, "You went to the grave site, Charlie, didn't you?" He becomes flushed, which also confirms for me he followed the press on the case so he'd know where his victim was buried. "You went because you didn't feel good about this particular murder. And you brought something with you to the cemetery and you put it right there on that grave."

The other prisoners are completely silent, listening with rapt attention. They've never seen Davis like this. I repeat, "You brought something to that grave. What did you bring, Charlie? You brought that picture, didn't you?" He just nods again and hangs his head.

This wasn't quite the witchcraft or pulling the rabbit out of the hat it might have seemed to the other prisoners. Obviously, I was guessing, but the guesses were based on a lot of background and research and experience my associates and I had logged by that time and continue to gather. For example, we'd learned that the old cliché about killers visiting the graves of their victims was often true, but not necessarily for the reasons we'd originally thought.

Behavior reflects personality.

One of the reasons our work is even necessary has to do with the changing nature of violent crime itself. We all know about the drug-related murders that plague most of our cities and the gun crimes that have become an everyday occurrence as well as a national disgrace. Yet it used to be that most crime, particularly most violent crime, happened between people who in some way knew each other.

We're not seeing that as much any longer. As recently as the 1960s, the solution rate to homicide in this country was well over 90 percent. We're not seeing that any longer, either. Now, despite impressive advances in science and technology, despite the advent of the computer age, despite many more police officers with far better and more sophisticated training and resources, the murder rate has been going up and the solution rate has been going down. More and more crimes are being committed by and against "strangers," and in many cases we have no motive to work with, at least no obvious or "logical" motive.

Traditionally, most murders and violent crimes were relatively easy for law enforcement officials to comprehend. They resulted from critically exaggerated manifestations of feelings we all experience: anger, greed, jealousy, profit, revenge. Once this emotional problem was taken care of, the crime or crime spree would end. Someone would be dead, but that was that and the police generally knew who and what they were looking for.

But a new type of violent criminal has surfaced in recent years—the serial offender, who often doesn't stop until he is caught or killed, who learns by experience and who tends to get better and better at what he does, constantly perfecting his scenario from one crime to the next. I say "surfaced" because, to some degree, he was probably with us all along, going back long before 1880s London and Jack the Ripper, generally considered the first modern serial killer. And I say "he" because, for reasons we'll get into a little later, virtually all real serial killers are male.

Serial murder may, in fact, be a much older phenomenon than we realize. The stories and legends that have filtered down about witches and werewolves and vampires may have been a way of explaining outrages so hideous that no one in the small and close-knit towns of Europe and early America could comprehend the perversities we now take for granted. Monsters had to be supernatural creatures. They couldn't be just like us.

Serial killers and rapists also tend to be the most bewildering, personally disturbing, and most difficult to catch of all violent criminals. This is, in part, because they tend to be motivated by far more complex factors than the basic ones I've just enumerated. This, in turn, makes their patterns more confusing and distances them from such other normal feelings as compassion, guilt, or remorse.

Sometimes, the only way to catch them is to learn how to think like they do.

Lest anyone think I will be giving away any closely guarded investigative secrets that could provide a "how-to" to would-be offenders, let me reassure you on that point right now. What I will be relating is how we developed the behavioral approach to criminal-personality profiling, crime analysis, and prosecutorial strategy, but I couldn't make this a how-to course even if I wanted to. For one thing, it takes as much as two years for us to train the already experienced, highly accomplished agents selected to come into my unit. For another, no matter how much the criminal thinks he knows, the more he does to try to evade detection or throw us off the track, the more behavioral clues he's going to give us to work with.

As Sir Arthur Conan Doyle had Sherlock Holmes say many decades ago, "Singularity is almost invariably a clue. The more featureless and commonplace a crime is, the more difficult it is to bring it home." In other words, the more behavior we have, the more complete the profile and analysis we can give to the local police. The better the profile the local police have to work with, the more they can slice down the potential suspect population and concentrate on finding the real guy.

Which brings me to the other disclaimer about our work. In the Investigative Support Unit, which is part of the FBI's National Center for the Analysis of Violent Crime at Quantico, we don't catch criminals. Let me repeat that: *we do not catch criminals.* Local police catch criminals, and considering the incredible pressures they're under, most of them do a pretty damn good job of it. What we try to do is *assist* local police in focusing their investigations, then suggest some proactive techniques that might help draw a criminal out. Once they catch him—and again, I emphasize *they,* not *we*— we will try to formulate a strategy to help the prosecutor bring out the defendant's true personality during the trial.

We're able to do this because of our research and our specialized experience. While a local midwestern police department faced with a serial-murder investigation might be seeing these horrors for the first time, my unit has probably handled hundreds, if not thousands, of similar crimes. I always tell my agents, "If you want to understand the artist, you have to look at the painting." We've looked at many "paintings" over the years and talked extensively to the most "accomplished" "artists."

We began methodically developing the work of the FBI's Behavioral Science Unit, and what later came to be the Investigative Support Unit, in the late 1970s and early 1980s. And though most of the books that dramatize and glorify what we do, such as Tom Harris's memorable *The Silence of the Lambs,* are somewhat fanciful and prone to dramatic license, our antecedents actually do go back to crime fiction more than crime fact. C. August Dupin, the amateur detective hero of Edgar Allan Poe's 1841 classic "The Murders in the Rue Morgue," may have been history's first behavioral profiler. This story may also represent the first use of a proactive technique by the profiler to flush out an unknown subject and vindicate an innocent man imprisoned for the killings.

Like the men and women in my unit a hundred and fifty years later, Poe understood the value of profiling when forensic evidence alone isn't enough to solve a particularly brutal and seemingly motiveless crime. "Deprived of ordinary resources," he wrote, "the analyst throws himself into the spirit of his opponent, identifies himself therewith, and not infrequently sees thus, at a glance, the sole methods by which he may seduce into error or hurry into miscalculation."

There's also another small similarity worth mentioning. Monsieur Dupin preferred to work alone in his room with the windows closed and the curtains drawn tight against the sunlight and the intrusion of the outside world. My colleagues and I have had no such choice in the matter. Our offices at the FBI Academy in Quantico are several stories underground, in a windowless space originally designed to serve as the secure headquarters for federal law enforcement authorities in the event of national emergency. We sometimes call ourselves the National *Cellar* for the Analysis of Violent Crime. At sixty feet below ground, we say we're ten times deeper than dead people.

The English novelist Wilkie Collins took up the profiling mantle in such pioneering works as *The Woman in White* (based on an actual case) and *The Moonstone.* But it was Sir Arthur Conan Doyle's immortal creation, Sherlock Holmes, who brought out this form of criminal investigative analysis for all the world to see in the shadowy gaslit world of Victorian London. The highest compliment any of us can be paid, it seems, is to be compared to this fictional character. I took it as a real honor some years back when, while I was working a murder case in Missouri, a headline in the *St. Louis Globe-Democrat* referred to me as the "FBI's Modern Sherlock Holmes."

It's interesting to note that at the same time Holmes was working his intricate and baffling cases, the real-life Jack the Ripper was killing prostitutes in London's East End. So completely have these two men on opposite sides of the law, and opposite sides of the boundary between reality and imagination, taken hold of the public consciousness that several "modern" Sherlock Holmes stories, written by Conan Doyle admirers, have thrown the detective into the unsolved Whitechapel murders.

Back in 1988, I was asked to analyze the Ripper murders for a nationally broadcast television program. I'll relate my conclusions about this most famous UNSUB in history later in this book.

It wasn't until more than a century after Poe's "Rue Morgue" and a half century after Sherlock Holmes that behavioral profiling moved off the pages of literature and into real life. By the mid-1950s, New York City was being rocked by the explosions of the "Mad Bomber," known to be responsible for more than thirty bombings over a fifteen-year period. He hit such public landmarks as Grand Central and Pennsylvania Stations and Radio City Music Hall. As a child in Brooklyn at the time, I remember this case very well.

At wit's end, the police in 1957 called in a Greenwich Village psychiatrist named Dr. James A. Brussel, who studied photographs of the bomb scenes and carefully analyzed the bomber's taunting letters to newspapers. He came to a number of detailed conclusions from the overall behavioral patterns he perceived, including the facts that the perpetrator was a paranoiac who hated his father, obsessively loved his mother, and lived in a city in Connecticut. At the end of his written profile, Brussel instructed the police:

> Look for a heavy man. Middle-aged. Foreign born. Roman Catholic. Single. Lives with a brother or sister. When you find him, chances are he'll be wearing a double-breasted suit. Buttoned.

From references in some of the letters, it seemed a good bet that the bomber was a disgruntled current or former employee of Consolidated Edison, the city's power company. Matching up the profile to this target population, police came up with the name of George Metesky, who had worked for Con Ed in the 1940s before the bombings began.

When they went up to Waterbury, Connecticut, one evening to arrest the heavy, single, middle-aged, foreign-born Roman Catholic, the only variation in the profile was that he lived not with one brother or sister but with two maiden sisters. After a police officer directed him to get dressed for the trip to the station, he emerged from his bedroom several minutes later wearing a double-breasted suit—buttoned.

Illuminating how he reached his uncannily accurate conclusions, Dr. Brussel explained that a psychiatrist normally examines an individual and then tries to make some reasonable predictions about how that person might react to some specific situation. In constructing his profile, Brussel stated, he reversed the process, trying to predict an individual from the evidence of his deeds.

Looking back on the Mad Bomber case from our perspective of nearly forty years, it actually seems a rather simple one to crack. But at the time, it was a real landmark in the development of what came to be called behavioral science in criminal investigation, and Dr. Brussel, who later worked with the Boston Police Department on the Boston Strangler case, was a true trailblazer in the field.

Though it is often referred to as *deduction,* what the fictional Dupin and Holmes, and real-life Brussel and those of us who followed, were doing was actually more *inductive*—that is, observing particular elements of a crime and drawing larger conclusions from them. When I came to Quantico in 1977, instructors in the Behavioral Science Unit, such as the pioneering Howard Teten, were starting to apply Dr. Brussel's ideas to cases brought to them in their National Academy classes by police professionals. But at the time, this was all anecdotal and had never been backed up by hard research. That was the state of things when I came into the story.

I've talked about how important it is for us to be able to step into the shoes and mind of the unknown killer. Through our research and experience, we've found it is equally important—as painful and harrowing as it might be—to be able to put ourselves in the place of the victim. Only when we have a firm idea of how the particular victim would have reacted to the horrible things that were happening to her or him can we truly understand the behavior and reactions of the perpetrator.

To know the offender, you have to look at the crime.

In the early 1980s, a disturbing case came to me from the police department of a small town in rural Georgia. A pretty fourteen-year-old girl, a majorette at the local junior high school, had been abducted from the school bus stop about a hundred yards from her house. Her partially clothed body was discovered some days later in a wooded lovers'-lane area about ten miles away. She had been sexually molested, and the cause of death was blunt-force trauma to the head. A large, blood-encrusted rock was lying nearby.

Before I could deliver my analysis, I had to know as much about this young girl as I could. I found out that though very cute and pretty, she was a fourteen-year-old who looked fourteen, not twenty-one as some teens do. Everyone who knew her assured me she was not promiscuous or a flirt, was not in any way involved with drugs or alcohol, and that she was warm and friendly to anyone who approached her. Autopsy analysis indicated she had been a virgin when raped.

This was all vital information to me, because it led me to understand how she would have reacted during and after the abduction and, therefore, how the offender would have reacted to her in the particular situation in which they found themselves. From this, I concluded that the murder had not been a *planned* outcome, but was a panicked reaction due to the surprise (based on the attacker's warped and delusional fantasy system) that the young girl did not welcome him with open arms. This, in turn, led me closer to the personality of the killer, and my profile led the police to focus on a suspect in a rape case from the year before in a nearby larger town. Understanding the victim also helped me construct a strategy for the police to use in interrogating this challenging suspect, who, as I predicted he would, had already passed a lie-detector test. I will discuss this fascinating and heartbreaking case in detail later on. But for now, suffice it to say that the individual ended up confessing both to the murder and the earlier rape. He was convicted and sentenced and, as of this writing, is on Georgia's death row.

When we teach the elements of criminal-personality profiling and crime-scene analysis to FBI agents or law enforcement professionals attending the National Academy, we try to get them to think of the entire story of the crime. My colleague Roy Hazelwood, who taught the basic profiling course for several years before retiring from the Bureau in 1993, used to divide the analysis into three distinct questions and phases—what, why, and who:

What took place? This includes everything that might be behaviorally significant about the crime.

Why did it happen the way it did? Why, for example, was there mutilation after death? Why was nothing of value taken? Why was there no forced entry? What are the reasons for every behaviorally significant factor in the crime?

And this, then, leads to:

Who would have committed this crime for these reasons? That is the task we set for ourselves.

Look for

MINDHUNTER

Wherever Paperback Books Are Sold

Coming mid-July from Pocket Star Books